PROSPECTS OF ECONOMIC GROWTH

PROBLEMS OF ECONOMIC GROWTH

PROSPECTS OF ECONOMIC GROWTH

Editors

S. K. KUIPERS and G. J. LANJOUW

University of Groningen, The Netherlands

1980

NORTH-HOLLAND PUBLISHING COMPANY
AMSTERDAM · NEW YORK · OXFORD

330.904
P966

ISBN for this volume: 0 444 85355 3

Publishers

NORTH-HOLLAND PUBLISHING COMPANY
AMSTERDAM · NEW YORK · OXFORD

Sole distributors for the U.S.A. and Canada

ELSEVIER NORTH-HOLLAND INC.
52 VANDERBILT AVENUE
NEW YORK, N.Y. 10017

Library of Congress Cataloging in Publication Data
Main entry under title:

Prospects of economic growth.

Papers presented at a conference organized by the Faculty of Economics of the University of Groningen, Sept. 7–8, 1978, in Gieten, Drenthe, The Netherlands.
Includes index.
1. Economic development—Congresses.
I. Kuipers, Simon Klass.   II. Lanjouw, G. J.
III. Groningen. Rijksuniversiteit. Faculteit der Economische Wetenschappen,
HD82.P75   330.9′04   79–19514
ISBN 0–444–85355–3

PRINTED IN GREAT BRITAIN

CONTENTS

PREFACE

The economies of the Western industrialized countries displayed very rapid growth in the first decades after the Second World War. However, in the middle of the Seventies this growth began to stagnate. The question then became pressing whether this stagnation should be considered a temporary or a more permanent phenomenon. In particular one would like to know whether one has to expect the rates of growth to be considerably lower in future decades than they were in the Fifties and in the Sixties. Future growth prospects will depend in particular on technical progress, availability of natural resources, pollution, changes in the economic order, both nationally and internationally, and changes in the international division of labour, as well as on the capacity of the industrialized countries to recover from external shocks (e.g. the oil crisis). Moreover, the slowdown of economic growth may also indicate that there is such a thing as a long wave, of which the downward phase was entered in the mid Seventies.

To assess what the prospects of economic growth are, the Faculty of Economics of the University of Groningen organized a conference on this subject on 7 and 8 September 1978 in Gieten, Drenthe, the Netherlands. In order to ensure that the different aspects of the growth problem were paid due attention, the programme committee, consisting of Mr. T. Huppes, Dr. S. K. Kuipers, Mr. G. J. Lanjouw, Dr. A. Nentjes and Mr. H. W. Plasmeijer, selected eight topics, for each of which an author and two discussants were invited. These subjects were:

(1) changes in the economic order at the national level and the relation with economic growth,
(2) changes in the economic order at the international level and their relation to economic growth,
(3) economic growth, technical progress and natural resources,
(4) economic growth and environment,
(5) prospects of employment growth,
(6) shifts in the sectoral pattern of production,
(7) the long wave in economic life, and
(8) the possibilities of long-run forecasting.

This volume consists of the papers and the comments dealing with these different topics. In the final chapter a summary and evaluation of the proceedings of the conference is given.

Editing the proceedings of a conference is not possible without the help of many others. In the first place, the editors have to thank their colleagues of the programme committee, Mr. T. Huppes, Dr. A. Nentjes and Mr. H. W. Plasmeijer, for their efficient and kind collaboration during the preparation of the conference. In the second place the assistance in the technical and administrative field should be mentioned. For as everybody knows, but not always realizes, this is not the least of the work to be done in organizing a conference and editing its proceedings. In this respect the editors are greatly indebted to Miss Johanna Broekhuizen for secretarial assistance, to Mr. H. van Ees for preparing the index and to Mr. J. P. Albers for reproduction of the various drafts of the papers. In the third place the editors should like to thank Mr. T. Preston for translation of some of the papers originally written in Dutch and for correction of the English language of the other papers. Last but not least, the contributors themselves must be thanked for the cooperative and precise way in which they were prepared to provide the various drafts of their papers. Because of this a quick publication of this volume has been possible.

The organization of a conference does not depend solely on the help of many people, it is moreover dependent on sufficient financial support. In this respect the editors gratefully acknowledge the financial contribution of the Faculty of Economics of the University of Groningen.

S. K. Kuipers
G. J. Lanjouw

LIST OF CONTRIBUTORS

C. P. A. Bartels, *University of Groningen, The Netherlands*
A. Bosman, *University of Groningen, The Netherlands*
F. van Dam, *University of Groningen, The Netherlands*
W. Driehuis, *University of Amsterdam, The Netherlands*
J. J. van Duijn, *Graduate School of Management, Delft, The Netherlands*
P. M. E. M. van der Grinten, *DSM, Heerlen and Technological University Eindhoven, The Netherlands*
H. de Haan, *University of Groningen, The Netherlands*
R. Hueting, *Central Bureau of Statistics, The Netherlands*
T. Huppes, *University of Groningen, The Netherlands*
Th. van de Klundert, *University of Tilburg, The Netherlands*
S. K. Kuipers, *University of Groningen, The Netherlands*
G. J. Lanjouw, *University of Groningen, The Netherlands*
P. S. H. Leeflang, *University of Groningen, The Netherlands*
H. Linnemann, *Free University of Amsterdam, The Netherlands*
J. A. H. Maks, *University of Groningen, The Netherlands*
F. Muller, *Erasmus University, Rotterdam, The Netherlands*
A. Nentjes, *Social Higher Education Friesland, University of Groningen, The Netherlands*
P. Nijkamp, *Free University, Amsterdam, The Netherlands*
J. B. Opschoor, *Free University, Amsterdam, The Netherlands*
H. W. Plasmeijer, *University of Groningen, The Netherlands*
D. B. J. Schouten, *University of Tilburg, The Netherlands*
J. Tinbergen, *Erasmus University, Rotterdam, The Netherlands*
H.-J. Wagener, *University of Groningen, The Netherlands*
J. Weitenberg, *Central Planning Bureau and University of Groningen, The Netherlands*
A.van der Zwan, *Erasmus University, Rotterdam, The Netherlands*
W. J. Zwezerijnen, *Erasmus University, Rotterdam, The Netherlands*

0510
1223
W. Europe

Chapter 1   *1-17*

WHAT HAS BECOME OF THE MARCH INTO SOCIALISM? SYSTEM DEVELOPMENTS IN POSTWAR EUROPE

H.-J. WAGENER

University of Groningen

This paper deals with major changes in economic systems of postwar Europe. Examples are the increased importance of state intervention and regulation, the concentration of capital, and the improved position of labour power. Although there is a trend towards more democratization in the politico–economic sphere, this is accompanied by a rapid centralization of decision-making. Some economic and social consequences of this development are indicated. Finally, it is asked whether this leads to stagnation. The systems observed seem to be in a very unstable situation due also to the absence of international control. But no convincing arguments for stagnation can be found.

1. Introduction

In the middle of the 1970s the capitalist economic system ran into its first major postwar crisis. Although individual countries had continually experienced ups and downs, general economic development since 1945 had been characterized by a relatively high degree of stability compared to the prewar period [cf. Lundberg (1968) and Verdoorn and Post (1969)].

The universal crisis which still persists may have been an accident (typical of capitalist economies) caused by cumulative processes that happened to occur in a synchronized manner. It may, however, indicate a more fundamental change in the stability behaviour of the system which can become chronic if left unchecked.

It is the purpose of this paper to identify and analyse some longer-term developments in postwar Western economies which could make for critical changes in their mode of operation. In order to link the postwar period with the past, we start in section 2 from the situation in 1945–1950, when it was strongly felt that a new epoch had begun. Several institutional innovations were the result of expectations and forecasts about the years to come.

Prospects of Economic Growth, edited by S. K. Kuipers and G. J. Lanjouw
© *North-Holland Publishing Company*

In sections 3 and 4 we acquaint ourselves with the major institutional changes experienced over the last 30 years or so. Above all, we have to analyse the continuous process of centralization manifesting itself in the changing role of the state and the concentration of decision-making power with the state, business, and the labour unions. This process has had some beneficial and some less advantageous consequences (section 5).

In section 6 we ask whether there are signs now of a more systemic or general crisis which might result from the institutional developments in the postwar period. Such signs are seen in the declining degree of pluralism and in stagnation. Be these fears justified or not, in section 7 we briefly look at some proposed ways out of a perceived dilemma. They are mostly inspired by the intention to reverse the process of centralization. After this it will be time to draw some conclusions.

2. The historical setting

The Second World War can be seen as the end of the great depression or as the starting point of a new epoch. It reshuffled the world in many respects, not least its economic conditions and relations. It has been argued [Weber (1947)] that the great depression was less a consequence of pure economic factors than the result of the fact that the framework of classical capitalism – the British world economy – had broken down since 1914.

It was expected that the vacuum would have to be filled by a new international framework – the "American world economy" – which, although equally monopoly capitalist, would avoid the destructive imperialist traits of the old system. Weber saw two central features of the American world economy in its major field of expansion, South-East Asia, and in its systemic confrontation and competition with the Soviet Union. As to Europe, he thought it would be exempted, and would be a field of historical indifference where different economic systems, namely different forms of socialism, could live next to each other and coexist. Restoration of capitalism, a return to free enterprise and competition – "all that, no doubt, is economic romanticism" [Weber (1947, p. 317)].

With the advantage of hindsight we may state that some kind of American world economy did indeed develop. However, it did so in two ways. One was the rather "pure economic" form of monopoly capitalism whose field of expansion was above all Western Europe. The other fell back on imperialism, though new forms of imperialism [cf. Magdoff (1969)], and spread mainly over South-East Asia and South America. The universal economic crisis of the Seventies corresponds to a crisis of the American world economy manifesting itself in the end of the Vietnam war and in the decline of the dollar.

As far as Europe is concerned things are not that easy, even if looked at in such a superficial way. In this context it might be useful to recall Schumpeter's scenario of "The march into socialism" (1950), which in many respects is similar to that of Weber. The march into socialism is defined by Schumpeter as "a conquest of private industry and trade by the state" [Schumpeter (1950, p. 446)]. He presents it as a consequence of social and cultural change from capitalist value systems with success and power uppermost, to postcapitalist value systems with security, equality, and stability as primary objectives.

After wars, we are told, it is inflation that accelerates social change most. And perennial inflationary pressure is built into a system where the generally accepted objectives demand a high level of employment and where the structure determines wages and thus the money costs of labour in a bargaining process between groups with different interests. Resulting conflicts, problems, and crises call for administrative or bureaucratic regulation. In general, the well-determined character of modern economic processes makes them accessible to administrative planning.

There can be no doubt that such developments can be found in the socio-economic history of Europe of the last 30 years. Those who for good, although normative, reasons advocated free enterprise and decentralization with more or less limited central controls [cf. for instance Verrijn Stuart (1947), Meade (1947), and Röpke (1948)] were immediately confronted with institutional changes that evidently pointed in a different direction: major nationalizations in Great Britain, the setting up of a planning office and indicative planning in France, the joint operation of a Central Planning Bureau and the Social and Economic Council (SER) in the Netherlands, for example.

It is arguable, however, whether it was really socialism that emerged. For free socialism, which was expected by Weber and which he characterized by the "setting-free of spontaneous self-determination . . . in the production process" [Weber (1947, p. 315)], certainly needed a different systemic framework than that developing in postwar Europe. Similarly, Schumpeter's idea that the dynamic forces which had propelled capitalism would dwindle away entered into conflict with his very own idea of epochal changes. The war had created such changes: destruction, demographic movements, innovations in aircraft, electronic and other industries, new management and planning techniques. In spite of growing state intervention and regulation there was ample scope for capitalist initiative to prove its superior dynamic properties. There was a considerable amount of free competition, though on a more international scale consistent with concentration at the national level. For whatever the bell tolled in the Fifties and Sixties, it did not toll for capitalism.

These inconclusive tendencies will have to be analysed more deeply in the following sections in order to be able to evaluate the postwar systemic development in Western Europe. Eastern Europe must be left aside, although the determination of its economic system – after some few years of indifference – by the confrontation of the two superpowers is plainly evident. However, we shall have to bear the existence of these types of socialism and the so-called "competition of systems" in mind. For it can partly explain the necessity of stabilization and growth in the Western systems.

3. The changing role of the state

The classical paradigm of the capitalist economic system is its autonomous and un-political functioning. The role of the state consisted in the neutral provision and en-forcement of laws, the monetary system, and internal and external security. Even if it ever was, such a paradigm can no longer be regarded as representative. The question, however, is to what extent the borderline between the economic system and the political system, the state, has been dissolved. Does the state have a universal power of intervention such that there is no sphere of autonomous private decision-making left, and what remains of private activity must be regarded as licensed autonomy or decentralized administration of orders [Offe (1974, p. 271)]? Or can we speak only of a complementary relationships between the capitalist economic system and the state such that the state has a general responsibility for the functioning of the economic system but may not directly participate in it except in cases where lack of profitability bars private enterprise [Habermas (1976, p. 287)]?

The first opinion seems to be going too far. It blurs the distinction between the modern capitalist state and its East European socialist counterpart, which is directly operative in the production process. There is no sound empirical basis for the statement that decisions in private enterprise derive from politics or public enterprise. However, the fields for public enterprise and politics have been widened and concomitantly the scope and extent of private property rights have been limited. But despite the all-pervasiveness of state regulations, the latter are still predominant in the economic spheres of production and circulation. The state has powerful instruments for regulating certain aspects of the design and quality of products, the location and shape of industrial settlements and housing, and the social and environmental qualities of production processes. And such regulations are certainly not cost-neutral. But the final decisions on what to produce, how much to produce and with which inputs, and whether or not to invest and in which assets, still rests with entrepreneurs or a managerial bureaucracy.

From this it follows that we can distinguish two areas of decision-making with respect to the economy: the political of the state and the economic of the enterprise. With different intensity a trend towards broader participation can be observed for both in the last decades. This has had a stabilizing effect: the general opposition to the capitalist system from the labour movement has lost some of its impact. Employed wage-earners as a class or a social group have gained in power since their specific interests became integrated through the competition of political parties, social "partnership" with fully acknowledged trade unions and co-determination at enterprise level. The actual distribution of decision-making power is hard to assess, and this is not the place to make such an attempt. The general tendency, however, can hardly be disputed.

This development necessarily has three major consequences in the field of economic decision-making:

(1) a quasistate-organ status of political parties and trade unions,

(2) a greater inflexibility as to changes, and

(3) a certain degree of selectivity as to interests.

While the first seems to be self-evident, let me explain the latter two kinds of consequences. A single entrepreneur with unrestricted private property rights will act only in accordance with his personal interests (which may be indirectly linked to other people's interests). He can react to changes and take risks at will. With broader participation in decision-making more interests will be directly represented. That is to say, more risks will have to be taken into account and the necessity for a certain unanimity will reduce flexibility. The corresponding stabilization effect is detrimental only if it leads to immobility.

In the welfare state's mass democracy with private enterprise, however, universal participation does not mean that all interests are equally well represented and served. For such interests as are capable of organization and enforcement will get preferential treatment [Offe (1974, p. 275 et seq.)]. Interests of more or less homogeneous status groups can be organized most easily, e.g. of farmers, workers, and doctors. And interests of groups in a more or less monopolistic position can be organized most effectively, since in a perfect competitive environment the activity of an individual or a group can by definition have no sanctionative effect. We therefore expect certain interests (of housewives or students, for instance) to exist for which the political regulation system offers inadequate provision.

Together with its increasing role in economic decision-making, the state has assumed responsibility for more and more functional aspects of the system. It has been said that there is a "general responsibility of the state for failures" [Habermas (1976, p. 289)]. The most severely felt failure of the classical capitalist system was its recurrent economic crisis. With the advent of Keynesian economic policy the state took responsibility for stable growth and full employment. Although the postwar record in that respect is not bad at all [cf. Lundberg (1968, p. 22 et seq.)], the instruments of monetary and fiscal policy do not seem to be a panacea.

Besides this more general aspect of modern state activity, several parts of the system have been identified in which the state increasingly participates. They have been called by Kuznets (1971, p. 253):

(a) the new industrial state,

  (b) the new military state,
  (c) the new welfare state, and
  (d) the new scientific state.

The new industrial state, which has extensively been dealt with by Galbraith (1969), is a result of structural and technological changes which led to large production units and called for regulation. The modern corporation has a quasipublic status. We return to the process of concentration in the following section. At the same time externalities and extreme scale factors or the shortsightedness of private interests made state activity necessary in certain fields.

The new military state is formed by the military–industrial complex. It is the result of increased international instability. Unlike the British world economy before 1914 the American world economy was unable to provide for a stable "pax americana" – not least because it reigned over only half of the world. The new welfare state is the best known and most directly felt aspect of the modern system development. Here we are thinking of mass education and health provision on an ever-increasing scale.

More generally one can state that the changed power situation in the economic system has made it possible to lower the individual and social costs of the capitalist production process to the workers or to compensate for them. Industrial safety measures, improvement of work, social security payments and guaranteed minimum wages are characteristic of this aspect of the modern welfare state. It has been said [for instance by Lindbeck (1977, p. 10)] that the state and other institutions have taken over services formerly provided by households: services for children, old people, the sick, and the physically and mentally handicapped. It certainly is true that the function of the family has changed. But the point to be made here is that only the capitalist production process has separated work and family life, produced and used wage labour, and for the rest has relied upon the family to provide an ever-increasing labour supply and to meet all socialization and personal security needs without compensation. It could be argued that the rapid postwar economic growth would have suffered from insufficient labour supply (especially of unskilled female labour) if the welfare state had not taken over social obligations from the family.

This point perhaps needs some further explanation. The strengthening of mass democracy almost tautologically meant an improvement in the social position of the working class. In nineteenth-century capitalism certain social costs of production (unemployment, industrial accidents, sickness, environmental pollution, for instance) had to be taken care of outside the economic system. The history of socio-economic legislation is certainly older than thirty years. But what we can observe over the last thirty years is an extremely rapid internalization of these social costs. Inside the economic system enterprises partly include these costs in the prices – a very important aspect of cost push – while a system of social insurance and transfer payments partly compensates for them. In this context it does not seem absurd to conclude that a great deal of what we call welfare is straight costs of social production. The improved position of the workers has made these costs explicit, has enforced their internalization, and has provided for their redistribution to some extent at the expense of profit income.

The new scientific state, finally, reflects the increasing role that science plays in economic growth. State activity in this respect derives both from the sheer size and risk of research and development investments and from the consideration that far-reaching inventions should be socially controlled. Seen from the other side, it also reflects the possibility that private enterprise has of externalizing certain costs of research and development.

We may conclude from this part of our analysis that up to now the state has not taken over economic activity from private enterprise. It has become active in certain fields but in general we are left with free market, private enterprise capitalism. The things that have changed, and in some instances drastically changed, are property rights and with them the cost situation of private enterprise and the social production process in general. State regulation and state activity have created new costs that were absent or minor – in education and social security for instance. Other costs have thus become internalized in the field of business: industrial safety and environmental pollution, for example. For some other costs it has become possible to externalize them from the private sphere: for instance, research and development and certain risks.

4. Concentration

The changing role of the state is one aspect of the very explicit trend towards centralization. The other aspect is the process of concentration, which has increased during the postwar period. Both aspects together are perhaps responsible for a number of consequences typical of the prevailing economic system.

The concentration of industrial firms is undisputed. The process has been going on for the whole capitalist epoch. It has accelerated over the last 30 years or so, especially in the last decade. This is not the place to discuss extensively the reasons for this development, although they might be most important for the conclusions to be drawn. The argument that this happened by force of (international) competition and that it can be taken as proof of an intact market rather than the opposite, is only half the story. The other half is that in most cases concentration is performed in order to circumvent the market or to avoid competition (also on an international scale). The fact that a big and more autarkic country like the US is no exception to the rule [see for instance Sherman (1976, p. 137 et seq.)] suggests that internal factors are certainly at work too. The most typical postwar development in this respect is the rise of the multinational corporation, which must also be seen as an attempt by private business to evade state regulation.

Even with strong though highly concentrated competition from abroad it is evident that the process of concentration leads to an oligopolistic or monopolistic market structure with increased degrees of freedom of action for the corporation. In the field of commerce and finance this has obvious advantages for big firms. Here it should be added that there is not only a formal process of concentration manifesting itself in a faster growth of big firms and in mergers but also an informal one in the guise of cartels, collusion, interlocking directorates, and bank control. It depends on national policy regulations whether the one or the other is more important: Great Britain seems to have more mergers than West Germany, France and Italy because of stricter legislation against restrictive trade practices [George and Ward (1975, pp. 25, 26)] or because in the latter countries trade policies are more antitrust oriented. But in itself this does not mean that business in these countries is less concentrated than in Great Britain.

Considering the increasing economic power of industrial firms one may ask whether the other parties constituting the market, workers and consumers, can keep up with that pace. For the consumers this may duly be questioned. The increasing power of the unions, however, is a commonplace for most conservative critics of the system. Judging by the criterion of union membership there are no significant changes in the period under investigation. Nevertheless, it would.be rash to conclude from this that unchanged power of the unions is confronted by a concentrated power of capital (the situation in the US on which Sherman (1977, pp. 154, 155) dwells is different from that in Western Europe). Indeed, labour is even more concentrated, it would seem, than capital. Here the quasistate-organ character of the unions already mentioned comes in. In collective bargaining they represent not only their members but also the total labour force. They do the same in near-government institutions like concerted action in West Germany or the SER in the Netherlands. Moreover, there is a certain relation between visible business and labour concentration, since in large monopolistic firms workers are concentrated in one place, which makes it easier to organize them [Sherman (1977, p. 162)].

The increased power of the workers is reflected not only in the market position of their unions. The changed role of the state in modern mass democracy also has something to do with it too. Labour-oriented political parties found wide support from the electorate and in many cases were able to participate in government, or to form it. This did not bring about an immediate revolution in the system, but certain system reforms in the fields of income distribution, social security and health and education may be ascribed to this fact.

5. Some consequences

When it comes to assessing the consequences and problems linked with the above developments in the system, we concentrate on the critical points rather than dwell on clearly positive results like greater security and better education. For probably it is the critical points that can explain some of the difficulties with which Western economies have to contend at present.

(1) *Greater stability and higher growth.* A couple of years ago this was listed among the unquestionably positive points mainly ascribed to an active state policy [cf. Lundberg (1968, pp. 24–26)]. With our recent experience the statement has to be qualified, although I think it still to be true. It depends on the variables which we consider (GNP, total consumption, individual consumption) and on our valuation of growth. Thus, growth rates decelerated and major unemployment again became a fact in the Seventies. Individual consumption, however, remained extraordinarily stable at the same time.

(2) *Inflation.* In contrast to classical nineteenth-century capitalism and also to the prewar period, prices have tended to rise permanently in the last 30 years. This is one of the major consequences of concentration in business which gives the firms strong price-fixing powers, with the effect that profits can be maintained even in periods of slowdown. On the other hand, there can be little doubt about the fact that concentration of labour power makes it possible for the second variant of cost-push inflation – wage inflation – to come into effect. It would be shortsighted, however, to consider only the latter and to disregard the former. The state, too, plays a role in this game, since it has to provide for the necessary quantity of money to finance inflation. There is little known about the manifest reasons for doing so. But, with the state's latent responsibility for stable growth, inflation seemed for a time to alleviate destabilizing social conflicts.

(3) *Efficiency.* In more general terms we might state that the control functions of the market have been reduced by concentration and state intervention. This will affect allocative efficiency. But nobody knows as yet the precise effects on what Leibenstein called X-efficiency and on dynamic efficiency. Perhaps even more important are the repercussions on informational efficiency. Centralization, in general, has a detrimental effect on this. But if we take uncertainty and risk into account, this statement becomes less self-evident [cf. Arrow (1974, p. 33 et seq.)].

Within the dualistic decision-making structure of the modern economic system, private business controls the bulk of economic information, which makes effective state regulation a rather doubtful affair. For the state will receive only such information as private business thinks necessary or advantageous to pass on.

(4) The remark by Lindbeck (1977, p. 14) must be taken along the same lines: "A national economy will be in serious trouble if the rate of return on bargaining with public authorities becomes higher than the rate of return on market activities." Although state intervention and regulation tends to remain general and nonspecific, the quasipublic status of big corporations counteracts such intentions.

(5) *Income distribution.* It is often held that increased labour power has changed functional income distribution in favour of labour. If labour power has indeed increased and if power is an income-determining factor, such a statement ought to be true. However, an important qualification must be added: evidence shows that the share of direct income from labour has not increased in the postwar period [cf. Glastetter (1977, p. 134) and Huppes (1977, pp. 62, 63)]. It is the share of social payments, which in a way compensate for the above-mentioned social costs of production, that has increased at the expense of profits.

In a private enterprise system this means that the firm's cost of employing labour has risen. Entrepreneurs will react with labour-substituting "rationalizations". These most probably will increase the social costs of production, and we enter a system-inherent vicious circle. In the longer run, however, its viciousness may be less obvious: if unskilled labour becomes too expensive because of minimum wage regulations, the better employment chances of skilled labour might increase the demand for qualifications and hence the cost of education. The final outcome will be a more even distribution of income and a higher stock of human capital.

Such a development is rather typical of postwar Europe. It has had the ultimate effect that even under minimum wage regulations there has been an insufficient supply of unskilled labour. This has led to the recruitment of foreign labour from less developed countries, forming a sizable proportion of the total labour force and coexisting with unemployment in times of a slowdown.

(6) *International interdependence.* Whereas concentration has given degrees of freedom to oligopolistic national firms, the increased international competition has decreased the degrees of freedom of the nation states. The high export dependence of most Western European economies makes an autonomous national policy almost impossible. Despite its increased importance in the economic system, the state's margin of action is narrow and in all its decisions and regulations it has to take into account the international competitiveness of the economy. If the market has loosened its control of the big corporations, it has gained control of the nation states.

(7) *Allocation.* In a private enterprise market economy the state has almost no income from production. It must finance its activities out of taxes and other derived incomes. The growing number of interventions and tasks performed by the state which are deemed necessary inevitably calls for a broadened income base of the state, that is to say for a higher degree of income diversion.

In principle there is no upper limit to the share of taxes and other such payments in national income. It is thought, however, that an "excessive" share might have detrimental effects on the allocative functions of the market. This will be the case if taxes and state regulations are non-neutral within the productive sphere of the economy, which sometimes (despite theories on lump-sum taxes and payments) is their outspoken intention. If allocative distortions then become too great, corrective countermeasures have to be taken, with the effect that state regulations call for further state regulations, etc.

(8) *Motivation.* One of the most complex problems in this respect concerns the increasing disjunction of income from labour and opportunities in life. The extended public provision for education and health, for instance, has greatly reduced the (intergenerational) income dependence of the satisfaction of these basic needs.

The allocative functions of the market would be more affected by a growing disconnection of performance and gratification. Without entering the extensive debate on this point, I would suggest that in an oligopolistic system where cost-plus pricing is the rule rather than the exception this might be a minor problem. About the motivational effects of such a gap, little can be said. They might turn out to be quite important as long as income is the only reward one gets from work. Again, X-efficiency, of which we know very little, seems to be the more important criterion.

(9) I now mention a final consequence of the systemic changes which has been pointed to by Offe (1974, p. 283). Nineteenth-century capitalism was characteristic of horizontal class differences determined by the control of the means of production. These differences greatly influenced the opportunities of individuals. Concentration, growing labour power, mass democracy and state intervention all had the effect of reducing the horizontal disproportionalities. In other words, social classes became less identifiable.

On the other hand, the problems of organization and enforcement of interests have created new disproportionalities which may be vertical or localized. This does not mean that capitalism has come to an end. It is still growth, the accumulation of capital, that reigns over our life. There is still a forceful element of private control over the means of production. The investment decisions of private business have remained untouched. But the conflicts in the system have become more impersonal: "With the compromise between classes built into the structure of late capitalism (almost) everybody is concerned and affected alike" [Habermas (1976, p. 310)].

6. Signs of a general crisis?

Looking at the socio-economic system of late capitalism, it is not far from the mark to describe it as "a coalition of Big Government, Big Business, and Big Unions" [Lindbeck (1977, p. 16)]. In this trilateral monopoly the state has the responsibility for the coherence and survival of the system. The high degree of concentration has two major effects on development: in the first instance decisions are taken at a very high level, and secondly any real conflict between the three would blow up the system which, as a matter of fact, would be in the interests of none of them.

Although we have stated that the interests of major groups of citizens are perhaps better represented in decision-making, this is not true of the individuals themselves. This can also be described in terms of a "high output versus a low input orientation" [Habermas (1976, p. 321)] of the individual. Because of a lack of participation at shop-floor level the gratification which one expects and derives from the social production process is mainly to be found in the sphere of consumption and not in the sphere of work. This is one of the system-inherent reasons why growth is necessary. With a long-term stagnation or decline of private consumption the motivation to contribute to the system would be drastically reduced. Thus, growth can be seen as the central *functional* problem of the system. However, all attempts to prove that accumulation leads internally to the stagnation of the capitalist system have thus far failed.

Like any bilateral monopoly, this trilateral one also constitutes a highly unstable situation. Workers and owners of capital can block the production process by strikes and lock-outs, and can do so on a nation-wide scale. By its nature government plays a more passive role. The three are tied together and must not rock the boat. That explains the above-mentioned compromise between classes.

The functional problem of the economic system can be specified in some greater detail:

(a) it has to satisfy the interests of the individual capitalist organization,

(b) it has to satisfy the interests of the production system as a whole, and

(c) it has to satisfy the interests of the mass of the population.

The interests of the individual capitalist organization are important insofar as at that level production in general and investments in particular are decided upon. We know very little about these investment decisions. We are told that they depend mainly on profit expectations. But whether profit expectations are influenced more by expected wage developments or by effective demand expected for the future makes for some differences in policy recommendations. Besides, the steadily growing share of exports in demand has increased the autonomous factors on which state intervention has little influence.

Thus, the interests of the production system as a whole – a matter of concern for all three parties, the general responsibility resting with the state – are determined by its international competitiveness and its stability. Total cost, the exchange rate, product quality and innovation, high employment and low inflation are crucial factors in this respect. The interests of the mass of the population are, as stated, mainly output-oriented. The legitimation of the state and hence the social stability of the system depend on a permanently growing output. (Incidentally, the Polish events of 1970 and 1976 showed that such problems are not unknown to Eastern European socialist systems either.)

Obviously, conflicts between the three spheres of interest can arise. They will be more fundamental between the last and the first two than for these two alone. Crises will occur within the existing system if conflicts are solved in such a way that one of these basic interests is neglected. In consequence the propensity to invest may decline, effective demand may be insufficient at a sectoral or a total level, government may become unstable or social unrest may even occur. A hypothesis of a permanent general crisis, however, must be able not only to explain the difficulties which the system managers have with the solution of their problems; it should also give the reason why in principle they are unable to solve them [cf. Habermas (1976, p. 318)].

Growth cum moderate inflation has proved a viable solution to most of the problems in the past. There is no inherent reason why growth cum moderate inflation should in principle be impossible for the future. The picture may change if we take external limits to growth into account, such as environmental limitations or exhausted natural resources. In such a case the system would need a lot more planning than seems consistent with its present structure.

7. Ways out of a dilemma?

The evaluation which the present state of the system gets from academic economists can best be read from their proposed changes deemed necessary to approach a more optimal situation. It is obvious that such proposals depend not only on the analytical insights but also on the political values of their proponents. Thus we have, for instance, the liberal view [e.g. Lindbeck (1977, pp. 19–24) and Bernholz (1977, pp. 588, 589)], the radical view [e.g. Sherman (1976, pp. 235–243)], and also the "intelligent radical" view [Meade (1975, pp. 14–16)], which is a more radical version of the liberal view. The basic difference between radicals and liberals lies in the importance liberals attach to private enterprise and the market mechanism, whereas radicals, though remaining extremely vague about the coordination mechanism, have a general preference for state activity and state control. Yet the recommendations concentrate on the same features of the present capitalist system.

The concentration of capital and economic decision-making power is the predominant point of concern. The radical solution to this problem is found in perfect centralization – the take-over of the economy by the state. The experience of Eastern Europe allows for certain doubts about the effectiveness of this solution. The more liberal proposals simply want to reverse the historical trend by breaking up big corporations, dissolving certain influential interest groups, and prohibiting collusive practices. Certain traits of naivety cannot be overlooked if it is proposed, for instance, that the persuasion of consumers be controlled by a tax on advertising [Bernholz (1977, p. 589)]. Since these authors do not interpret the process of concentration as a system-inherent development, they also fail to indicate the institutional changes by which such a reversal of the trend could be accomplished. Experience with antitrust legislation and other direct state intervention in the past is certainly not convincing. One has only to recall the breaking-up of the world's biggest chemical trust (IG Farben) into its three major constituent parts, which now are the world's three biggest chemical corporations, having partitioned the market among themselves.

Spreading the titles to ownership of these capital concentrations more evenly between households would probably make the system "more socially acceptable" [Lindbeck (1977, p. 22)]. But it does not change the inherent logic of capital accumulation, which functions independently of ownership relations as long as the system of property rights allows of a high degree of contractual freedom. Today, the capital market plays a minor role in financing private business. Thus, a redistribution of private wealth will perhaps have less effect on the operation of the economy than some people expect. This is, it seems, the dividing line between more conservative and more democratic liberals. The first prefer capital as the central control unit, seeking more pluralism in a better distribution of wealth [cf. Bernholz (1977, p. 589)]. The second prefer people as the central control unit, demanding a broader participation inside organizations and a broader base for recruiting managers of organizations [cf. Lindbeck (1977, pp. 21, 22)].

As far as the role of the state is concerned, the general philosophy is still greatly influenced by Hayek's "The road to serfdom" (1944). At the same time, however, recommendations tend to reflect the paradigm of an "optimum regime", as developed by Tinbergen (1959). Despite its theoretical foundations in normative welfare the optimum regime seems rather to be a rationalization and description of existing mixed systems in Western Europe with certain corrective proposals. Besides external and scale economies, public goods, the provision of equal opportunity and a general stabilization policy, more recent deliberations stress the necessity of coping with the uncertainties of the future by means of governmental indicative planning and of preparing major structural changes through central planning [cf. Meade (1975, pp. 102–109)].

Judging by these opinions in the literature one gets the impression that a broad group of economists is not basically discontented with the prevailing trends in postwar development and does not see in the changed role of the state a threat to future growth. On the contrary, it rather seems to be a precondition for more stable growth and innovations, as it has been during the last decades. Only the followers of Hayek's extreme individualism would like to see the nineteenth-century state return. The proposed deflation of social services resembles in a way the price deflation policies during the great depression and would probably have the same fatal effects.

8. Conclusions

When it comes to drawing conclusions we may ask: what has become of the march into socialism? The answer cannot be a simple one. It is evident that Schumpeter's rather pessimistic forecast did not come true: bureaucratic administration did not replace the market mechanism, although it should not be overlooked that the concentration process has greatly extended the field for bureaucratic administration inside organizations. But in terms of information, coordination and control, the price mechanism still seems to be a quite efficient system despite its distributional and stability disadvantages. Or, as Meade has put it: "the price mechanism is the worst possible form of economic system except the others" (1975, p. 123).

State activity has emerged not as a substitute for but as a complement to the market, with the result that the system of property rights has undergone major modifications. Compared with the prewar situation, the societies of Western Europe have already travelled a long way on the road to socialism. But, together with concentration of capital and labour power, the tendency towards centralization obstructed, if not prevented, a free and independent participation of individuals in the social production process, which was deemed a central feature of the evolving new socialist system by Weber.

The success story of postwar economies has been a story of the market mechanism complemented by state regulation and intervention. Private business and competition provided the dynamic forces while the state attended to the fulfilment of minimum distributional and stability requirements. An important point to be made concerns the permanent widening of the market beyond the borderlines of the nation states through growing international interdependence. The checking of autonomous market forces by national economic policies stops at the border. The great international markets or the world market in general operate under typically prewar conditions: there is no powerful institution to control the autonomous unfolding of the competitive forces, with the consequence of major instabilities and injustices. What obviously would be needed is a legitimized international order with the effective power to regulate and intervene in the development of the market on a supranational level.

It is only very recently that the problems of centralization have been recognized. But they demand major system reforms in order to be solved. For at present we are travelling in the opposite direction. Although the distribution of power has been changed through a strengthening of the labour side, no diversification has occurred, only a highly concentrated confrontation. The inherent conflict must be kept latent for the sake of maintenance of the system. Its only possibility of showing up is inflation, the sign of an unsuccessful attempt to squeeze the share of the others. If, however, the system's environment, for instance international competition, makes inflation more or less impossible, the conflicting expectations may lead to an open economic crisis. With flexible exchange rates this reasoning is less stringent.

Shares play a less important role if the absolute amounts possessed by everybody are increasing. Thus, growth has become the best lubricant and the basic criterion of legitimation for the postwar economic systems. On the whole they did very well in this respect when compared with any other previous period. There has been so much growth that as a system objective growth even became a point of debate. Yet, if our analysis is correct, growth is not a freely chosen objective but a structural function of the system. If you decide that growth is no longer desirable, you have to change the system.

At this point I bring into discussion Keynes's vision of fifty years ago: "The economic problem may be solved, or be at least within sight of solution, within a hundred years. ... If the economic problem is solved, mankind will be deprived of its traditional purpose" [Keynes (1972, pp. 326–327)]. The basic needs will be provided for more or less universally, technical progress will make traditional production work a scarce activity. The consequences of such developments are not only a change of the economic system. They ask for a complete reorientation of the social and personality systems. The step "out of the tunnel of economic necessity into daylight" [Keynes (1972, p. 331)] will be taken gradually, and Keynes may have been mistaken about the period involved, as were those two other economists who predicted it in almost the same wording some eighty years before him. We are now through half the period indicated by Keynes, and as far as material welfare and hours of work are concerned, a great deal of his optimistic predictions have come true. The accompanying systemic changes, however, seem to be oriented rather exclusively towards the traditional economic purpose and, moreover, they are slow. And this may explain the fact that in relative abundance we repeatedly suffer from economic crises.

References

Arrow, K. J., 1974, The limits of organization (Norton, New York).

Bernholz, P., 1977, Freiheit, Staat und Wirtschaft: Auf der Suche nach einer neuen Ordnung, Zeitschrift für die gesamte Staatswissenschaft 133, 575–590.

Galbraith, J. K. 1969, The new industrial state (Houghton Mifflin, Boston).

George, K. D. and T. S. Ward, 1975, The structure of industry in the EEC, an international comparison (Cambridge University Press, Cambridge).

Glastetter, W., 1977, Die wirtschaftliche Entwicklung der Bundesrepublik Deutschland im Zeitraum 1950 bis 1975 (Springer, Berlin, Heidelberg, New York).

Habermas, J., 1976, Zur Rekonstruktion des Historischen Materialismus (Suhrkamp, Frankfurt).

Hayek, F. A. von, 1944, The road to serfdom (Chicago University Press, Chicago).

Huppes, T., 1977, Inkomensverdeling en institutionele structuur (Stenfert Kroese, Leiden).

Keynes, J. M., 1972, Economic possibilities for our grandchildren, in: Essays in persuasion, The collected writings of John Maynard Keynes, vol. IX (Macmillan, London) pp. 321–332.

Kuznets, S., 1971, Notes on stage of economic growth as a system determinant, in: A. Eckstein, ed., Comparison of economic systems, Theoretical and methodological approaches (University of California Press, Berkeley, Los Angeles, London) pp. 243–267.

Lindbeck, A., 1977, Can pluralism survive? (The University of Michigan, Michigan).

Lundberg, E., 1968, Instability and economic growth (Yale University Press, New Haven).

Magdoff, H., 1969, The age of imperialism (Monthly Review Press, New York, London).

Meade, J. E., 1947, Planning and the price mechanism (Allen & Unwin, London).

Meade, J. E., 1975, The intelligent radical's guide to economic policy, The mixed economy (Allen & Unwin, London).

Offe, C., 1974, Politische Herrschaft und Klassenstrukturen, Zur Analyse spätkapitalistischer Gesellschaftssysteme, in: H. P. Widmaier, ed., Politische Ökonomie des Wohlfahrtsstaates (Fischer-Athenäum, Frankfurt) pp. 264–293.

Röpke, W., 1948, Die natürliche Ordnung, Die neue Phase der wirtschaftspolitischen Diskussion, Kyklos 2, 211–232.

Schumpeter, J. A., 1950, The march into socialism, American Economic Review, Papers and Proceedings 40, 446–456.

Sherman, H. J., 1976, Stagflation, A radical theory of unemployment and inflation (Harper & Row, New York).

Tinbergen, J., 1959, The theory of the optimum regime, in: Collected Papers (North-Holland, Amsterdam) pp. 264–309.

Verdoorn, P. J. and J. J. Post, 1969, Comparison of the prewar and postwar business cycles in the Netherlands: An experiment in econometrics, in: M. Bronfenbrenner, ed., Is the business cycle obsolete? (Wiley, New York) pp. 436–466.

Verrijn Stuart, C. A., 1947, Die Ursache des Strebens nach Wirtschaftsordnung, Kyklos 1, 131–150.

Wagener, H.-J., 1979, Zur Analyse von Wirtschaftssystemen (Springer, Berlin, Heidelberg, New York).

Weber, A., 1947, Kapitalistische Weltwirtschaft und Sozialismus, Kyklos 1, 299–320.

Chapter 2

p. 1 =

COMMENT ON WAGENER'S PAPER

T. HUPPES

19·23

University of Groningen

The main purpose of Wagener's paper is:

(a) to identify some longer-term developments in postwar Western countries, in particular the major institutional changes; and

(b) to investigate whether there are signs of a general crisis resulting from these institutional developments.

The author conceives of the institutional developments as a continuous process of centralization manifesting itself in:

(a) increasing state intervention in economic decision-making;

(b) a concentration of industrial firms, leading to an oligopolistic or monopolistic market structure; and

(c) greater power of the trade unions.

These developments lead Wagener to characterize the socio-economic system of late capitalism as "a trilateral monopoly" or, as Lindbeck calls it, "a coalition of Big Government, Big Business and Big Unions".

So far Wagener's paper evokes little comment. Few will challenge the fact that state activity has extended considerably in the last few decades. Nor will there be many likely to deny that firms have concentrated and that the unions have become more powerful. It is the second part of Wagener's paper, in which he analyses "the consequences of the postwar system developments" and the related "signs of a general crisis", to which I object. His list of consequences include high growth rates, permanent inflation, increasing government expenditure, greater social security and decreasing profits. Now there is no doubt that these phenomena are among the more salient aspects of postwar economic development. It is open to doubt, however, whether they should be regarded as the consequences of the trend towards centralization. A provisional confrontation with some facts will show that such a relation may be considered questionable.

Prospects of Economic Growth, edited by S. K. Kuipers and G. J. Lanjouw
© *North-Holland Publishing Company*

(1) *Economic growth*. Between 1955 and 1970 the average growth rate in West Germany, Italy and the Netherlands was twice that in the United Kingdom and the US. I wonder whether this difference can be accounted for by the fact that these countries had different system developments (in terms of state intervention or concentration of industrial firms). Numerical data might shed some light here.

(2) *Inflation*. The average rate of inflation between 1955 and 1970 also varied considerably: the US and West Germany display significantly lower rates (about 2.3 percent) than for instance the Netherlands and Sweden (about 3.7 percent). Again, I wonder whether Wagener would be able to show a satisfying cross-nation correlation between these rates and figures on concentration trends in the various countries.

(3) *Government expenditure*. Although the state has extended its power over economic life, the fact remains that in most Western countries the share of government expenditure in national income has risen by only a few percent. The growth of the collective sector (government expenditure plus social security payments) is almost wholly due to the rise in social security payments.

(4) *Social security payments and profits*. The drastic rise in social payments is indeed one of the most significant aspects of postwar economic development, the more so because of its remarkable consequences for profits. As Wagener remarks quite rightly, social payments rose at the expense of profits: the sum of the share of social payments and the share of profits remained virtually constant, just like the share of direct income from labour. In my book *Inkomensverdeling en institutionele structuur* (1977) I have pointed to these developments and shown that growth rates and the rise of social payments may be considered closely related, theoretically as well as empirically. Wagener seems to reject these findings, and instead offers a rather vague explanation of the rise of social payments in terms of "a compensation for the social costs of the capitalist production process" and "the changed power situation in the economic system". I return to these matters at the end of this comment.

First, however, I will discuss the part which, according to Wagener, has been played by postwar growth and inflation in maintaining late capitalism and preventing a general crisis. His view bears some resemblance to the Frankfurter Marxism à la Habermas. We are told that the trilateral monopoly between Government, Business and Unions constitutes "a very unstable situation, . . . any real conflict between the three would blow up the system". Thanks to economic growth such fatal conflicts have been avoided so far. Wagener: "Because of a lack of participation at shop-floor level . . . the interests of the mass of the population are . . . mainly output-oriented. The legitimation of the state and hence the social stability of the system depend on a permanently growing output." It will be clear that Wagener regards economic growth as "a system-inherent necessity".

Postwar inflation is another factor which has helped to stabilize Western economies: ". . . inflation seemed for a time to alleviate destabilizing social conflicts . . . . If the system's environment, for instance international competition, makes inflation more or less impossible, the conflicting expectations may lead to an open economic crisis." It is not surprising, therefore, to find that in section 6 Wagener comes to the conclusion that economic growth and inflation have prevented a general crisis. In the future, too, growth and inflation seem to him to offer a viable solution to "the inherent conflicts of late capitalism". It follows that zero growth in the present system is impracticable: ". . . growth is not a freely chosen objective but a structural function of the system. If you decide that growth is no longer desirable, you have to change the system."

My main objection to this kind of reasoning is that it can hardly be falsified. As long as growth and inflation continue – and there is every appearance that they will for some time – it is possible for Wagener to maintain his point of view. Unless of course his argument implies that different growth and inflation rates are attended by different numerical values of stability or conflict indicators. But I assume that the author would regard this implication as too specific. If so the dispute will remain unsettled. Needless to say, I do not share his a priori view of society.

Although space is limited, I will submit some of my own views on the matter as a counterbalance. It is my view that the postwar development of Western countries should be qualified as historically unique, more than anything else, mainly because of three marked characteristics:

(1) an unprecedented economic growth, which as often as not caused the real income per head to be doubled or even tripled;

(2) an unprecedented rise in social security payments, coupled with a complementary fall in the share of profits; and

(3) an unprecedented, permanent inflation.

Both theoretically and empirically these processes seem interdependent. The theoretical relation between characteristics (1) and (2), discussed in *Inkomensverdeling en institutionele structuur*, may be found with the aid of the evolutionary paradigm from institutional economics, which regards the development of science and technology, or economic growth, as the main cause of institutional change (see table 2.1).

There is method in these changes, for they tend in the direction of social equalization. For instance, Myrdal (1976): ". . . in the Western countries social equalization goes together with economic growth in circular causation and with cumulative effects". In sociology, too, this tendency is recognized: "Among the factors believed to bring about the decline of social inequality, a special place is generally assigned to economic growth ... The faith in the equalizing effect of economic growth is shared alike by adherents of socialism and capitalism" [Béteille (1969, p. 364)]. Thus, the rise in social payments may be regarded as an aspect of social equalization: those who, through no fault of their own, are incapable of providing for themselves, have come to be considered equal fellow-citizens, entitled to financial independence. In the long run it is

Table 2.1

Some major postwar trends in selected Western countries (growth, social payments, inflation), 1955–1970.

Countries	ΔQ Average growth (ind. prod.) [a]	ΔS increase in social payments (% nat. inc.) [b]	ΔP average inflation [c]
Canada	4.9	7.2	2.40
West Germany	6.7	7.1	2.42
Italy	7.2	6.9	2.93
The Netherlands	6.6	9.3	3.66
Sweden	6.2	8.4	3.81
UK	2.9	4.6	(3.67)
US	3.5	5.4	2.34

[a] Source: *Economic Survey of Europe* (UN, New York, 1969 Part 1, 1970);
   The Growth of World Industry, vol. 1 (UN, New York, 1974).
[b] Source: *The Cost of Social Security* (ILO, Geneva, 1961, 1964, 1967, 1972, 1976).
[c] Source: *Economic Survey of Europe* (UN, New York, 1970 Part II, 1973, 1976);
   Main Economic Indicators (OECD, Paris, 1960, 1967, 1972).

"the general views of society about what is fair and equitable" [United Nations (1967, ch. 5, p. 33)] manipulated by the state and unions with varying success which determine the course of social payments. This leads one to expect a greater rise in fast-growing countries than in countries with low growth rates. The facts do not refute this relation: the cross-nation correlation for a number of prominent Western countries (including the Netherlands) between 1955 and 1970 is 0.85

$$\Delta S = 2.08\Delta Q + 3.86 \qquad (R = 0.85).$$
$$(t = 3.26) \tag{1}$$

The relation between characteristics (2) and (3) is easier to grasp. As stated, the sum of the share of profits and the share of social payments has remained constant in the last few decades, as has the remaining share of direct labour income (= share of labour minus social security payments). This implies that wage increases have kept abreast of the rise in labour productivity. In other words, the rise in wage costs has been caused solely by the rise in social payments. Thus, it stands to reason that the differences in inflation between the various countries are related to the divergent rise in social payments (or the divergent decrease in profits). Here, too, the relation is not refuted by the facts. Apart from the UK, whose inflation was much increased by the sharp devaluation of the pound, the cross-nation correlation for the years between 1955 and 1970 is 0.84:

$$\Delta P = 11.69\Delta S + 2.45 \qquad (R = 0.84).$$
$$(t = 3.02) \tag{2}$$

In summary, I agree with Wagener that the institutional changes in postwar Western countries have been many and comprehensive. On the matter of the nature and the direction of these changes, however, our ways part: while acknowledging the trend towards centralization, it is my view that the trend towards equalization (foreseen by Schumpeter) should be considered at least as important. Finally, with regard to the relation between institutional changes and the main economic processes, such as economic growth, our views are incompatible.

References

Béteille, A., ed., 1969, Social inequality (Penguin, Harmondsworth).
Huppes, T., 1977, Inkomensverdeling en institutionele structuur (Stenfert Kroese, Leiden).
Myrdal, G., 1976, Chairman's introduction, in: A. de Beuck and J. Knight, eds., Caste and race (Churchill, London).
United Nations, 1967, Incomes in post-war Europe (UN Publications, New York).

Chapter 3

p. 1:

COMMENT ON WAGENER'S PAPER

J. WEITENBERG

25 - 33

Central Planning Bureau/University of Groningen

1. Introduction

It is hard to disagree with Wagener when he describes the trends during the postwar period in the economic systems of the industrialized countries in Western Europe. He is right when he establishes a tendency towards concentration among private enterprises in the market sector. This concentration refers especially to the command of capital, i.e. to the decision-making process in the business sector. He is also right when he notes that the power of the unions has strongly increased, notwithstanding the fact that the degree of union membership by employed persons has not increased at all. Finally, it cannot be denied that the concentration among both capital and labour has been accompanied by increasing state regulation and intervention.

Wagener even concludes that these three tendencies have amounted to a trilateral monopoly, between which an unstable balance exists. Both capital and labour could take action that would disturb this balance. This, however, would imply the destruction of the economic system as such, in which neither these two parties nor the state are interested. It is considered the special responsibility of the state to attend to the continuation of the economic system. This would require the state to maintain the subtle balance between capital and labour. The potential conflicts between capital and labour, which are due to divergent interests, do not become manifest provided there is sufficient economic growth. Inflation too can contribute to keeping these conflicts below the surface. From this the author concludes that growth cum moderate inflation is essential to the survival of the economic system in the Western world.

As I have said, it is hard to disagree with Wagener's description of postwar developments. An agreement with facts, however, does not necessarily imply that the analysis of the underlying factors behind the facts is endorsed, nor that the in-

Prospects of Economic Growth, edited by S. K. Kuipers and G. J. Lanjouw
© *North-Holland Publishing Company*

terdependencies between the facts are subscribed to. In his analysis Wagener remains somewhat vague and leaves the reader much room for speculation. Without stating this explicitly, he suggests that the tendencies described are inherent in the market system. My basic objection to Wagener's analysis is that he fails to draw the inescapable conclusion from his analysis. If the tendencies are inextricably bound up with the capitalist system, they will continue as long as such a system exists. More and more regulations and intervention by the state would be required. Inevitably this would be accompanied by a further restriction of individual freedom, both in the field of property rights and in the domain of civil contracts. Under those circumstances not only are the essential characteristics of the market economy expunged, but the market system also loses its dynamic properties. It then indeed becomes doubtful whether the Western economies will be able to continue their economic growth. The basic condition for the survival of the market system would in that case no longer be fulfilled.

If the tendencies described are not immanent, which I hope to demonstrate, a more optimistic view with respect to continuation of the market system is justified. For, if the concentration and centralization tendencies happen not to be bound up with the market mechanism, policies and institutional modifications to reverse the trends described may be considered.

To answer the question raised above, the tendencies mentioned have to be investigated very thoroughly. In particular, attention has to be paid to common elements in the concentration and centralization processes. This will be done in the following sections. Some conclusions will end this comment.

2. Some tendencies during the postwar period

The concentration of industrial firms is undisputed, Wagener states. He argues that it has always been an essential feature of the capitalist system, but this process has accelerated tremendously during the postwar period. Wagener does not go into the reasons behind the accelerated process of concentration, although he admits that this might be most important for the conclusions to be drawn. He adheres to the inconclusive statement that on the one hand the process of concentration has been stimulated by closer international competition, but that on the other the avoidance of free competition has at the same time also contributed to faster growth of already large firms. In both cases an oligopolistic or monopolistic market structure has been the result, and consequently individual firms have acquired more opportunities to manipulate their prices.

First, it has to be shown that concentration is inherent in the capitalist system. As far as concentration stems from economies of scale, this may be seriously doubted. To realize such scale effects, concentration is inevitable, independently of the ruling economic system. It is a fact that the basic industries (oil refining, bulk chemistry, metallurgical industries), electrical industries and the transport facilities industries (cars, ships, aircraft) have undergone a more than average rate of growth since the Second World War. In all those branches of industry positive scale effects play a dominant role. It then goes without saying that this has been accompanied by more concentration within the industrial sector as a whole. Efficiency rather than price considerations underlies this development. Of course, governments should be aware that consumers too take advantage of these scale effects. A favourable condition was that during the same postwar period protective barriers were demolished, so that competition no longer stopped at national borders.

In this context it is striking that Wagener does not mention the founding of the European Community, the birth of the European Free Trade Association and the various GATT rounds. Through these developments markets were enlarged and national firms were able to make larger product series, which also contributed to lowering costs. Anyhow, statistics do not confirm that profit margins have become extraordinarily high in the large-scale sectors. If anything the opposite is the case.

There are other motives for concentration besides economies of scale. Concentration will also occur in sectors where large amounts have to be invested in research and development. Fine chemicals and electronics are sectors that put much effort into research, and here too concentration tendencies are at work. Again it is not the economic system but the technical character of the production process that determines the concentration tendency.

Another motive for concentration is the spreading of risks. Monoproduction makes a firm more vulnerable to cyclical and structural developments, which can considerably differ from sector to sector. Diversification of activities and enlarging the number of markets (countries) served may reduce these risks. If I am correct, this factor played a dominant role in the postwar concentration process. Mergers and take-overs often had to do with the combining of dissimilar activities. This kind of concentration seems typical of the capitalist system. In general it does not involve monopolistic or oligopolistic pricing. Experience shows that sooner or later quite a large number of mergers of this kind prove unsuccessful, not to say failures. Each activity requires its own expertise, and activities that are not identical cannot simply be combined. Against this background it is understandable that an intensification of legislation in the field of mergers is taken into consideration.

A last motive for concentration is the abolition of fair price-competition. This motive cannot be denied, but it has not caused major problems in the postwar period. Extension of the relevant legislation, improvement of information and sometimes moral suasion have been able to prevent the abuse of concentration for this purpose.

What conclusions can be drawn from the preceding description? First, in order to realize economies of scale there has been a lot of concentration in the Western economies. This was not only promoted by changes in the composition of industrial activities, but was also fostered by the enlargement of markets. Concentration also became manifest in technologically advanced sectors, where a great deal of effort is put into research and development. Secondly, both phenomena have a technical background, and are not typical of the capitalist system. Thirdly, concentration occurred to diversify risks or to manipulate prices. These latter motives seem inherent in the capitalist system, but either proved to be unsuccessful or were combated by adequate legislation or regulation by the state.

3. Has labour become more powerful?

Has labour become more powerful in the postwar period, as observed by Wagener? I think so, but I am not certain whether or not we share the same line of reasoning. However, first the facts have to be looked at.

What are the signs that indicate a more powerful position of labour in general, and the unions in particular? It is indeed a fact that the degree of union membership by employed persons has hardly changed at all. About one-third of employed persons nowadays belong to a union – a participation rate that does not differ significantly from the situation in the early Fifties. Yet the power of the unions has increased. One indication is the closer cooperation between individual unions. There is nowadays a limited number of big federations of unions, while the natural differences in strategy between the nondenominational and the denominational unions have lost their sharp edges in the course of the time. Through this the traditional weapons of labour have become more effective, without causing higher costs.

A second hint is that the scope of collective wage agreements has been extended. Not only are hourly wage rates, overtime payments, etc. settled in the contracts, but more and more attention has been paid to fringe benefits and the like. For purposes of illustration the following items may serve: arrangements for special leave and early retirement, working conditions on the job, procedures in the event of layoffs, managerial and board appointments, the provision of information with respect to investment decisions, mergers, etc. All of these conditions are aimed at improving the position of the worker. By declaring these agreements legally binding, employees can go to court if conditions are infringed by the employer.

These settlements were initially meant to protect the position of the low-paid workers. In the course of time the better-paid employees were also brought under collective wage agreements. So the extension refers both to the scope of the settlements and to the number of employees who can base their rights on these contracts.

One more clue can be mentioned. As observed correctly by Wagener, the character of the unions has changed. Nowadays they feel themselves responsible for the more spiritual interests of their members. They try to influence the politicians in their political decision-making process, in order to change society in a direction which is more acceptable to their members. Apart from moral suasion and their willingness to cooperate in the field of wage policies, unions have threatened in the past to use their traditional weapons (strikes, boycotts, etc.), and sometimes did in order to "convince" the politicians of the importance they attach to certain social reforms. Indeed, from this it may be concluded that the unions have acquired a semipublic status.

All these facts confirm that the power of the unions has grown during the postwar period. This, however, does not explain how this could happen. Was it only a natural reaction to the more concentrated power of capital, just to cope with the new situation? This reasoning is incomplete and I agree with Wagener when he points out that political parties became aware of the interests of the employed wage-earners. Because of the progress of political democracy, the electorate became more conscious of its political power. Political parties had to compete more severely for votes by paying explicit attention to the interests of numerically important groups. Personally I consider this factor of the utmost importance. Through this process the power of the unions increased tremendously, the more so because the share of employed wage-earners in the total labour force had been continuously growing.

But there are additional explanations. Young graduates have entered the unions, which has resulted in more professional strategies. Moreover, the composition of the union members has changed. The proportion of workers employed in the nonmarket sectors (education, health, social welfare, government administration) has grown. These sectors are not faced with a price mechanism, nor do they suffer from international competition. Consequently, the general attitude with respect to economic laws has gradually altered. Finally, the increased relations between the various branches of industry have to be mentioned. Actions with low input costs for the unions therefore caused higher output effects for society as a whole.

The conclusion of this section is that the power of labour during the postwar period has strongly increased, far more than that of capital. The most important factor seems to me the progress of democracy, which forced political parties to pay a great deal more attention to the interests of employed wage-earners. But other factors, like a more professional management of the unions, intensified relations between sectors and a declining share of employment in the market sectors played a role too.

4. The changed role of the state

I agree with Wagener when he declares that the role of the state has changed since the Second World War. The state has become far more responsible for the operation of the economy. The decision-making processes in politics and economics have been much more integrated. Wagener indicates that the increased role of the state was necessary for the survival of our economic system. The balance between Big Business and Big Unions is so unstable that a Big Government is required to take care of the problems and the conflicts between these two big powers. This suggests that government is rather passive and reacts only to changes in the relations between capital and labour. However, this view ignores the fact that the size and the power of the state are affected by other factors too. An investigation of the determinants behind the evolution of the public sector may therefore be useful.

It cannot be denied that the public sector has grown substantially. Wagener mentions four domains of increased state activity, namely industry, defence, welfare provisions and scientific research. Again I agree with him, but this enumeration does not explain why the state became more involved in these areas. To me the growth of state activities has to do with the following factors:

(a) economic growth: the government supplies goods and provisions with a higher than average income elasticity;

(b) increased complexity: as a consequence of the increased specialization, the urbanization, the population density and the changed character of industrial activities (pollution, safety, etc.), more regulation is required for a smooth functioning of society;

(c) changed attitudes: owing to improved education and information the shortcomings of society are examined more closely; this has resulted in a replacement of private activities by public activities (health, social security, etc.); and

(d) the decision-making process in the public sector: the weighing of benefits and costs has become looser because the interests of groups who pay little or no tax have been better protected by the politicians.

Progress of democracy, advance in technology and growth of welfare appear to be decisive elements in the explanation of the expansion of the public sector. In many Western countries close to 50 percent, and for some countries even more, of the national income is nowadays skimmed off by taxation and spent or transferred by the public sector. Immediately after the Second World War this share was something like 25 percent. From this it will be clear that the direct impact of the public sector on the economy has increased substantially. This impact not only refers to stabilization of the economy, but also holds for allocation and distribution. Allocative and distributive effects can be distinguished, but cannot be separated. Changes in allocation do have distributive effects, and – conversely – changes in distribution affect allocation. The allocative and distributive effects in their mutual relations will be touched upon in the last section, in which the functioning of the economic system will be analysed.

To end this section some attention should be paid to the attitude of the state with respect to the concentration tendencies in the market sector. Two quite distinct lines of conduct are possible. On the one hand it may be imagined that the state drafts laws, prescriptions, prohibitions, etc. and also supervises compliance with them in order to regulate the positions of both capital and labour. Apart from the provision of purely public goods, the public sector does not participate in the economy. Under these circumstances tax rates can be kept low, and intervention in the operation of the economic system will be only modest. The desired allocative effects are brought about by changes in costs and prices. There is no clear reason why such a system could not function in practice. The scope for distributive policies, however, will be limited in this system.

When distributive considerations come to the fore, quite a different economic system is required. Regulations are no longer sufficient and the state has to participate more actively in the economy in order to attain the desired distributive aims. In this situation a considerable share of national income has to be guided to the public sector. The discrepancies between gross and net incomes may become so large, especially in marginal terms, that the market mechanism no longer functions. Even with perfect freedom of contracts, pure property rights and free entry to the markets, an economy cannot operate when combined marginal rates of the public sector (taxes, contributions and income-tied public prices) come close to 100 percent.

During the postwar period Western economies in general, and the Dutch economy in particular, have faced a development in which much stress was laid on the distributive targets. The doubling of the share of the public sector which occurred during that period was entirely due to the tremendous growth of transfer expenditure. Once more, it is not the economic system that can be blamed for this rise. There is no clear-cut relation between the skewness of the income distribution and the economic system that is in force. In his contribution Wagener gives no evidence that he is aware of this.

5. Will capitalism survive?

Will the coalition of Big Business, Big Unions and Big Government be prolonged in the decades to come? That is the basis question. Wagener is quite optimistic, although he considers economic growth to be an essential condition. I am not that optimistic, because economic growth is not independent of the ruling economic system. The functioning of this system has to be investigated before a prediction about the chances of survival can be made.

To me the prolongation of our economic system depends on the incentives it offers to the various economic agents. An important incentive to capital is the rate of return. This rate has continuously declined since the early Sixties, at least at the macroeconomic level. Measured after depreciation, but before tax, something like 3 percent per annum results nowadays as a "real" rate of return. Looking at the past, such an outcome is extremely low. A doubling may be necessary to ensure that enterprises continue to invest and, by doing so, create the conditions for future growth.

Will the required improvement of the rate of return be acceptable to labour? The implication would be that the labour income ratio should drop from 90 to about 80 percent. This is not impossible, but then something in return should be offered to labour. Probably unions will insist on far-reaching co-determination with respect to investment plans, stricter employment guarantees, and more profit sharing. I seriously doubt whether these social reforms will be agreed to by the entrepreneurs, who are not necessarily the same persons as the owners of capital. The entrepreneurs will certainly resist these reforms, unless similar modifications of the economic system take place in other countries. But even then much opposition can be expected, because undoubtedly entrepreneurs will fear a rigidity in the decision-making process. They also will stress the question of responsibility: who has to be blamed for the decisions when these prove, after all, to be wrong?

Next, what will be the reactions of the savers? Are they inclined to accept profit sharing? I really do not know. Their real interest rate after tax might even become higher, once profit sharing has been introduced. This of course depends on the necessary recovery of profit margins. Here again these are opportunities for investing abroad.

Finally, how will the workers react? It is clear that a substantial drop in the labour income ratio leaves no margin for any improvement in real disposable income. By stating this, I take it for granted that economic growth will be only modest and that a lessening of the burden of taxes and social security contributions is impossible. Underlying the latter assumption is that no real decrease in the transferred incomes will be agreed upon for the time being. Consequently the benefits of social reforms have to be compared with the costs of no improvement and possibly a decline in purchasing power.

To be fair, I do not believe that unions or politicians will be able to convince the workers that they should choose the social reforms. Besides, such a choice would deteriorate the functioning of the labour market. The incentives to participate in the labour force and to contribute as efficiently as possible to production would be frustrated. This point has to be stressed more if the assumption is correct that a real decrease in transferred incomes will be considered only as an ultimate remedy.

The dilemma is clear. The will to invest can be improved by a substantial lowering of the labour income ratio, but at the same time the will of the workers to participate in the production process would decline. Economic growth cannot offer a solution, because there will be no growth. Under those circumstances the income transfer programmes and policies have to be reconsidered. Then a distinction has to be made between programmes that are tied to demographic characteristics – pensions for old people and widows, allowances for large families, etc. – and programmes which supply income when people become ill, disabled, unemployed, etc. The conditions of the latter programmes in particular will then probably be revised, because here there is a relation with participation rates and effort.

Otherwise the prophecy of Stevers (1978) may be borne out. Our economic system and our democracy have to die, and we have to face dictatorship of either the Left or the Right. Because this would run counter to our long-lived cultural tradition, ultimately it will be decided to revise the social security system.

Reference

Stevers, Th., 1978, Antwoord Stevers, in: H. Daudt and H. van der Wolk, eds., Bedreigde democratie?, Intermediair 14 (1/2), 23.

4000
Global

Chapter 4

CHANGES AT INTERNATIONAL LEVEL OF THE SOCIO-ECONOMIC ORDER AND POWER STRUCTURE

J. TINBERGEN   35 - 43

Erasmus University, Rotterdam

The most important changes in the international social order have been the establishment of the Group of 77, the creation of the Organization of Petroleum Exporting Countries, the attempts at geographical integration in Western Europe, Latin America and Africa, and the shifts of manufacturing from developed to developing countries, partly as a consequence of the activities of transnational enterprises, and partly as a natural process of development.

1. Definition of the socio-economic order, in particular its international aspects

In this paper I will deal with the international aspects of the socio-economic order and the power structure. This implies that national socio-economic orders and power structures cannot and should not be ignored. The relations between the inhabitants of the world and the world's institutions constitute an intricate network that can hardly be split up into national and international relationships. Trade between two countries with a different socio-economic order cannot be organized without taking into account features of their national order and power structures. Although I try to avoid duplication with the subjects treated by others, this may not always be possible. I hope that in any case a basis for useful discussions can be offered.

The socio-economic order of a national, or of another geographical entity, is a concept of a multidimensional character. In my opinion Lindbeck's list of these dimensions has been well chosen [Lindbeck (1975)]. It contains:

(a) the structure of decision-making, ranging from decentralization to centralization; Van den Doel (1971) restricts the use of these words to the private sector and uses the phrases deconcentration versus concentration for the public sector;

(b) the mechanism of information, allocation of means, coordination of decisions, ranging from a free market to an administrative mechanism;

Prospects of Economic Growth, edited by S. K. Kuipers and G. J. Lanjouw
© *North-Holland Publishing Company*

(c) property rights, ranging from private to public owernship;

(d) the mechanism for encouraging enterprises to observe well-advised social behaviour;

(e) relations between individuals and firms taking decisions, ranging from monopolies to competition;

(f) the degree of openness towards the rest of the world (percentage of national consumption imported, degree of freedom to immigrate, etc.).

I now add a dimension containing information about

(g) the technology and organization of work; technology ranging from capital-intensive to labour-intensive, and the organization of work (apart from its degree of centralization, mentioned under (a)) assuming such forms as admitting a right to work (and to receive income) or an obligation to work (no work, no income) or related arrangements.

As stated, I concentrate on the aspects which are most relevant to international relations. A limited importance can be attached to a simple summing-up of the socio-economic systems of the nations of the world, since international relations are much influenced by the degree of similarity in socio-economic order. Some features of the socio-economic order are more or less homogeneous within the main political "blocs", such as Eastern Europe or the Western countries. It seems to be more interesting to adapt the definitions of aspects (a) to (g) to the world at large. Thus, we may think of a supranational or international public sector, comparable to one within a nation mentioned under (a) and (c). Similarly, a mechanism (b) may apply to commodity agreements as an example of an administrative procedure in the international sphere. Property rights, mentioned under (c), may apply to such objects as the natural resources in the oceans, or even to all mineral riches or to all scientific knowledge. Mechanisms for encouraging positive social behaviour may apply not only to firms [for instance, transnational enterprises (TNEs)], but also to governments or their citizens vis-à-vis the rest of the world. Equally, the situation of monopoloid attitudes may be applied to groups of nations, whether geographical (common markets) or functional (suppliers of capital, knowledge, or oil). By definition aspect (f) does not make sense for the world at large. The aspect (g) of technology may be a world characteristic when applied to international relations, such as transportation and communication. Air traffic has replaced passenger transportation by sea over long distances; container ships have penetrated everywhere; and so have communication technologies (telephone, telegraph, satellites).

The examples mentioned illustrate the continual change in the socio-economic order, both inside and between countries. Looking at the world community in a "macro" way, the recent changes that deserve most attention for the future are those to be expected as consequences of the "new scarcities", or ecological aspects. But also several of the "older" aspects of the socio-economic order, such as trade relations, financial transfers and the transfer of technology, are in need of a change.

2. Definition of power structure

The concept of power too is a multifaceted one. There are at least five, maybe more, components of power.

(a) Physical violence, whether exerted legally (structural violence) or illegally (revolutionary violence). Legal need not, of course, be identical with ethically justified: it is a factual characterization.

(b) Economic power originating from the possession of scarce commodities or endowments (capital goods, capabilities).

(c) Economic power originating from organized scarcity as distinct from "natural" scarcity (monopoly power), where the dividing line between natural and organized is less clear than it might seem at first sight.

(d) Power of ideas, whether rational (e.g. scientific knowledge or argument) or ethical (moral).

(e) Power of custom or habit, recognized by lawyers as a legal basis in numerous cases.

Sticking to this multidimensional character of power, some characteristics of the present world power structure may be listed, as an illustration.

(i) Military structural power is concentrated in the US and the Soviet Union but extends further to the nations with nuclear arms and those on their way to having them.

(ii) Revolutionary power is building up as a consequence of social tensions in several nations, among them many less developed countries (LDCs) showing great inequalities.

(iii) Economic power as a consequence of the possession of scarce commodities or capabilities can be found in the wealthy countries and in groups of wealthy people in poor countries; additionally, in the sector of science and technology, strongly concentrated in the developed countries (DCs) and in groups of countries such as the Organization of Petroleum Exporting Countries (OPEC).

(iv) Economic power as a consequence of organized scarcity cannot be clearly distinguished from the previous type of power, to the extent that natural scarcity is sometimes openly used as a basis for organization (OPEC), and sometimes used as an almost unconscious basis for like-minded mentalities. TNEs are in each instance an organization of talent and capital, but TNEs, however powerful in micro-economics, are not explicitly organized in one body. Their common problems do create similar behaviour. Trade unions too can be powerful within single countries; in DCs they actually are. But their international federations are not (yet) examples of world power.

(v) The power of ideas is particularly strong if they take the form of ideologies, i.e. uncritical acceptance of doctrines. These may be social or nationalistic. Examples are "laissez-faire" on the one hand and communism on the other as social ideologies. Nationalistic ideologies are too numerous to list. In a few important cases new ideas have had an impact on the course of history, for instance the arguments used by Jean Monnet in favour of European integration, the ideas of Raúl Prebisch on the necessary cooperation between LDCs, or the ideas on the "new scarcities" spread by the Club of Rome with the aid of their own members or of invited outsiders [Meadows and Meadows et al. (1972), Mesarović and Pestel (1974), Tinbergen with the RIO group (1976)]. The latter group coined the ideas of "new coalitions" which may change the power structure. These new coalitions are coalitions of groups with identical interests of which they had not been sufficiently aware so far. Examples are Western consumers and industrial workers in developing countries (common interest: imports of cheap manufactures from LDCs into DCs); Western farmers and marginal farmers in LDCs (common interest: high and stable prices of food grains); and Western producers of equipment and the unemployed in LDCs (common interest: more financial transfers from DCs to LDCs in order to create industrial employment).

3. Interrelations at international level between socio-economic order and power structure

In various ways socio-economic order and power structure may influence each other. Limiting myself to the international aspect of the relationship, I illustrate my thesis with some examples.

An international order in which large financial transfers from DCs are made available to LDCs may accelerate the process of capital accumulation in the latter and so increase their ownership of capital goods and their power. Similarly, an international order in which a large flow of knowledge is transmitted from DCs to LDCs may increase the capabilities of citizens of LDCs and hence raise their power.

A second set of examples concerns an international order in which imports from LDCs into DCs are increased. This may enhance the processing of their own natural resources, with the aid of indigenous labour, by LDCs and so increase both national income and employment. The latter will improve – i.e. render less unequal – the income distribution as well as general well-being, and hence again the country's power.

So much for the impact of the socio-economic order on the power structure. The latter of course clearly affects the socio-economic order. Each nation is governed by its leading elite which has come into power by force, as in the case of authoritarian regimes, or by the voting of the people, as in a democracy. Also, the group in power may be the big landowners' group, as in a feudal society. Or, it may be the owners of capital, as in early capitalism. Then, again, it may be a managerial group, as in developed capitalism. In a postindustrial society, according to several scholars, more power will be in the hands of technicians or scientists, or both. The example of successive socio-economic orders and their power structures again illustrates the interrelation between socio-economic order and power structure. This interrelation does not apply only to the situation within nations. In an international community it will be the economic order and power structure of the most powerful nations that will determine, to a considerable extent, the corresponding features of the world or the part of the world considered.

4. Changes, at international level, of socio-economic order and power structure

Recently some important changes in socio-economic order and power structure have taken place at the international level. A brief description will be given. In the world of LDCs the need for a common policy vis-à-vis the DCs has increasingly been felt. Raúl Prebisch's activities included the creation of the United Nations Conference on Trade and Development (UNCTAD) where LDCs felt more "at home" than in the General Agreement on Tariffs and Trade (GATT), which partly covered the same ground. Similarly, the United Nations Industrial Development Organization (UNIDO) has become a place where the LDCs are influential. Among many other activities, they set the target that by the year 2000 they should have one-quarter of the world's manufacturing capacity. So far the "Group of Seventy-Seven", with now over a hundred non-aligned member nations, has succeeded in formulating a common policy vis-à-vis the two blocs ("East" and "West") of industrialized countries. This has not changed even after the success of the oil-exporting countries in raising the oil price, making some of them richer than several DCs.

A change in power structure was also aimed at by a group of Western European countries, namely those that established the European Communities (EC) and those that later joined the original six. The world has become accustomed to the existence of the EC and has experienced some aspects of the power they exert. The integration process has come to a standstill, however, during the last five years or so and the prestige of the EC has suffered from their lack of unity on a number of policy items.

More generally, the socio-economic order of industrialized countries is continuing its transformation into what some call a postindustrial society. Among the characteristics are a relative decline of the manufacturing sector and a movement in the direction of service activities, both old and new. But many more aspects are under discussion.

Considerable changes in thinking have been brought about by the discovery of possible "limits to growth", related to what ecologists had maintained earlier and dramatized by the serious food shortages in South-East Asia and Central Africa as well as by the sudden awareness of a possibly imminent energy shortage. Changes in thinking also emerged from the frustration experienced by the LDCs as a consequence of the unwillingness of the DCs to play their part in the world development process as laid out in the objectives of the Development Decade 1961–1970 and the Second Development Decade 1971–1980; both having been solemnly adopted by the United Nations General Assembly (in 1961 and 1970, respectively), but hardly taken into account by the most important industrialized countries. The LDCs frustration led them to emphasize a need to be more self-reliant and to propose the establishment of a New International Economic Order (NIEO). Their proposal was adopted by the 1974 General Assembly Special Session, at about the same time as the adoption of the Charter of the Rights and Duties of Nations.

At present we are in the midst of an intensive dialogue between both governments and individuals on this new order, one of the last manifestations of this dialogue having been the series of meetings, held in Paris, of the Conference on International Economic Cooperation (CIEC). Among the most important issues are questions of vital interest to the world's population as a whole. Some examples may be quoted.

(i) Can we hope for cooperation in organized form of the world as a whole, i.e. West, East and South (where South stands for the LDCs)? Or must there be a choice between West and South or East and South, meaning that the LDCs should turn communist?

(ii) If full cooperation in all matters of importance is out of the question, can we seek issues on which some cooperation remains possible? Some scholars maintain that "purely technical" tasks, for instance, can indeed be accomplished by bodies with supranational power; such as matters of communication [dealt with by the Universal Postal Union (UPU)], of public health [of which the World Health Organization (WHO) is in charge] and – possibly in the future – environment, the task of the United Nations Environmental Programme (UNEP). Closely related to the last subject, but in fact of much wider scope, is the future management of the oceans, discussed in a series of conferences on the Law of the Seas. In 1970 the principle was formulated by the UN General Assembly that the oceans beyond the territorial zones (at some 12 miles' distance from the coast), not having been claimed so far by any nation, should constitute a "common heritage of mankind". Unfortunately, a real tragedy is developing in a stepwise claiming by most coastal nations of sovereignty over an "Exclusive Economic Zone" (EEZ) of 200 miles around the continents. This in fact boils down to the situation that almost the whole of oil and gas under the continental shelves (i.e. areas with a sea no deeper than 200 m) has now been appropriated by the coastal countries. The same fate threatens to apply to the riches known as metal ore nodules, on the bottom of the deeper parts of the ocean. This again means that the rich countries, who have the technology to exploit them, claim property rights to oil and other minerals outside their coastlines, these parts of the "common heritage of mankind" fully escaping use in favour of LDCs.

(iii) To what extent should future production, division of labour, and trade be planned and to what extent can it be handled by market forces? Should we aim at a maximum or at a minimum of trade between DCs and LDCs or, put another way, should the LDCs "opt out" of the present world trade system, or some alternative system?

The general picture of the world seems to be that in the end the group of LDCs will become more self-reliant, and begin to assume a trade union mentality, comparable to what the workers in the DCs did a century ago. OPEC is a good example, common markets may become more successful; the non or semi-industrialized world is "waking up".

5. Influence of economic growth on the power of LDCs

A question to be dealt with here is how economic growth will affect the power structure of the world. In an attempt to answer this we must distinguish between short- and long-term growth and between growth of the DCs and the LDCs.

In the short run growth of production in the industrialized world is a necessity for both worlds. After the hesitation of the stagflation period the time has come deliberately to expand demand, at the same time keeping incomes under control. The demand expansion has to come from the surplus countries, e.g. Germany, Japan and a number of oil-exporting countries. This is not the place to suggest how the former two countries could be convinced to change their minds on these issues. But no doubt such a policy would be salutary to the world at large. No important changes in power structure can be expected in the short run.

I now assume that this revival will be organized; in part it may come about spontaneously.

Coming, then, to the longer-term growth we must aim at, it may be wise to plan for and expect a lower rate of growth for the future decades than the growth we experienced between 1950 and 1970; this growth was quicker than ever before and could confront us with insoluble problems, as far as we can judge today. The clearest problems are those of pollution and of energy. But there are others. It must be repeated that our knowledge is restricted and that further research in many directions is indispensable. Even so it can be stated that many Western countries suffer from too high a consumption, thereby jeopardizing the health of many. Consumption per capita higher than optimal can be observed at present with regard to alcoholic beverages, tobacco products, meat and fats, not to mention drugs. Consumers must be protected against themselves: in several countries on each packet of cigarettes a warning has to be printed about the dangers of smoking; in France, for lack of private organizations who do so in Holland, a government campaign is being conducted warning against too much consumption of alcohol. In their own interest DCs should reduce their consumption. The modest growth recommended above is meant to further a less unequal income (and hence consumption) distribution. For cultural reasons too a new life style is urgently needed if Western civilization is to be saved and to be maintained as a meaningful concept.

In fact the long-term growth rate of rich countries should be considerably lower than the growth rates of the poorer countries. This is the only way to attain a better political stability than today's disequilibrated world shows. It is implicit that this will change the world's power structure, because precisely less inequality of power among LDCs and DCs is needed for more stability.

6. Influence of power of LDCs on economic growth

Finally, I briefly discuss the impact of greater power of the Third World on economic growth. The plea for a new international order is based on the inequalities in power between LDCs and DCs. If policies can be designed and carried out to arrive at a new international order, the LDCs' power will increase at the expense of the DCs' power.

Recalling the similarity between the labour movement of the nineteenth and twentieth centuries and the present self-reliance movement of the Third – and, if you like, Fourth and Fifth – World(s), we may say that a more balanced power position between workers and other social groups in the industrialized world was the aim of the labour movement. The power of workers' organizations is the basis on which today's social security rests, and it confirms the change in power position. Returning to the world scene we may restate, then, that the effect of more power possessed by the LDCs will similarly lead to a better equilibrium between the power of the various "blocs". Its effect on growth will give better opportunities for socio-economic development in the poorer part of the world. Hence, the simplest way to characterize the impact of a better distribution of power among DCs and LDCs as to economic growth is that this growth itself will be better distributed. Since the total margin left for the whole world's growth is uncertain and possibly small, if not negative, a better distribution is the best we can strive for. This is the moment again to realize that precise knowledge on the possibilities for growth is lacking.

Let me conclude by reiterating, therefore, the vital need for more research and for a less materialistic life cycle.

References

Doel, J. van den, 1971, Konvergentie en evolutie (Van Gorcum & Co., Assen).
Lindbeck, A., 1975, Economic systems and the economics of the New Left, Reprint Series no. 42 (Institute

for International Economics Studies, University of Stockholm, Stockholm).

Meadows, D. H. and D. L. Meadows, et al., 1972, The limits to growth (Universe Books, New York).

Mesarović, M. and E. Pestel, 1974, De mensheid op een kruispunt (Agon-Elsevier, Amsterdam).

Tinbergen, J. (coörd.), 1976, Naar een rechtvaardiger internationale orde (R IO) (Elsevier, Amsterdam/Brussel).

4000
Global

Chapter 5   *p. 35*

COMMENT ON TINBERGEN'S PAPER

F. VAN DAM   *45-50*

University of Groningen

1. Introduction

In his paper Tinbergen analyses several factors that cause changes in the international order and power structure. Amongst them are the following.

(a) Since 1964 the developing countries have been operating as a bloc vis-à-vis the rich countries; they have assumed a trade union mentality and have created organizations in which they are influential (UNCTAD).

(b) An intensive dialogue is taking place on the realization of a New International Economic Order.

The bloc policy of the developing countries has been reasonably effective at the level of formulation of development strategies (DD I, DD II, NIEO) and of international law ("Charter of Economic Rights and Duties of States"). As a consequence a "climate of opinion" has been created which, for example, allowed the OPEC countries to increase the oil prices by unilateral action.

At the level of negotiations on concrete economic problems (aid levels, commodity prices, access to markets, etc.) the results of the bloc policy of the developing countries have been negative. Since 1964 aid has been decreasing (as a percentage of BNP of the rich countries) and no structural measures have been taken to improve the economic position of the poor countries.

The possibilities of a bloc policy for the poor countries are decreasing, for three reasons:

(a) the differentiation between developing countries (see section 2);

(b) the interdependence of developing and developed countries (see section 3); and

(c) the disappearance of the borderline between developing and developed countries (see section 4).

Prospects of Economic Growth, edited by S. K. Kuipers and G. J. Lanjouw
© *North-Holland Publishing Company*

2. Differentiation

Traditionally, the developing nations had been predominantly exporters of primary products: leaving aside oil, their exports of primary products in 1963 amounted to $18 billion and their imports to $6 billion. The balance has now shifted considerably, for by 1976 Third World exports of primary products (again excluding oil) amounted to $56 billion and their imports to $38 billion.

Similarly, the developing nations by tradition had been predominantly importers of manufactured goods, but here too there has been a change: the share of primary products in Third World exports fell from 82 percent in 1963 to 56 percent in 1976, while that of manufactures rose from 18 to 44 percent over the same period.

For several years now the developing countries have had access to the international capital markets to finance their balance-of-payments deficits. While ten years ago the poorer nations had little chance of obtaining long-term commercial credit, by 1976 they were financing some 30 percent of their balance-of-payments deficits with such loans.

Until a few years ago the developing nations were involved with the multinationals only as host countries for the subsidiaries of Western firms: now they themselves are establishing multinationals which seek and find business elsewhere in the world.

The changes in the economic situation of the developing countries have varied very considerably from country to country, and as a result the developing nations' bloc has split de facto into groups of states with conflicting interests.

The oil price rise has benefited the countries of OPEC but given rise to a large deficit on the oil-importing countries' balance of payments.

The exporting industries of the Third World are concentrated in a small group of countries (Korea, China, Taiwan, Hong Kong, Singapore, Brazil and Mexico and, on a limited scale, Argentina, India, Pakistan and Malaysia), in which, however, three-quarters of all the population of developing countries live. Certain of these countries now in the process of industrialization – India, for instance – already export more manufactures than they import, and such countries clearly benefit from high prices for these goods: equally clearly, other developing countries benefit from low prices.

The increasing imports of primary products are also concentrated in a small group of countries, coinciding partly with the group now in the process of industrialization. Certain developing countries are already on balance importers of primary products, while others have remained exporters, and this has given rise to a conflict of interests as regards price levels.

The same applies to access to the capital market, which is enjoyed by only a limited number of countries. Those lacking such access advocate general debt-relief arrangements, while others, who use capital market funds to finance a large part of their balance-of-payments deficit, do not want such arrangements, since they fear that the result would be the loss of their entrée to the capital market.

Finally, the growth of multinational firms in the Third World is also restricted to a small (but important) group of countries, among them Brazil, India, Mexico, Taiwan and OPEC countries.

The economic divergence of the developing countries into groups with conflicting interests means that they can no longer operate as a homogeneous bloc in their relations with the rich nations.

3. Interdependence

The growth of trade between rich and poor countries (in particular in manufactures), the increased role of the developing countries on the capital market (supply by OPEC countries, access by newly industrializing countries), the accumulation of investments by the rich in poor countries, and the creation of multinational firms by developing countries have caused a growing interdependence of rich and poor.

Interdependence implies that their relations with the developing countries have become part and parcel of the economic policy of the rich countries. The traditional bloc relationship, based on confrontation and solidarity, has been replaced by a relation based on a search for common interests. The stagnation in the developed countries underlines the importance of using their ties with the poor countries for their economic interests.

Instances of possible common interests are:

(a) increase of exports by developed to developing countries (possible measures: more aid, debt-relief, access of the poor countries to the international capital market, increase of export guarantees and growth of trade);

(b) increased investments (surpluses of capital and technology of the developed countries will be used on a profitable basis; shortages of capital and technology of the developing countries will be covered).

The interdependence is not of a general nature. For example, the relations between developed countries and OPEC countries, developed countries and newly industrializing countries, and developed countries and exporters of primary commodities are of a different nature. This differentiation impedes a bloc policy by both the poor countries and the rich countries.

4. Disappearance of the borderline

Problems that until recently were a monopoly of the poor countries, such as stagnation, inflation, unemployment and deficits on the balance of payments, are these days the privilege of the rich countries too. The growing similarity, for example between countries of Southern Europe and Latin America, makes the concept of two different homogeneous blocs futile. For a further theoretical analysis reference may be made to recent publications by Dudley Seers. For practical illustration the application by Argentina and Columbia for membership of OECD may be instanced.

5. Negotiations

At present no negotiations between developed and developing countries are taking place, except about a Common Fund for the financing of buffer stocks of commodity agreements. The prospects for such agreements are gloomy. Only for rubber has some progress been made. In fact, the agenda for negotiations for the realization of the New International Economic Order is blank.

The lack of negotiations is caused by the still prevailing bloc policy and by a change in the relations between rich and poor countries. The pattern of these relations was formerly one of poor, dependent countries requesting aid on the one hand and rich countries on the other. The picture was characterized by feelings of domination, confrontation and calls for solidarity. This has changed: relations between rich and poor countries have become matter-of-fact and businesslike, for the following reasons:

(1) The completion of the process of decolonization and the end of the tensions caused by domination and demands for freedom, so that the former colonies and colonial powers are freer in the positions they can adopt with regard to one another.

(2) The developing countries' policies of self-reliance (which have made them more critical of everything connected with rich countries), trade with the rich countries, the multinationals and also aid.

(3) The oil crisis, when a large group of developing countries had to content with balance-of-payments deficits which were not cushioned by the rich countries, while at the same time the rich countries began working towards a policy of self-sufficiency.

(4) The recession in North America and Western Europe and the structural unemployment there have meant that the countries involved have been more concerned than before with their internal problems: they are less likely to accept, for example, the transfer of industries to developing countries because this would mean unemployment at home.

(5) The external policies of the EEC are less and less concerned with Asia and Latin America owing to the extension of the association to virtually all African countries, the overall policy on the Mediterranean region, and the Euro-Arab dialogue.

(6) Half the developing countries are no longer recipients of aid: their relations with the rich countries are therefore more free.

(7) Revival of conservative thinking on the part of Western countries has led,

among other things, to their paying less attention to problems outside their purview.

(8) The economic interdependence of rich and poor countries.

For all these reasons relations between rich and poor countries have become more realistic, and consequently in the years ahead these relations will have to be based primarily on common interests. Given that the reasons are mostly of an enduring nature, the new attitudes are also likely to be long-term.

The differentiation, the interdependence, the disappearance of the borderline between developing and developed countries and the businesslike character of their relations imply that the existing negotiating structures (North–South dialogue) and negotiating programmes (New International Economic Order), which are based on the premise of the developing countries' unity, are consequently no longer of significance. Indeed, they actually have a paralysing effect, since they compel the developing countries to adopt common standpoints which are untenable given their conflicting interests. In other words, the North–South dialogue no longer exists in any real sense.

The involvement of different groups of countries in the various aspects of economic activity has become complex. The 1960 stereotype, with the poor countries on the one side of the markets and the rich countries on the other, has disappeared. This applies not only to raw materials and finished products, but also to markets in capital and food. In all these cases the dividing line now runs right across rather than between the traditional rich and poor blocs.

These new relationships and complicated involvement necessitate the adaptation of decision-making structures. If the problems are to be manageable, this adaptation must be in the direction of negotiations and decisions on a problem-by-problem basis. For the decision-making process to be meaningful and effective, participation should be limited to the countries directly concerned with the particular subject, and this should be so arranged that world power balances are reflected as well as the power structures immediately relevant to the subject under discussion. Consultations on regulations for the market in cereals should involve only the major importers and exporters, and their weight in the decision-making process should be determined by two factors: the economic balance of power on the world scale and the power structures immediately relevant to the cereals market.

In a number of cases consultations have already occurred and decisions been taken in such limited forums. An example is provided by the process which led to the creation of the Witteveen facility: the IMF invited only the potential contributors to take part in discussions, and this resulted in decisions being reached quickly and effectively.

The present situation is very much the opposite of this: general discussions are held several times a year, and concrete negotiations fail to materialize. The effect is suffocating: generalities are repeated endlessly but have no practical result. Since 1972 we have had UNCTAD III, the Sixth and Seventh Special Sessions of the United Nations, UNIDO II, the North–South dialogue, UNCTAD IV, the World Employment Conference and the various declarations drawn up by governmental and non-governmental groups – the Dakar Declaration, the Algiers Declaration, the Belmont Statement and the Cocoyoc Declaration.

In the case of a thematic approach the combination of countries and interests involved will depend on the issue under discussion. For this reason different issues should not be assembled into packages, since this would inevitably lead to the outcome reflecting the lowest common denominator – as witness the North–South dialogue in Paris which was doomed from the start because of this linking together of problems.

On the basis of these considerations we arrive at the following guidelines for future negotiations:

(1) each issue should be negotiated separately;

(2) a forum should be chosen or created for each issue;

(3) agreements should not be linked together in packages;

(4) only the parties directly concerned should take part in the negotiations;

(5) the negotiating procedures should reflect the economic balance of forces in the world and in the markets concerned;

(6) negotiations involving rich countries, OPEC countries and newly industrializing countries should cover only those issues which involve, for each of the parties, an interest which can be satisfied during the negotiations;

(7) the agreements to be reached should accord no special facilities to OPEC countries and the newly industrializing countries – they should occupy a position similar to the rich countries; and

(8) an old-style aid link should be maintained with real "poverty countries", taking the form, wherever possible, of specific programmes.

Finally, economic growth and power in today's world are not subject to redistribution. Both are the results of countries' own efforts and of international policies and agreements based on parallel interests. Solidarity by the rich towards the poor as a factor in international policy applies only to extremely poor countries presenting no economic or military threat. In fact, such countries are to be found only in Africa and parts of South Asia. In these countries a minority of the population of the developing countries live.

There is no guarantee that the increased power of the developing countries will result in increased stability.

4000
Global

Chapter 6 p. 35:

COMMENT ON TINBERGEN'S PAPER

H. DE HAAN and G. J. LANJOUW

University of Groningen   51 - 55

1. Introduction

In this comment the following matters relative to Tinbergen's interesting and stimulating paper will be dealt with. First, attention will be paid to the definitions of the international economic order and the international power structure (section 2). Next a sketch will be given of the postwar international economic order (section 3). In this section a distinction is made between two ways in which the international economic order can change: as a result of actions at official level and as a result of developments at private level. As an example of a subject related to the first level the question of a New International Economic Order is dealt with (section 4). After that some developments at the second level are discussed (section 5). Finally some conclusions are drawn (section 6). As will be clear from the above, we have taken the liberty of not strictly following the line of Tinbergen's paper.

2. The definitions of the international economic order and the international power structure

Following Lindbeck, the concept of the socio-economic order is defined by Tinbergen on the basis of a number of aspects. As a consequence the concept becomes rather vague and in some cases even ambiguous. An example may help to elucidate this. An increase of imports form LDCs into DCs is connected by Tinbergen with a change in the international order. If the more traditional and narrower definition of the economic order based solely on the mechanism of coordination of decisions is used, an increase of imports from LDCs is rather the expression of a more consistent application of the rules of the *present* order (see also sections 3 and 4). In what follows we use the narrow definition of the economic order.

Prospects of Economic Growth, edited by S. K. Kuipers and G. J. Lanjouw
© *North-Holland Publishing Company*

In his paper Tinbergen subsequently tries to adapt the seven aspects of the socio-economic order at national level to the world at large. One difficulty, however, is that there are different institutional arrangements for the economic relations between the various countries of the world. International trade between East and West takes place within a different framework from that of international trade between countries of the same bloc. For this reason it seems to be preferable to make a distinction between the group of countries with (some variant of) a system in which market forces play a predominant role and the group of countries with (some variant of) a centrally planned economy. Conceived in this way, there is no such thing as a world economic order.

With respect to the concept of power it may be observed that Tinbergen does not give a definition of it. Only a classification of different kinds of power is given. A possible and, in our opinion, workable definition is the following: power is the capacity to influence the behaviour of others in a way not desired by them. The exercise of power can take place at two levels: private and official. The latter concerns the relations between governments and other official bodies. Defined in this way, power finds expression in the *relations* between either private parties or official bodies. Next we can define economic power as a subcategory of power in general which refers to economic relations. If international trade relations are taken as an example of economic relations, it can be maintained that the power position of a country depends on the importance to its trading partners of its export products. This importance will, for instance, be greater as the proportion of products for which no substitutes exist is greater. The most obvious example of such products is, of course, petroleum, on which the economic power of the OPEC countries is based. Put differently, the power position of a country in international trade depends on the degree of competition in the markets of its export products.

The above indicates that the economic power of a country cannot simply be measured by its national product, as is suggested by Tinbergen.

A closer look at the above definitions of economic power and economic order brings to light the relationship between the two concepts. For example, a monopoly indicates a strong position of the supplier of the goods in question while at the same time monopoly elements have a bearing on the economic order in the sense that they affect the working of the market mechanism.

3. The postwar international economic order

The present Western system of international trade and payments is still based on the principles as laid down in the General Agreement on Tariffs and Trade and the Bretton Woods agreement by which the International Monetary Fund was brought into existence. In the field of trade the main elements are liberalization and non-discrimination; in the monetary field the main principle is convertibility of currencies. In our opinion, this liberal international economic order reflects the predominant position of the Western countries after the Second World War. Liberalization of trade, non-discrimination and convertibility were in their interest.

For many economists the presence of the above principles is one of the factors considered to be responsible for the rapid economic growth in the Western countries after the Second World War.

After the process of decolonization the principles were challenged by the LDCs. This has in the course of time resulted in a number of interesting resolutions by bodies of the UN family. Especially those concerning a New International Economic Order and the Charter of the Rights and Duties of Nations have to be mentioned here. They are examples of attempts to change the international economic order by action at the *official level*. We shall return to this subject in the next section. In addition, however, the international economic order can change as a result of developments at the *private level*. These developments will be dealt with in section 5.

At the end of this section we call attention to the fact that Tinbergen's paper focuses on the North–South relation, thereby ignoring the growing importance of the economic relations between East and West. In these relations the Western principles mentioned above do not apply. It would be worthwhile inquiring to what extent increasing economic contacts between countries with different economic systems can stimulate economic growth. That, however, is, outside the scope of this short comment.

4. A New International Economic Order?

The LDCs have acquired a very considerable voting power in the United Nations. Until now they have not, however, been able to achieve a fundamental change in the international economic order. In this connection it is worthwhile taking a closer look at the UN resolution regarding a New International Economic Order. The integrated programme for raw materials as devised by Gamani Corea is one of the most essential elements of this order [UNCTAD (1974)]. It is doubtful whether the proposals in question, such as those regarding the system of buffer stocks, cooperation between producer countries, multilateral trade contracts, and compensatory financing schemes grosso modo imply a fundamental departure from the present international economic order. With the exception of the multilateral trade contracts they leave the working of the market mechanism more or less unaffected. Besides, a number of experts hold that, if proposals of this kind were put into practice, their effectiveness would be dubious. [See, inter alia, Kebschull et al. (1977), Meier (1968) and Johnson (1967).]

In our opinion, policies based on transfer of technology, processing by LDCs of their own raw materials, formation of customs unions by LDCs and the like are more capable of success, provided that the decisions concerning production are guided by comparative cost differences. The success of this sort of strategy does not require a change in the international economic order, but rather depends on the continuation of the present order, especially the liberalization of international trade. An increase of protectionism in the Western world would be very harmful in this respect.

It is hard to predict whether the improvements of the international division of labour implicit in the above strategy would promote welfare or economic growth in our second-best world. In any case, the international distribution of welfare would become more equitable and, like Tinbergen, we consider this necessary. In this connection attention must be paid to the UN study *The future of the world economy* [Leontief et al. (1977)]. They show that "if the minimum targets of growth for the developing countries, as set by the International Development Strategy, were implemented continuously throughout the remaining decades of this century, and if growth rates prevailing in the developed countries during the past two decades were to be retained in the future, then the gap in per capita gross product between these two groups of countries, which was 12 to 1 on the average in 1970, would not start diminishing even by the year 2000" [Leontief et al. (1977, p. 3)]. Leontief et al. demonstrate, however, that under an alternative scenario the gap can be reduced to 7 to 1. In a preliminary study they show that this target can be achieved by a gradual disarmament combined with a moderate transfer of the released resources to the LDCs. In our view, this line of thought is more promising than a plea for a reduction of consumption of tobacco products and alcoholic beverages as is made by Tinbergen.

At the end of this section we consider one of the examples Tinbergen uses to show that there have lately been important changes in the socio-economic order and the power structure. OPEC is quoted as an example of the strengthening position of the LDCs. Tinbergen does not, however, mention the fact that the rise in oil prices has been very harmful to many LDCs. For this reason we do not believe that the parallel drawn between the labour movement and the Third World is very appropriate: the interests of the various (groups of) LDCs diverge.

5. Changes at the private level

In Tinbergen's paper hardly any attention is paid to changes of the international economic order as a result of developments at the private level. In our view these may have had a greater impact than actions at the official level. A notable example is the growing importance of multinational enterprises. Characteristic of these enterprises is, among other things, that they have advanced technology at their disposal and that they sell their products in monopolistic or oligopolistic markets. An increasing part of world trade takes place within multinational enterprises, implying that this part of trade is no longer subject to market forces. In our terminology this means a change in the international economic order.

Until now attempts to effect a code of conduct for multinationals in order to reduce the negative aspects of their behaviour and further to develop the positive aspects have not been successful.

Another development at the private level worth noting concerns the field of international finance. Both the centrally planned economies and the LDCs increasingly call on private financial markets to cover their payments imbalances. The Euro-currency market plays a particularly important role in this respect. It is outside the scope of this comment to discuss the pros and cons of this development. It is only mentioned as another example of the important developments taking place at the private level.

6. Conclusions

(1) As Tinbergen's definitions of the socio-economic order and the power structure are rather vague it is rather difficult to use them to describe developments in the real world.

(2) Tinbergen has not been very successful in indicating the changes in the essential elements of the international economic order as a result of actions at the official level.

(3) Changes in the international economic order as a result of developments at the private level should have been discussed.

(4) Tinbergen's plea for a new life style would become more substantial if the transfer of resources released by disarmament were made part of it.

(5) We agree with Tinbergen that too little is known about the interrelations of the international order, the international power structure and economic growth, and that more research is needed.

References

Johnson, H. G., 1967, Economic policies towards less developed countries (George Allen and Unwin, London).

Kebschull, D., W. Künne and K. W. Menck, 1977, Das integrierte Rohstoff-programm (HWWA, Hamburg).

Leontief, W., A. P. Carter and P. A. Petri, 1977, The future of the world economy: A United Nations study (Oxford University Press, New York).

Meier, G. M., 1968, The international economics of development (Harper and Row, New York).

UNCTAD, 1974, An integrated programme for commodities: The role of multilateral commitments in international commodity trade, TD/B/C. 1/166 (Geneva).

In Volume XIX

Chapter 7

ECONOMIC GROWTH, TECHNICAL PROGRESS AND NATURAL RESOURCES*

H. LINNEMANN

Free University of Amsterdam

57-77

In this century the availability of stock-renewable resources (primarily agricultural produce) and of stock-material resources (minerals except fossil fuels) will not constitute a bottleneck for continued economic growth of the industrialized countries, although their relative prices might increase somewhat. Prospects for continued material growth, however, depend in significant measure on the future energy situation. During the second half of the 1980s supply problems might become acute because of the limited availability of stock-energy resources and the slow development of "new" sources (flow energy). Government policies may lessen the impact of probable shortages (energy conservation, energy price increases, reorientation of growth). A slowing down of material growth is to be valued positively.

1. Natural resources in economic theory

Production, and hence economic growth, requires the use of production factors: labour, capital and natural resources. This paper focuses on the availability of natural resources for the future growth of the world economy, and of the industrialized countries in particular. It attempts to shed some light on the issue of a possible shortage of natural resources as an impediment to economic growth in times to come. The conclusion of the paper will presumably not be surprising to most readers: the question whether natural resources will set an upper limit to world production and economic growth in the foreseeable future cannot be answered by a simple and straightforward yes or no.

Natural resources are, in some form or other, essential for production; it is inconceivable that they should be entirely replaced by nonmaterial inputs. Their importance springs to the eye most immediately in the primary sectors of production: agriculture and mining. Manufacturing and construction could not exist without inputs from the primary sectors. The same is true for tertiary (or higher-ranking) activities, even though the natural resources input share may be relatively low in many cases. As

* This paper is a slightly expanded version of an article published in *De Economist* 125 (1977), 465–483.

Prospects of Economic Growth, edited by S. K. Kuipers and G. J. Lanjouw
© *North-Holland Publishing Company*

the consumption and production structure changes with increases in the level of per capita income, the natural resources component in total production will change as well, and will usually tend to decrease relative to total output. The relative weight of natural resources as a production factor is also influenced by technological change. Technical progress may reduce the input of natural resources per unit of output, although savings in one direction (e.g. land in agriculture, raw materials in manufacturing industry) often imply additional requirements of another natural resource (e.g. by using more energy).

Changes in the production structure, technical progress, and substitution between the various natural resources themselves may and do modify our dependence on natural resources for production and economic growth. Consequently, it is a flexible dependence – but dependence it is. Recent publications (most conspicuously *The Limits to Growth* study by D. L. Meadows and associates) and recent events (in particular the actions of the OPEC cartel) have increased our awareness of the vital importance of natural resources to world economy and society, now and in the future. What, then, are the prospects of economic growth from the point of view of the future availability of these natural resources? Classical economic theory had little doubt as to the long-term prospects of economic growth. Scarcity of natural resources would lead, in its view, ultimately (Malthus) or presently (Ricardo), to diminishing returns to productive efforts. Consequently, any process of economic growth would sooner or later slow down and grind to a halt. In fact, this view on scarcity became a doctrine, as Barnett and Morse (1965, pp. 1–2) have pointed out: the "doctrine that an inherently limited availability of natural resources sets an upper bound to economic growth and welfare". This doctrine gained for economics its reputation as the "dismal science".

J. S. Mill elaborated on the Ricardian approach, and added an important qualification. Technology and institutions may change as a consequence of progress of civilization. The law of diminishing returns certainly holds, also in Mill's view, but "(t)his law may, however, be suspended, or temporarily controlled, by whatever adds to the general power of mankind over nature; and especially by any extension of their knowledge, and their consequent command, of the properties and powers of natural agents".[1] Mill's plea not to push man's interference with natural living space too far, in order to preserve the beauty of nature, has received less attention than his statement on the role to be played by technical progress in reducing scarcity.

Although the law of diminishing returns has kept its place in economic theory ever since Ricardo, the doctrine of increasing natural resources scarcity faded away. The progress of science and technology since the middle of the 19th century, the opening up of 'new' continents, the revolutions in the field of communication and transportation, the economies of scale to be realized in large production units, are among the factors that made the notion of scarcity of natural resources seem to be a distant one. In economic theory, hardly any interest was shown in the (aggregate) relation between

[1] Mill (1929, p. 188), as quoted by Barnett and Morse (1965, p. 69).

natural resources and economic growth. At most, some attention was paid to the discrepancy between private and social criteria for exploiting natural resources.

By and large, modern economists came to hold an optimistic view of natural resources availability. They assumed, often implicitly, that technical progress and increased substitution possibilities would in fact solve the problem, except perhaps for the scarcity of agricultural land in densely populated countries or regions. Of course, the development of additional and new resources would involve costs – but costs of a magnitude that could be borne without much pain. Most economists were inclined to agree with E. Zimmerman, the well-known expert on the world's resources, when he wrote in 1951: "Resources are highly dynamic functional concepts; they *are not, they become,* they evolve out of the triune interaction of nature, man, and culture. . . . The problem of resource adequacy for the ages to come will involve human wisdom more than limits set by nature" [Zimmerman (1951, p. 814)].

This optimistic view still prevails to date, but it is meeting with growing opposition.[2] The concept of natural resources is indeed a dynamic one, but that does not change the fact that it pertains to a limited physical space. Important resources may indeed come close to exhaustion in the not too distant future (oil). Concern for environmental quality may impose constraints on the use, or the rate of exploitation, of several resources. In general, the social costs of developing and using resources may be much higher than had been anticipated earlier. On the potential magnitude of accessible mineral resources, geologists and mining engineers often take a less optimistic stand than most economists. The uneven distribution of resources over the earth, the great disparities in resource consumption levels between countries, and political factors influencing exploration, exploitation and trade complicate the picture even more. It seems likely that the general optimism of the last hundred years or so concerning the availability of natural resources will be undermined further in the years ahead.

2. Aspects of resource availability

Unrestrained optimism regarding future availability of resources is not justified and therefore dangerous; on the other hand, overall pessimism is equally one-sided and unwarranted. A realistic assessment is necessarily more complex, and will eventually involve dealing with specific individual resources. Within the scope of this article it is impossible to go into such detail; we have to limit ourselves to certain broad categories of resources, and to try and formulate a (usually tentative) conclusion for each category. Before doing so, it is useful to list summarily some of the more important aspects that have to be taken into account in assessing the future adequacy of natural resources for

[2] For a survey of recent (economic) literature on resources, see Peterson and Fisher (1977) and Fisher (1977).

economic growth. This list must include many noneconomic factors, in order to do justice (at least partly) to the broader context of the issue at stake.

2.1. Physical and biological aspects

Since we are dealing with natural resources, an assessment of their potential availability has to start from theories and data belonging to the realm of the natural sciences. Information is needed concerning the composition of the atmosphere, lithosphere and hydrosphere in terms of the "dead matter" potentially available as resource. Estimates of the average composition are quite inadequate as far as the lithosphere is concerned; what is needed is a frequency distribution of all sorts of materials (say, ores) by grade of concentration in the higher layers of the crust of the earth. This again involves theories on the genesis of the various deposits. An assessment of the physical availability of different materials in the earth's crust is therefore a complex matter fraught with uncertainties.

No less complicated is the question of the potential availability of living matter, a resource reproducing itself under appropriate conditions. The quantity of vegetal material that could be produced and used by man for food and other requirements depends in biological terms inter alia on the area of cultivable land, water availability, the quantity of nutrients in the soil, and the losses due to pests and diseases. Again, a simple and straightforward answer as to the potential production of living matter is not available.

2.2. Technological aspects

Even if certain resources are known to exist, their accessibility and use will depend on technological knowledge. Without technical know-how, most resources would not even be resources. Modern agricultural technology has achieved astonishing increases in yields per hectare. Metallurgical technology has, in just over a century, changed the role of aluminium from that of a curiosity at the Paris Exhibition of 1855 to that of a leading metal surpassed in industrial importance only by iron. Mining of nodules on the ocean floor will increase considerably the known reserves of several metals. Why, then, should we worry about limited natural resources as long as the technologists are with us to do their job?

For several reasons it is not quite as simple as that. First, technology can be developed and introduced only at a cost, and this cost may be very considerable – not only in economic but also in ecological terms. Secondly, the direction that technological research and development will take is often the outcome of a host of factors and forces operative within transnational and national enterprises and governmental bodies, and it is therefore by no means certain that the "proper" developments will occur at the "proper" time. Thirdly, while technological developments may and will alleviate problems of growing scarcity in one area, these developments may at the same time create or increase future problems in another field owing to its input requirements, or its output of residuals or other negative external effects.

Consequently, technical and technological progress will be a very important factor in the future availability of natural resources, but such progress should not be conceived of as the key to a cornucopia of resources. For the future of modern societies as we know them today, finding access to new and "lasting" sources of energy (solar energy, nuclear fusion) would seem to be the most crucial issue for sustained material growth. Whether or not the energy-supply problem can be solved in the long run without fundamental changes in the structure of society and in individual behaviour remains uncertain.

2.3. Economic aspects

Although demand and supply factors are different for different resources, the markets for natural resource products have some characteristics in common. On the demand side, primary commodity markets usually display an income elasticity of demand lower than one. For industrial raw materials the same phenomenon is often formulated in terms of the decreasing intensity of use per unit of GNP at increasing levels of GNP per capita. However, this decreasing intensity of use manifests itself only at higher income levels: during the earlier stages of the industrialization process the intensity of use (e.g. of base metals) increases. To be sure, not all natural resource products necessarily show a less than proportionate increase in demand at higher income levels: the total demand for energy may well increase at a rate higher than that of GNP growth, even at high GNP levels. Also, substitution processes (e.g. between metals) may lead temporarily to increasing intensity of use per unit of GNP for the relatively cheaper or more suitable material.

It is virtually impossible to make a general statement about the level of the price elasticity of demand for (products of) natural resources since there are differences both between products and between different uses of the same product. Owing to the possibility of substitution between different resources, which frequently occurs, the price elasticity of an individual natural resource product may be rather high whereas for a package of related products with mutual substitutability it is much lower, and in fact often close to zero in the short run.

On the supply side, the markets for most natural resource products show the well-known rigidity in the short run, since production cannot adapt itself at once to changing market conditions. Agricultural processes are in time controlled by the rhythm and vagaries of nature, and expansion of the production of minerals and energy requires long lead times. Price fluctuations and stock manipulation are the associated market phenomena. From the point of view of the future availability of resources for economic growth, these short- to medium-term characteristics are of less importance than the long-term prospects for increasing supply of natural resource products, and the economic prerequisites for such increased supply. The latter issue will be taken up below.

2.4. Political aspects

So far a regular supply of raw materials at low or at least reasonable prices has been a major concern for most nations, since it is of vital importance for economic and military power. The recent use of the oil weapon has reminded oil-importing countries of their vulnerability on this point. Resource-rich countries may try to use their particular resource or resources to strengthen their position in the international political arena by using their sovereign rights to restrict the rate of exploitation and the volume of supply, or even to cut supply to zero for some or all customers. In a world with sharp conflicts between nations, political interference with the use of natural resources and their products is a fact of life.

2.5. Cultural and ethical aspects

Concern for a healthy biosphere and awareness of the finiteness of the Earth are among the factors that may induce a different attitude towards material growth and the use of natural resources for that purpose. Ecological considerations are already gaining importance in production and consumption decisions, although they still carry relatively little weight. A minority of people, particularly in the rich countries, feel that the very uncertainty and lack of knowledge about the complex and dynamic equilibria in nature should make man much more careful in his relations and interference with the biosphere of which he himself forms part. The fact that natural resources in dead-matter form (minerals) are in the last instance exhaustible adds to their inclination towards a materially simpler life style. The ethical consideration that the generations to come are also entitled to a world in which human life is worth living strengthens their arguments. If this minority view should gradually gain wider acceptance, future demand for natural resources would obviously slow down considerably.

The above aspects of the issue of future adequacy of natural resources have been touched upon merely to illustrate the complexity of the problem and the near-impossibility of a clear-cut answer. Of course, things get simpler when the analysis is limited to a relatively short period of, say, ten to fifteen years, but even in this case many provisos will have to qualify the conclusion. In the subsequent pages we shall focus on the question of whether or not economic growth in the industrialized market economies of the West in the years till 1990 will be hampered by a shortage of natural resources. In doing so, we obviously need to know also what the global situation as regards natural resources is likely to be in the near future.

As mentioned above, in the context of this article we cannot deal with all individual (products of) natural resources. We shall discuss them groupwise, and distinguish between renewable and exhaustible resources; energy will be dealt with separately. Borrowing the terminology of Pearce (1976, p. 145), the following four categories of natural resources will be discussed: (a) stock-renewable resources, (b) stock-material resources, and energy resources, both (c) stock-energy resources and (d) flow-energy resources.

3. Stock-renewable resources

In Pearce's definition, this category of resources has a fixed stock at any point in time, but the stock is renewable through biological reproduction. It comprises agricultural produce, livestock (largely based on agriculture), and marine resources. If current consumption of these products does not, for a series of years, exceed the increase by reproduction of the available quantity of the commodity concerned, the resource itself will not be depleted. This presupposes that the resource will not be mismanaged otherwise (as, for example, in the case of land degradation and erosion), so that its reproductive capacity is maintained.

Let us turn to agriculture first. Is agricultural output likely to hit an upper limit in the near future? This question has been studied recently in some detail by a team of soil scientists and plant physiologists of the Agricultural University at Wageningen [see Buringh et al. (1975)], as part of a larger study on world agriculture to be mentioned below. On the basis of soil and climate characteristics, the world's total land area was subdivided into 222 broad soil regions, and for each soil region its suitability for agricultural production was assessed. It was found that only about 40 percent of all potentially arable land is actually being cultivated. This finding is in line with the results of an earlier study by the United States President's Science Advisory Committee;[3] only in the regional breakdowns do the two studies show certain discrepancies. Thus, agricultural production could be increased substantially by enlarging the area under cultivation. More important, however, is the possibility of increasing output by raising

---

[3] *The World Food Problem* (1967).

yields per hectare; here the unused potential is – for the world at large – much greater, while at the same time intensification of cultivation is more attractive from an ecological point of view.

The magnitude of the unused potential for agricultural production is relatively smaller in the industrialized countries than in the developing countries; nevertheless, it is still quite considerable, notably in North America, Australia and the industrialized socialist countries, less so in Western Europe, and least of all in Japan. To what extent the unused potential will be used in the years to come depends on the development of the world markets for agricultural products and on the national policy objectives of the individual countries, or groups of countries like the European Community. Together with a large group of colleagues the present author has tried to analyse the world food situation with the help of a large computer model MOIRA developed for this purpose [Linnemann et al. (1979)]. The main findings have already been published [De Hoogh et al. (1976)]; for the period up to 1990 many of the simulation runs (based on alternative assumptions concerning growth rates of population and nonagricultural GDP and concerning international and national food policy objectives) show rather similar developments of food production in the Western industrialized countries. For instance, North America is likely to remain by far the most important food exporter over this period; in these simulation runs, the self-sufficiency ratio for food (as measured in this study) of the European Community increases from about 60 in 1975 to 70–75 in 1990. It should be noted, however, that MOIRA has not been developed or used primarily for prognostic purposes; also, in other simulation runs (characterized by a slow growth rate outside agriculture, and a deliberate change in national policies in the rich countries in order to stimulate agricultural production increases in the poor countries) the self-sufficiency ratios of the Western countries are lower – by the West's own decision, in fact.

All this points in one direction: there need be no fear of a food scarcity in the industrialized countries in the foreseeable future. To the extent that an international food policy would aim at a relatively high world food price level (as a precondition or stimulus for stepping up food production in the Third World), national food prices in the rich countries might also show a slight tendency to rise. For nonfood agriculture, the supply potential is likewise very great; for these commodities the dependency of the industrialized countries on Third World producers is considerable, but deliberate interruption of supply and cartel-like price manipulation are not likely to be effective policy instruments for the producers (otherwise the negotiations about the various commodity agreements that have been proposed would less frequently have failed altogether).

It is true that the rather bright picture concerning agricultural resources presented here is a simplified one. It does not distinguish between individual agricultural commodities, it assumes that the necessary inputs (fertilizer, energy) will be available, and it disregards disturbances that might be caused by adverse weather conditions or outbreaks of particular plant diseases. Detailed discussion of these points would not lead to a conclusion that is basically different, however. As to the commodity breakdown, one aspect that deserves explicit mention is the time lag or gestation period involved in some of the production processes (e.g. tree crops). In the particular case of timber, it is possible that, owing to this gestation period and to inadequate replanting in the past, a relative shortage might develop.

The discussion about the other stock-renewable resources will have to be very brief. The supply of animal food is based on vegetal production; if the latter does not present a basic problem, the same holds for the former. The situation is different for animal resources from the sea and from inland waters. The latter have been seriously affected by water pollution in many parts of the world, and the production from the sea is stagnating or declining for several species because of mismanagement of the resource concerned (overfishing, and sometimes again pollution). The economic effects might be considerable, but mostly so at the local level. Economic growth prospects in the industrialized countries as a whole will not be strongly affected by it, although it remains a sad example of human misuse of nature and natural resources.

4. Stock-material resources

For this category of resources, total stock and total supply in time are fixed. The extraction effort applied to them determines the rate of flow at which the given stock is being tapped. Future availability can be increased only by abstaining from present consumption. However, unless the extracted commodity is transformed in the subsequent production stages in a form which makes it nonrecoverable, recycling and reuse of the material are possible. Pearce (1976, p. 145) includes water as a stock-material resource with a very high level of recycling. (Stock-energy resources are discussed in section 5.)

The mineral resources we are dealing with here may be subdivided again into metallic and nonmetallic minerals, but even if we were to introduce this distinction the heterogeneity between the resources would remain very great. The common denominator that exists in the case of renewable resources – the process of photosynthesis underlying all vegetal production – is lacking in the case of mineral resources; in the words of a recent study on world mineral supplies, "a sound genetic theory . . . is an objective which must be worked for with all possible means at our disposal" [Vokes (1976, p. 95)]. For the time being "(r)eliability comparable to that of estimates of biological resources is obtainable only for the relatively few important dissolved salts in well-mixed oceans of known dimensions, and perhaps for fossil fuels and a few other sedimentary mineral deposits (gypsum and salt, for example)" [Lovering (1969, p. 109)]. General statements about the future availability of stock-material resources are hard to make, for this reason, and the conclusion that we will arrive at in this section is fraught with more uncertainty than that of the preceding section.

Nevertheless, a few things stand out clearly. First of all, figures about the so-called reserves of the various minerals do not say much about long-term availability. In the words of Chapman (1969, p. 34), a "reserve refers to that proportion of a resource that is known with reasonable certainty to be available under prevailing technical, economic, and other societal conditions". Published reserve figures are frequently of the order of magnitude of, say, twenty times annual extraction levels since such reserve magnitudes are adequate from the point of view of the planning perspective of mining companies (and governments, one might add). Unless the annual extraction level were to exceed the annual rate at which resources are changed into (new) reserves, the reserve position would not worsen. Reserves may be increased by (i) exploration leading to the identification of additional or new deposits, (ii) technological progress leading to a lowering of the minimum acceptable grade of concentration (cut-off grade), to greater depth of mining in-situ, etc., and (iii) price increases which make exploitation of submarginal deposits economically feasible. These three factors might work simultaneously; in the past, factors (i) and (ii) have been by far the most important forces, and for many metals relative prices have gone down rather than up.

For how long could this process of turning resources into reserves go on? In other words, what is the magnitude of present-day reserves (or present-day extraction levels) in relation to the stock-total of the resources? On this point opinions differ, since it is not clear what the most meaningful definition of the total resource stock is. Crustal abundance (i.e. the total quantity of a chemical element in the earth's crust) is obviously much too high a figure: the continental earth crust measures on the average 36 km in depth, and not only open-pit mining (500 m) but also solution mining (present maximum 3 km) cannot penetrate that far below the surface. The fact that crustal abundance is a million or more times annual extraction levels cannot guarantee the adequacy of future reserves. Using a simple method suggested in the Geological Survey Professional Paper 820 [Brobst and Pratt (1973)], Nordhaus (1974, p. 23) introduced the concept of ultimate recoverable resources defined as 0.01 percent of the total amount of each element available to a depth of 1 km. Given this somewhat arbitrary definition, ultimate recoverable resources vary in magnitude from 100 (gold) to 68,000 (aluminium) times the present levels of annual resource extraction.

A group, of which the present author formed part, has used another approach: the method of McKelvey/Erickson as presented in the same Geological Survey Professional Paper 820. In this approach it is assumed that potential recoverable resources of all (metallic) minerals will be the same fraction of crustal abundance as the fraction that the known reserves of those metals most diligently sought for in the US constitute of US crustal abundance. Or, quoting Erickson (1973, p. 24), "if we search for an element hard enough, we find it in about the quantities we might expect". The working party using this method concluded that the ratio between potential recoverable resources and annual extraction was about 200 to 300 for relatively scarce metals (copper, lead, mercury, silver, tin) and only for gold (150) lower than that.[4]

The above figures are optimistic in the sense that, even if the resources do exist in the assumed quantity, they still need to be found. Also, it is implicitly assumed that energy will be available, that ecological considerations do not preclude their exploitation, etc. At the same time, the figures are pessimistic, since they disregard possible technological progress and the consequences of possible price increases for the commodity concerned. As regards the latter point, the report of the working party mentioned above refers to a "price elasticity of the volume of reserves" in the range of 1.5 to 2, but adds that for various ores this elasticity may well be smaller than one.[5] This "price elasticity of the volume of reserves" has been estimated from "step-cost functions" indicating how much of the various mineral reserves are likely to be available at different levels of extraction costs. Using such step-cost functions, the UN study on *The Future of the World Economy* [Leontief et al. (1977, pp. 45 and 73–74)] computes in its initial or basic scenario a slight increase in the relative prices of some base metals up to 1990, and a doubling of relative prices in the decade 1990–2000; however, as this study explicitly states, this scenario "assumes a pessimistic estimate of mineral reserves". In a scenario based on more generous resource endowments, relative metal prices in 2000 are only about 20 percent higher than in 1970.

Over the next 10 to 20 years, the stock-material resources required for continued economic growth will therefore, on the whole, not constitute a bottleneck – even though their relative price level might increase somewhat. Of course, this does not exclude the possibility of shorter-term supply problems for specific individual commodities, but a general and overall shortage of mineral resource products is very unlikely to emerge in the more immediate future. In fact, if the mining of deep-sea resources were to gain momentum in the 1980s – which is as yet still uncertain – the markets for the metals found in the manganese nodules (nickel, copper, cobalt, manganese, molybdenum) might be in danger of disruption owing to potential oversupply towards the end of the decade.

If, for any individual commodity, a shortage of a more structural nature should tend to develop, for whatever reason, such shortage (and price increase) will often induce substitution processes using cheaper materials, and increase recycling of the material in short supply whenever possible. For base metals, present-day levels of recycling are often around one-third of total annual supply, and certainly not at their maximum.

The possibilities of substitution and of recycling that exist for many modes of metal use, the often rather large number of countries producing a particular mineral resource product and the consequent heterogeneity among them in socio-political orientation,

---

[4] *Recommendation on the Future Availability of Metallic Minerals* (1975, p. 32).
[5] Ibid., p. 39.

and the initially weak economic and financial position of most developing countries exporting mineral resources, are among the factors that effectively limit the market power of producer cartels for mineral resource products other than oil. It is not to be expected that for any metallic mineral resource a producer cartel could be as successful as the OPEC cartel, and it would most certainly not have the impact on the economies of the Western (and other!) countries that OPEC has had and still has.[6] It is true that for most mineral resources the industrialized countries of the West, taken together, are net importers,[7] but in spite of the apparent dependency of the West on raw material imports from mineral-resource exporting developing countries the overall economic position of the latter countries makes them dependent on the industrialized countries rather than the other way round [Coppens (1972, pp. 145–146)].

Summarizing, it is hardly likely that the availability of stock-material resources will constitute a bottleneck for continued material growth of the Western countries in the immediate future. Relative prices of some minerals may display an upward tendency towards the end of the century – say, after 1990. For individual minerals, short-term instability of prices may continue in the future as it did in the past. In the particular case of water (both for industrial and for domestic use), it is likely that the last memories of its former status of an (almost) free commodity will disappear quickly in view of tightening supply problems.

5. Stock-energy and flow-energy resources

There is no need to explain the crucial importance of energy to the present-day world economy. The structure and working of contemporary human society are inextricably connected with the availability and use of large quantities of nonhuman energy. The rather optimistic picture given above concerning the availability of stock-renewable and stock-material resources – optimistic at least in the short and medium term – is based on the assumption of an adequate energy supply on conditions as prevailing today. Is it justified, however, to assume the continued availability of energy in ever-growing quantities, in the various forms and at the prices now prevailing? The answer is no, in fact – particularly in the long run.

World supply and consumption of primary energy (excluding human and animal energy) originate in their quasitotality from stock-energy resources; coal (31 percent), oil (45 percent) and natural gas (21 percent) together accounted for about 97 percent of energy supply in 1974–75. Nuclear fission (largely also stock-energy) contributed about 0.5 percent, while the remainder originated from flow-energy resources, mostly in the form of hydro-electricity (just over 2 percent). For individual countries the

[6] *Recommendation on the Future Availability of Metallic Minerals* (1975, p. 51).
[7] Ibid., pp. 18–19.

relative importance of the various sources of energy differs; nevertheless, as the industrialized countries together consume more than 85 percent of world energy production the above percentage distribution over the various energy resources also holds, by and large, for the energy consumption in the Western countries as a group.

The historical record shows a close relationship between the rate of growth of GNP and that of energy consumption for virtually all countries [Darmstadter (1972, pp. 181–185)]. Still, the energy–GNP elasticity coefficient varies between countries and in time. During the transition stage from a predominantly agricultural society to an industrialized economy the elasticity coefficient is clearly larger than one; also, differences in the structure of manufacturing industry lead to different energy–GNP elasticities between industrialized countries. For the United States, the elasticity coefficient may be smaller than (but still close to) one; in many other industrialized countries it is larger than one [Darmstadter (1972, pp. 181–185); see also Biswas (1974, p. 12)]. On the average, assuming an energy–GNP elasticity of one for all Western economies together probably implies a conservative estimate of energy requirements in relation to GNP growth for the years to come.[8]

In several respects, this is obviously a crude analysis of energy needs. Energy is not a homogeneous commodity, neither in terms of the primary sources, nor in terms of its end uses. Government policies may change the energy–GNP relationships as observed in the past, although such changes are likely to be slow. The most "straightforward" component of an energy policy is presumably energy-pricing policy; yet there is considerable uncertainty as to the price elasticity of overall energy demand. A recent RFF study [Ridker et al. (1977, p. 1)] assumes for the United States a long-run price elasticity of demand for energy of −0.25 (low possibility of substituting other inputs for energy) or, alternatively, −0.75 (high substitution). For industrialized countries other than the US the lower absolute value might be the more realistic estimate.

So far we have examined some market characteristics on the demand side. On the supply side, the uncertainties would seem to be even greater. As to the physical availability of the number one energy resource to date, crude oil, continuation of extraction rates increasing annually by 5 percent or more would exhaust the ultimately recoverable reserves by 2010 or so. If annual extraction of oil were to remain constant at its present level, the ultimately recoverable reserves would be used up only in the second half of the next century. Supply policy of the major oil producers will perhaps aim at a future course of development in between these two alternatives. Extraction rates may be expected to increase further (depending on the rate of growth of demand) till 1985 or 1990, when the level of oil production may be stabilized so as to avoid investment in additional capacity expansion that would not pay off any longer. By the year 2000 annual production levels might start falling gradually. Of course, it remains speculative

---

[8] Note, however, that the OECD has lowered its estimate for the period till 1985 from 0.98 to 0.83; see *World Energy Outlook* (1977, p. 32).

to assume a supply policy along these lines, but it is probably the most reasonable assumption one can make at the present time.

For natural gas, the situation is not unlike that for oil. Middle East oil producers may be expected to acquire a larger share in world production of natural gas, though part of it will be used locally in the region. Again, stabilization of the production level may be aimed at after an initial expansion of output. As the ultimately recoverable reserves of natural gas are probably close to half those of crude oil (in terms of energy content), the share of gas in total world supply is expected to remain about half as large as the share of oil, or even a bit lower.

Of the fossil fuels, coal is by far the most abundant resource in relation to its actual level of use. Known reserves are estimated to be 200 times its annual extraction level, and the ultimately recoverable reserves might surpass the known reserves by a factor of 20. Physical availability is not a problem for the time being – but problems there are, nevertheless, and in many respects: environmental pollution (both in production and in use), technical problems in mining and in transportation, high costs of converting coal into gas or oil, large investment outlays, long lead times, and – as a consequence of all this – political hesitation to opt for the coal alternative. The USSR and the US have the largest reserves and are the largest producers, and the future role of coal is strongly influenced, therefore, by (energy) policy decisions of these two countries. A similar uncertainty, and a dependence on policy decisions, exists with respect to future use of oil shale and tar sands for oil production. These large reserves are located almost entirely in North America; their commercial exploitation is not attractive at the moment, since production costs are (perhaps) 1.5 times the present world market oil price level.

The picture that emerges from the above supply considerations is that at a moderate-to-high rate of economic growth in the industrialized countries – say, at 4 percent growth per annum, but perhaps already at 3 percent, or maybe only at 5 percent – overall demand for energy will increase rapidly enough to start outpacing the increased supply of stock-energy resources by 1985 (or at most a few years later). Further increases in the energy price, and a slowing down of economic growth, would then become inevitable. Both factors will facilitate the major oil producers' decision effectively to stabilize their level of supply. This – admittedly impressionistic rather than minute – picture of the energy situation in the 1980s requires some further comments and clarification.

First, it is implied that in the coming 10 to 15 years "new" sources of energy will not alleviate the supply constraints to a considerable extent. The share of flow-energy resources in total supply will increase but remain modest in the near future. The recent OECD energy study[9] expects an increase to 6 percent of total supply by 1985, chiefly

---

[9] *World Energy Outlook* (1977, pp. 80–100). The percentages refer to total world supply, which is not explicitly stated in the OECD report itself but can be derived from it, as is done, for example, in *Advies inzake besparing op het huishoudelijk energieverbruik* (1977, bijlage 1).

in the form of hydro-electricity. The same study assumes a share of nuclear energy of about 7 percent in 1985 – a figure considerably lower than that of the earlier OECD study *Energy Prospects to 1985* (1974), but in the opinion of the present author still likely to be an overestimate of the contribution to be expected from nuclear power.

Secondly, energy conservation measures might reduce the energy–GNP elasticity coefficient and lower the rate of growth of energy demand. The OECD study referred to above estimates a conservation potential of 16–19 percent of total energy requirements (on the basis of the 1973 situation) that could be realized by 1985 in the OECD countries. The effect of such measures would be to postpone the tightening of the world energy market till after 1990, and to buy time for the switch-over to new energy sources. The largest contribution to energy conservation might come, according to the OECD report, from the transportation sector, while industrial and residential/commercial energy uses rank second and third with about the same energy-saving potential. There are, however, as yet few signs that governments will launch strong energy-conservation programmes.

Thirdly, the picture of a supply shortage of oil and gas emerging somewhere between 1985 and 1990 assumes that the (relative) energy prices in the Western countries remain more or less unchanged until then. Deliberate domestic energy price increases – and preferably as soon as possible – might curb growing energy demand. Short-term effects might be modest, and even the long-term elasticity may not be too high (see above); a substantial increase, phased out over a number of years but announced beforehand, would therefore be indicated. Obviously, a price rise of energy will affect – both directly and indirectly – the general price level and thus strengthen inflationary pressures. Nevertheless, a gradual price increase is to be preferred to a much more disruptive price jump around 1985. Again, a more smooth transition to the "new energy" situation – whatever the new resource or resources will be – could be effectuated.[10]

In sum, the prospects for continued material growth of the industrialized countries of the West depend in significant measure on the future energy situation. About this situation, however, considerable uncertainty obtains – particularly with regard to the future development of supply. During the second half of the 1980s energy supply problems might become acute. Early government policies may postpone and lessen the impact of probable shortages. A "wise" policy package might include measures such as (a) stimulation of energy conservation, (b) energy price increases, (c) reorientation of production towards less energy-intensive processes and products, and (d) stimulation of R&D in the field of energy production (particularly flow energy) and use. Moreover, as the socio-cultural climate in the West may be developing in a direction that permits a de-emphasizing of material growth, a slowing down of growth rates is to be valued positively.

[10] The case for anticipatory energy price increases is also argued in Labohm (1977).

6. Technical progress

In the above sections, reference has been made several times to the role played by technical progress in the "creation" and utilization of natural resources. Some additional comments may be in place as regards the relative importance of future technical progress in the area of the various resource categories. Such progress may take place not only in the production (and distribution) of the resources, but also in the efficiency of their use.

Agriculture, the most conspicuous amongst the stock-renewable resources, is characterized in most parts of the world by a slow and gradual adoption of improved technologies. Owing to the predominance of small-scale production units, of behaviour patterns rooted in cultural tradition, of poor access to financial resources, and so on, there is in fact a considerable reservoir of technical improvements in agriculture waiting for actual application by an increasing number of producers. This is particularly true of developing countries, even if we take into account the need for adaptation to local conditions, but it also applies to agriculture in the industrialized countries. To put it in the form of a slight overstatement: the technology to be used for considerably improving agricultural yields in the remaining decades of this century is known, grosso modo. The constraints for increasing output lie in the inherent "sluggishness" of the agricultural sector (as indicated above) and in the socio-economic set-up that should provide adequate incentives for output increases. It may be noted in passing that there is also considerable scope for reducing postharvest losses, especially as regards food production in developing countries; again, the techniques are known but the investment funds are lacking.

In order to avoid the impression that in the field of agricultural technology all problems are already solved, it should be added that the environmental consequences of modern and modernizing agriculture deserve further study and may require modification of present-day approaches. As already observed above, yield increases are most probably to be preferred to expansion of cultivated area, from an ecological point of view. Environmental aspects of increased production in general are discussed in the companion paper by Hueting, and we will not pursue this matter here.

With respect to natural resources other than agriculture, R&D and technical progress are to a much greater extent controlled and directed by (large) private enterprises; as a consequence, the unused stock of potential technical improvements tends to be much smaller. It is estimated that 90–95 percent of all metal mining outside the centrally planned countries is in the hands of some 150 Western companies, operating in all parts of the world.[11] Over the past decades, technical progress has brought down per-unit production costs (also as a consequence of increased size of the individual technical unit) and production has become more capital-intensive. As Nordhaus (1974,

---

[11] *Recommendation on the Future Availability of Metallic Minerals* (1975, p. 12).

p. 24) has pointed out, most metal prices have gone down considerably since 1900 in relation to the general wage level in industry. There are some signs, however, that relative prices have been falling more slowly in recent years; moreover, in the past "cost and price figures have not taken account of the 'external' costs of extraction, transportation, and processing of raw materials" [Peterson and Fisher (1977, p. 711)] (largely environmental costs). It is not unlikely that the rate of technical progress in mining will be lower in the future than it has been in past decades, and that technological improvements will have to be orientated in substantial measure towards reducing the negative environmental side-effects of mining and metal production.

It is interesting to note that there may be a certain "competition", within each mining company's research budget, between allocations for new exploration and funds for technological research. From a recent report we quote:

> Technical advances with regard to the minimum acceptable ore content have the advantage that the exploitable proportion of all known locations is raised; the increase in exploitable reserves that can be achieved in this way will usually be much bigger than that resulting from the discovery of a new location. Moreover, every new location is, of course, tied to one place, whereas technical improvements can be applied primarily where this is considered most desirable for economic and political reasons. Now that the national governments in many developing countries are taking a more critical attitude towards Western mining companies, it would seem not unlikely that these companies will lay greater stress on technological research than on exploration in developing countries.[12]

The consequence of this would be that in the long run the potential mineral reserves would be located more and more in the developing countries.

The area in which technical progress seems to be moving fastest at present is that of offshore technology, and in the particular case of metals this is primarily deep-ocean mining (nodules). As already observed, successful mining of nodules would change the market prospects for certain metals quite considerably. As far as the use of mineral end-products (metals, etc.) is concerned, further economies may be expected in the form of lower material inputs and increased recycling – depending, of course, on the future price developments for the materials concerned.

Of decisive importance is, for obvious reasons, the future development of energy production. Which energy resources are going to replace oil and natural gas in due course? Here a multitude of views and opinions exist. In the context of this article it is impossible to give a detailed account of potential or probable technological developments in the future, and their pros and cons. We can only repeat and summarize here what would seem to be the common wisdom at the moment of writing – but nevertheless common wisdom as perceived by the present author. Com-

[12] *Recommendation on the Future Availability of Metallic Minerals* (1974, p. 49).

mon wisdom, then, "assumes" that in the more distant future an acceptable (though perhaps costly) solution of the energy supply problem will be found, i.e. it is assumed that well after the year 2000 virtually inexhaustible, reasonably priced and environmentally acceptable energy from new sources will be available in large quantities. The two most serious candidates are energy from nuclear fusion and solar energy plus, in a minor role, geothermal energy and bio-energy. If this assumption is accepted, the problem becomes one of bridging the period between, say, 1990 (when oil and natural gas supplies may slow down in growth) and 2030 or 2050, when the new sources will hopefully come to full maturity. During this transition period fission energy was until recently supposed to play an important part in energy supply, but is now lagging behind the initial time schedules for several reasons, including popular worries and public protests. It looks as if coal (both as a boiler fuel and as the raw material for synthetic oil and gas) will be a more important energy source for the transition period, in spite of its environmental drawbacks.

Already the oversimplified picture given above presents a R&D task of colossal magnitude, and its realization – if possible – will furthermore require investment outlays of huge dimensions.[13] The technological and economic tasks lying ahead of us in the field of energy supply are probably so great that one cannot help wondering about the apparent equanimity of most governments and policy-makers on this point.

7. Concluding remarks

A thorough investigation of the relationship between economic growth and natural resources availability requires a book-length treatment and a multidisciplinary team of authors. The present analysis is neither profound nor original; it is hoped that it will stimulate others to do a better job in the rather neglected field of natural resources. The tentative conclusions we arrived at in this article are largely in line with those of McCracken et al. reported recently to the OECD.[14] Analysing the feasibility of continued growth, also in view of the supply of energy, food and raw materials, the OECD expert group states:

Our overall conclusion is that for the most part there are no major technical constraints impeding continuing growth. . . . Compared with what was achieved during the 1960s, potential growth rates will probably be somewhat lower. . . . (F)or the

[13] To quote Chynoweth (1976) on the American situation: "The energy sector alone has generally commanded about 22 per cent of the available US investment capital in the past, and over the coming years some predict that it may need as much as 30 per cent or more."

[14] McCracken et al. (1977, pp. 152–153). For an analysis focusing on the raw materials position of the Netherlands, see *Advies inzake het te voeren grondstoffenbeleid* (1978).

next five years potential output in the OECD area as a whole may be growing up to 1 per cent less rapidly than the 5 per cent rate of the 1960s. This seems to us to be a plausible assumption. Looking further ahead, however, one cannot rule out the possibility that a problem of overall energy supplies could emerge which could inhibit the growth of supply potential.

The McCracken report deliberately uses the term "growth potential", since the actual growth performance might well remain below the potential. Contrary to the McCracken report, the present author would welcome a less-than-potential growth rate of the industrialized countries (accompanied, of course, by otherwise desirable and appropriate social and economic policies). The reasons for this preference for a slow rate of material growth in the rich countries are twofold. For one thing, the ecological and environmental side-effects of ever-increasing material production have undesirable and sometimes even dangerous consequences for life on earth. True, some of these negative effects could perhaps be avoided. Also, it remains uncertain how wide the margin is between a healthy and a dying biosphere, and where within this margin we find ourselves to date. But given this uncertainty and the chance – however small, perhaps – of a truly serious threat to human and other forms of life, it is doubtful whether our rich societies really need more-of-the-same that badly.

A second point, related to the first, involves the time horizon of our decisions and is, as such, familiar to economists. At a nonzero discount rate, the future no longer matters beyond the present generation. Apart from oil and natural gas, nonrenewable resources are likely to be adequate for our lifetime – so why worry? On ethical grounds such a stand can and should be queried. Admittedly we cannot foresee all problems that the coming generations will have to face (and even less solve these problems!), but it is not beyond our control to try to keep options open to them. One way of doing this is to economize on the use of stock resources – also by slowing down and eventually halting the rate of material growth.

It is beyond the scope of this paper to discuss the implications of slower growth or "zero growth" for the industrialized countries. It goes without saying that the reorientation of economies and societies towards new or at least reformulated goals will be and has to be a gradual process – not only because of the required adaptations in the social framework of the industrialized countries themselves but also in view of the fact that the rich countries still function in part as the engine of the growth process in the developing countries. In the latter countries material growth should continue for decades to come, but there, too, the direction of growth will (have to) differ from the pattern of the past and the role of the Western engine stimulating export-orientated growth will probably be reduced.

Material growth in the Western countries is still possible in the years immediately ahead, and will remain possible for a much longer period if the energy issue can be solved satisfactorily. Whether it would be wise to make maximum use of this possibility is a different question altogether – but a question that deserves serious attention, also from economists.

References

Advies inzake besparing op het huishoudelijk energieverbruik, 1977 (Voorlopige Algemene Energie Raad, Den Haag).

Advies inzake het te voeren grondstoffenbeleid, 1978 (Sociaal-Economische Raad, Den Haag).

Barnett, H. J. and Ch. Morse, 1965, Scarcity and growth (Johns Hopkins, Baltimore).

Biswas, A. K., 1974, Energy and the environment (Environment Canada, Ottawa).

Brobst, D. A. and W. P. Pratt, eds., 1973, United States mineral resources – Geological survey professional paper 820 (Government Printing Office, Washington, D.C.).

Buringh, P., H. D. J. van Heemst and G. J. Staring, 1975, Computation of the absolute maximum food production of the world (Agricultural University, Wageningen).

Chapman, J. D., 1969, Interaction between man and his resources, in: P. Cloud et al., Resources and man (Freeman, San Francisco) pp. 31–42.

Chynoweth, A. G., 1976, Materials conservation – A technologist's viewpoint, Economic impact 16, 27–33.

Coppens, H. A. J., 1972, The European Community and the developing countries seen in global perspective, in: Ph.P. Everts, ed., The European Community in the world (Rotterdam University Press, Rotterdam) pp. 135–183.

Darmstadter, J., 1972, Energy consumption: Trends and patterns, in: S. H. Schurr, ed., Energy, economic growth, and the environment (Johns Hopkins, Baltimore) pp. 155–223.

Energy prospects to 1985, 1974 (OECD, Paris).

Erickson, R. L., 1973, Crustal abundance of elements, and mineral reserves and resources, in: Brobst and Pratt, eds., 1973, pp. 21–25.

Fisher, A. C., 1977, On measures of natural resource scarcity (International Institute for Applied Systems Analysis, Laxenburg).

Hoogh, J. de, M. A. Keyzer, H. Linnemann and H. D. J. van Heemst, 1976, Food for a growing world population: Some of the main findings of a study on the long-term prospects of the world food situation, European Review of Agricultural Economics 3, 459–499.

Labohm, H. H. J., 1977, De afwendbaarheid van een wereldolietekort, Economisch-Statistische Berichten 62, 864–866.

Leontief, W. et al., 1977, The future of the world economy (Oxford University Press, New York).

Linnemann, H., J. de Hoogh, M. A. Keyzer and H. D. J. van Heemst, 1979, MOIRA – Model of international relations in agriculture (North-Holland, Amsterdam).

Lovering, T. S., 1969, Mineral resources from the land, in: P. Cloud et al., eds., Resources and man (Freeman, San Francisco) pp. 109–134.

McCracken, P., et al., 1977, Towards full employment and price stability (OECD, Paris).

Meadows, D. H., D. L. Meadows, J. Randers and W. W. Behrens, 1972, The limits to growth (Universe Books, New York).

Mill, J. S., 1929, Principles of political economy (Longmans & Green, London).

Nordhaus, W. D., 1974, Resources as a constraint on growth, American Economic Review, Papers and Proceedings 64, 22–26.

Pearce, D. W., 1976, Environmental economics (Longman, London).

Peterson, F. M. and A. C. Fisher, 1977, The exploitation of extractive resources, Economic Journal 87, 681–721.

Recommendation on the future availability of metallic minerals, 1975 (National Advisory Council for Development Cooperation, The Hague).

Ridker, R., W. Watson and A. Shapanka, 1977, Economic, energy, and environmental consequences of alternative energy regimes – An application of the RFF/SEAS modelling system (Resources for the Future, Washington D.C.).

Vokes, F. M., 1976, The abundance and availability of mineral resources, in: G. J. S. Govett and M. H. Govett, eds., World mineral supplies – Assessment and perspective (Elsevier, Amsterdam).
World energy outlook, 1977 (OECD, Paris).
The world food problem, 1967 (Government Printing Office, Washington D.C.).
Zimmerman, E. W., 1951, World resources and industries (Harper, New York).

Chapter 8   *p. 57:*

COMMENT ON LINNEMANN'S PAPER

P. M. E. M. VAN DER GRINTEN

DSM, Heerlen and Technological University, Eindhoven

79-82

1. Supply of and demand for resources

In broad outline I agree with Linnemann's argument. Expressed in different terms, the point he has made is that for the present there is little danger of an economically paralysing scarcity of natural resources because:

(a) methods of extracting may yet be considerably improved;

(b) the (re)processing may become more economical and efficient; and

(c) the pricing system is expected to effect still more substitution and optimization.

An exception is rightly made for the *energy* raw materials, which are far less price-elastic. Indeed, these resources may be so scarce before the year 2000 that everything must be done to find alternative energy sources as soon as possible; at the same time drastic economies will also be essential.

It is remarkable, however, to observe how most models (including world models) for the supply of energy and resources show again and again the powerful effects of adaptive and "feedback" policies. Indeed, these models actually assume that technological progress is not going to be paralysed by scarcity situations.

2. Technological progress

This brings me to the role of technological progress. In my opinion Linnemann has placed too little emphasis on the tasks and possibilities of technological progress and of technological innovation in particular. Science, technology and industry will play a dominant part in the changes, adjustments and innovations necessary in the near future. This will, in the first place, involve a substitution of new for fairly old products and processes. In its struggle for continuity, the manufacturing industry has for a long

Prospects of Economic Growth, edited by S. K. Kuipers and G. J. Lanjouw
© *North-Holland Publishing Company*

time observed the *life-cycle* principle of process–product–market combinations, by bringing its new, semi- and fully-developed activities into proper balance.

Particularly important is the possibility of dropping old processes and products that have reached advanced maturity and replacing them by new products under development, which are cheaper or better and which may therefore penetrate markets and develop rapidly. Economies of scale and breakthroughs in technology or in the marketplace may subsequently result in a major productivity increase. This phenomenon will continue to be present in the future, probably even at a more rapid pace. In practice it may involve the utilization of cheaper (= more abundant) resources such as the oceans, minerals and agricultural base materials; the development of other processes, including biochemical syntheses, photosynthesis, equipment for extreme conditions of temperature and pressure (new materials!) and large-scale recycling.

Secondly, markets in the Western world will certainly display a shift towards a demand for better-quality products of a higher added value, based on more know-how and with a high degree of service performances. Thus, a qualitative rather than a quantitative growth can be expected, initiated by a distinct change in welfare standards.

The substitutions and adjustments described above will almost certainly also be accompanied by changes in and optimization of the world's industrial patterns. Generally speaking, it is most advisable for industries using appreciable quantities of base materials and capital to be established where quantities of commodities are actually available (the Middle East, for instance); activities which require appreciable know-how and marketing skills, on the other hand, will be quite compatible with conditions in the West. This, as well as the changes initiated in the labour-intensive industries a long time ago, is indicative of a thorough restructuring process. Actually it can again be regarded as the completion of a life cycle and, therefore, as part of the normal and acceptable dynamic development of society.

3. Consequences in terms of business economics

It has been argued above that products or even industries will eventually reach their saturation point because, for example, the costs of labour and raw materials make the product too expensive for further penetration. This will cause growth to slow down and, consequently, the productivity and margins to be reduced.

Criteria that are frequently used such as the gross profit per dollar of wages (G/W) and the gross profit per dollar of assets (G/A) will then display a steady fall, which is an indication that the related activities are no longer compatible with the prevailing social and economic climate [Van der Grinten (1978)]. The company concerned may then try to change over to products of a higher added value, which will open up prospects of a new life cycle and increases of productivities of capital and labour. Forward integration is often part of this change.

By way of illustration the following tables show the 1970 and 1976 sales and asset profiles of a typical European company producing bulk chemicals; they relate to a period which showed a slowdown of the enormous growth of the Sixties, resulting from the rapidly rising cost of basic materials and labour (energy crisis, wage explosion). See tables 8.1 and 8.2.

Table 8.1

Sales profile of a typical European chemical company.

	1970	1976	Price growth (% p.a.)	Volume growth (% p.a.)
S (sales)	100	100	7	10
C (cost of supplies)	52	64.5	11	9.9
D (depreciation)	8	7	8	6
W (wages)	25	22	13	2
G (gross profit)	15	6.5		

Table 8.2

Balance sheet data of a typical European chemical company.

	1970	1976	Growth (% p.a.)
A (assets)	100	100	8
E (equity)	40	30	3
L (loans)	60	70	11
S/A (sales : assets)	0.9	1.4	8
G/A (gross profit : assets)	0.14	0.1	−5

These tables clearly show that, despite the continuing volume growth of sales and productivity, the cost increases have been such that a dramatic narrowing of the gross profit margin (G/S) has resulted. This is not compensated for by sufficient improvement of the nominal labour productivity (S/W) and capital productivity (S/A), so that the above ratios $(G/W, G/A)$ in fact decline, as is shown in table 8.3.

Table 8.3

Development of return on wages and on assets.

	1970	1976
$\frac{G}{W}=\frac{G}{S}\times\frac{S}{W}$	$\frac{15}{100}\times\frac{100}{25}=0.6$	$\frac{6.5}{100}\times\frac{100}{22}=0.3$
$\frac{G}{A}=\frac{G}{S}\times\frac{S}{A}$	$\frac{15}{100}\times 0.9=0.14$	$\frac{6.5}{100}\times 1.4=0.09$

Let us now start from the data of a producer of performance and fine chemicals. In 1970 these products were still in their development stage. Their ratios show the reverse trend to those of the bulk chemical producers, which is due to higher added values (i.e. a smaller component for energy and raw materials), to an increased volume growth and to the accompanying increase in productivity. See table 8.4.

The G/W ratio thus rises from 0.25 to 0.34. With a turnover rate S/A increasing from 1.5 to 2 the return on assets G/A increases from 0.15 to 0.23, which compares very favourably with the "old" bulk chemicals.

Table 8.4

Sales profile of performance chemicals.

	1970	1976	% growth per annum	
			price	volume
S (sales)	100	100	7	15
C (costs of supplies)	35	42	11	15
D (depreciation)	15	13	8	11
W (wages)	40	33.5	11	7
G (gross profit)	10	11.5		

4. Summary

Although the traditional industries, which include the basic industries, will show a decline in growth and a tendency towards consolidation, our industrial companies must be able to effect changes in the pattern of their activities such that their continuity is ensured by innovation, specialization and switching to products with a substantial know-how requirement and a high degree of service performance.

Reference

Grinten, P. M. E. M. van der, 1978, Strategic planning in a large company, in: C. van Dam, ed., Trends in financial decision making (Martinus Nijhoff, Leiden/Boston) pp. 50–71.

Chapter 9   *p. 57:*

COMMENT ON LINNEMANN'S PAPER

A. NENTJES   *83 - 86*

University of Groningen

In the concluding pages of his paper Linnemann remarks that "a thorough investigation of the relationship between economic growth and natural resource availability
requires a book-length treatment and a multidisciplinary team of authors". This should
not, however, obscure the merit of Linnemann's contribution as a praiseworthy review
of recent opinion on the possibility of future scarcity of natural resources.

   Before commenting on specific categories of resources, three general remarks are
called for.

   (1) The uncertainty which surrounds any prediction regarding the future availability
of natural resources has been mentioned but needs very strong emphasis: uncertainties
concern the future development of demand patterns, increases in known reserves of
nonrenewable resources, and shifts in the marginal cost of extraction and production.
As a consequence, "common opinion" in the field of natural resources is neither
homogeneous nor stable: estimates of how long the supply of petroleum will remain
available range from a low of 17 years to a high of 100 years, and the remaining
supplies of conventional petroleum have been estimated at anywhere between a low of
285×10^9 tons and a high of 400×10^9 tons [Govett and Govett (1977)]. As indicated
by Linnemann, opinion on resource availability in the last ten years has swung from
buoyant optimism in the 1960s to the bleak pessimism in *The Limits to Growth* and
back to today's reserved optimism. As a lesson from this we should learn not to place
too much trust in our own opinions on natural resource availability.

   (2) Another point concerns the definition of natural resource shortage. Although
taken for granted in Linnemann's paper, more explicit attention could have been paid
to the fact that it is not shortage in an absolute physical sense which is the interesting
phenomenon, but rather the economic concept of scarcity as exhibited by the marginal
costs at which natural resources are available. In the face of a pressing demand a
looming physical shortage will make itself felt through increasing marginal costs of

exploration, extraction and production of resources, increasing marginal user cost and probably also increasing environmental costs. If the availability of natural resources should become a main problem, it will show up in a dramatic rise in resource prices.

(3) In connection with the above, a third point should be made. In the paper hardly any attention is devoted to the mechanism which links natural resource scarcity to a decline in the rate of economic growth. I should have liked to see more light shed on this question. Does resource scarcity make itself felt only by a decrease in the rate of growth of *potential* output, as seems to be suggested in the concluding remarks? In the very long run, after the structure of production has adapted to new scarcities, this might be true. In the short and intermediate period rising relative prices of resources will affect balances of payments, inflation and effective demand, even to the point of general underemployment of labour and capital. The aftermath of the 1973 rise in oil prices may be cited as a vivid illustration.

Availability of agricultural produce is not expected to constitute a bottleneck for continued economic growth of the industrial countries for the next two decades or so. This conclusion is based on MOIRA – an important piece of research in which Linnemann participated. It is comforting to see this projection supported by the findings of Leontief et al. (1977), as published in *The Future of the World Economy*, although they forecast a somewhat lower rate of agricultural growth. The increase of agricultural output has to come from an increase in the yields per hectare. This development is also preferred from an ecological point of view. We should not, however, close our eyes to the enormous destruction of landscapes which seems to be the inseparable companion of the intensification of cultivation. There is a need for conservationist policies in this field. One wonders about the extent to which such policies will hamper further increases in land productivity.

For the category of mineral, nonenergy resources, Linnemann gives a bright picture. An overall shortage of mineral resources is not expected to emerge in the immediate future. Supply problems for specific minerals may occur, but these should not constitute a bottleneck for continued economic growth. The publications from which this prospect is derived all draw their information about resource availability from the United States Bureau of Mines resource appraisals, so that one should not be very surprised to find parallel results in the publications quoted. This again illustrates the small data base for research in this field.

Prospects for economic growth depend significantly on the future energy situation. Linnemann sees the possibility of serious problems of supply during the second half of the 1980s.[1] He narrows the problem down to scarcity of two specific energy resources: oil and natural gas. I prefer the following diagnosis. If bottlenecks do appear, which is still uncertain, the problem will primarily be one of reallocation from oil-based energy

[1] In addition to Linnemann's references the following studies are of significance: WAES, Wilson et al. (1977), Häfele and Sassin (1977), and WEC (1978).

production to coal-based energy production. In the field of electricity generation and manufacturing the possibilities of substituting coal for oil do not seem too bad. A cross-price elasticity between coal and oil of 0.5 was found by Griffin (1977) and one of 0.6–0.7 in manufacturing by Halvorsen (1977). Both report an own price elasticity for oil demand in electricity generation and manufacturing of about −3. In addition energy-saving has been drastically bringing down the energy–GNP elasticities in industrialized countries. From International Energy Agency data the energy–GNP elasticities shown in table 9.1 have been derived.[2]

Table 9.1

	1960–1972	1972–1977
German Federal Republic	1.0	0.3
Japan	1.0	0.7
United States	1.1	0.3
The Netherlands	1.6	0.4
IEA countries	1.0	0.5

This is not to deny that there may be serious sectoral problems. Road transport especially, with little prospect in the near future of interfuel substitution or fuel saving, may be seriously affected. However, I do not visualize the industrialized world grinding to a halt because of a general shortage of energy. It is interesting to note that in Leontief's scenarios there is more than a doubling of oil prices between 1980 and 1990, while coal prices show a slight decrease; gross domestic product maintains an annual rate of growth in the region of 3–4 percent.

Intensification of coal burning will indeed cause serious environmental problems. There is, however (with reason) a much greater and growing concern in Western Europe about the environmental and political impact of nuclear energy. Its future as an oil substitute has now become very uncertain. I share Linnemann's hope that non-exhaustible and clean energy sources will become available in the long run.

Although the prospects for agricultural and nonenergy mineral production seem bright, this may no longer be true if energy were in fact to become very scarce. Modern agriculture has become highly dependent on fertilizers, and among these nitrogen is very energy-intensive in production. The energy-intensity of the extraction of minerals increases very strongly with the decreasing degrees of purity of the ores. Production of metallic magnesium, aluminium and steel, to give a few examples, takes a lot of energy. (In the Netherlands the production of iron and steel, aluminium and ammonia accounts for 40 percent of industry's use of energy.) In many cases recycling consumes more energy than the extraction and production of new materials. It is an interesting and important question to what extent rising prices of energy would affect the structure and level of demand for primary products.

[2] *International Herald Tribune,* 24 April 1978.

References

Conservation Committee of the World Energy Conference, 1978, World energy resources 1985–2000 (Guildford).

Govett, M. H. and G. J. S. Govett, 1977, Scarcity of basic materials and fuels: Assessment and implications, in: D. W. Pearce and I. Walter, eds., Resource conservation, social and economic dimensions of recycling (New York University Press, New York).

Griffin, J. M., 1977, Inter-fuel substitution possibilities: A translog application to intercountry data, International Economic Review 3, 755–773.

Häfele, W. and W. Sassin, 1977, Future energy scenarios (Invited paper at the Tenth World Energy Conference, Istanbul, 19–23 September, 1977).

Halvorsen, R., 1977, Energy substitution in U.S. manufacturing, Review of Economics and Statistics 4, 381–389.

Leontief, W. et al., 1977, The future of the world economy (Oxford University Press, New York).

Wilson, C. L. et al., 1977, Energy, global prospects 1985–2000. Report of the Workshop on Alternative Energy Strategies (WAES) (McGraw-Hill, New York).

Chapter 10

ENVIRONMENT AND GROWTH: EXPECTATIONS AND SCENARIOS*

R. HUETING   *87-103*

Central Bureau of Statistics, Voorburg

Starting from the subject-matter of economics, economic growth can mean only one thing: an increase of the satisfaction of wants (welfare). This is assumed to depend on the available quantity of scarce goods. The latter include both produced goods and now scarce environmental goods (water, soil, air and plant and animal species). It proves impossible to place both categories of goods under the same denominator (e.g. money). Consequently, extrapolation of national income on the strength of the expected development of productivity is not permitted. Decisions can best be taken on the basis of scenarios. Probably continued growth of production will have disastrous effects on the environment. Prevention of these creates a considerable amount of permanent employment but exerts a permanent check on the growth of production.

1. The concept of growth

A discussion of expectations with regard to economic growth and environment (including the use of space) is not feasible without a definition of concepts. In the hope that I will not insult the reader, I first of all recall that economic theory concerns itself with the problems that occur when making a choice between the scarce resources that can meet man's wants. The satisfaction derived from the availability of scarce goods is called welfare. The theory assumes that in our dealings with scarce resources we try to maximize our welfare. This is regarded as the aim of economic action. Economic growth must therefore amount to an increase in welfare, the enhancement of the pleasure derived from having scarce goods at one's disposal.

The great difficulty of economic theory in general, and this volume in particular, seems to me the impossibility of measuring welfare (the satisfaction of wants). The latter is not directly observable "from outside" and thus is not a cardinal measurable quantity in itself. In practice we therefore try to measure the factors which in our opinion influence welfare and *do* lend themselves to measurement. In doing so we start

* This paper originally appeared in *Denken en Meten* published by the Centraal Bureau voor de Statistiek, Voorburg, Holland.

Propects of Economic Growth, edited by S. K. Kuipers and G. J. Lanjouw
© *North-Holland Publishing Company*

from a number of assumptions that we then often forget again, which does not help to clarify discussions on growth.

Of the factors that influence our welfare, the following seem to me to be the most important: the size of the package of goods at our disposal, the quantity of goods at the disposal of others (the degree of income inequality), working conditions and the extent to which desired and actual work coincide (preferably no involuntary unemployment; flexible working hours would, on the other hand, be welcomed). Of these welfare parameters, the size of the package of goods has acquired such a great emphasis in economic theory and economic policy that in everyday practice we have come to designate the increase in the package of goods as economic growth.

And yet throughout the years doubt has been cast on the value of this indicator, for a variety of reasons. For instance, the question whether welfare is properly represented by the package of goods has for more than 40 years been a topic at international congresses of National Accounts people, whereby it has proved impossible to arrive at unanimity. The question has now popped up again in the fashionable but misleading concept "selective growth" (which we shall consider below). The answer is in my opinion simple but unfortunately rather long-winded: the changes in the package of goods form a highly important (but not unique) indicator of welfare as long as we make the following assumptions.

(1) Wants grow less than proportionately to the increase in the goods becoming available.

(2) Changes in the package of goods form a reasonable reflection of the changes in relative preferences, while the factors of production in the reference year are capable of producing more than the package of goods in the base year.

(3) Corrections are made for reductions of the package of goods as a result of factors beyond man's control, such as natural disasters.

(4) Corrections are likewise made for reductions of the package of goods as a result of factors for which man is responsible.

In the discussion on environmental deterioration the opinion may sometimes be heard that in the wealthy countries wants are almost saturated and obtaining still more goods does not make people any happier. It is also occasionally argued that we are trapped in a production and consumption structure that compels us to acquire all kinds of goods which do not satisfy our deeper ("real") wants. (Formerly there were two bicycles outside the door, now two cars, and this has not made us any the happier.) For those holding such opinions the changes in the package of goods do not of course have the slightest significance as an indication of the trend of welfare. This view (which is defended among others by a number of leading Dutch economists and statisticians[1]) cannot be "proved" any more than can the opposite. It is a matter of

---

[1] H. K. van Tuinen (personal communication) and J. B. Opschoor in a discussion during the symposium "Economische groei" (Economic growth) of the Institute for International Studies on 13 October 1976 in the Academiegebouw, Leiden.

plausibility of points of departure. One of the consequences of rejecting the parallelism between changes in the package of goods and welfare is that – at least in the margin – the goods are not scarce. The sacrifice of potential growth of production on behalf of the environment therefore does not form an economic sacrifice (cost). The emphasis of the discussions on growth – in this volume also – should shift considerably, probably towards the wants side. For of course a considerable piece of real economic growth can be achieved if our wants change in the sense that – independently of environmental considerations – we come to prefer cycling to driving and a sweater to high room temperatures (and at the same time a small family to a large one).

I am assuming here that there is consistency between wants and actions. People do broadly what they want, so that we can go by their behaviour, in so far as the preferences can express themselves in that. In my opinion we would not keep on exerting ourselves at often unpleasant or dangerous work if the goods we obtained as a result always proved a disappointment afterwards. Moreover, many wants are still unsatisfied, for by no means everybody has a house with a garden or a motor yacht, or holidays in other continents. As regards the first point, parallelism between the size of the package of goods and the level of satisfaction of wants seems the most plausible point of departure.

The second point of departure is also plausible. For by increasing productivity we have the choice between more of the same goods, more new goods, or a combination. In terms of economic growth "more" means not only more in quantity, but also more in quality and variety. The question whether new products generate new wants cannot be answered. Have people always wanted to fly, or did this want come into being with the invention of the aeroplane? The fact that man has tried for centuries to propel himself through the air suggests that the former is the case. However, what is decisive is the existence of a possibility of choice with respect to the composition of the package of goods.

In welfare comparisons in time, utilizing the changes in the quantity of economic goods that have become available, it seems in any case necessary to make allowance for the third aspect. A natural disaster may destroy goods; the threat of war and an increase in (violent) crime may reduce safety.[2] The production elicited by this serves only to restore the level of satisfaction of wants that had already been attained before the external factor occurred. Realization of the functional classification advocated by some (a classification by purpose) for the National Accounts will enable the users to apply such a correction if desired. Another solution is to consider series in peacetime without disasters and further to confine oneself to what are called surprise-free future surveys.

The fourth point presents insurmountable difficulties: the environmental deteriora-

---

[2] A difficulty with the example of threat of war is the uncertainty whether the factor is indeed an external one. In the course of history there have been countries that stepped up their expenditure on armaments to extend their territory or sphere of influence. In that case one can hardly speak of an "external" factor. Moreover, there are minorities who consider that safety does not increase but decreases as a result of arming.

tion caused by man may be regarded as a loss of scarce goods which can only exceptionally be quantified in a (shadow) price that is directly comparable with the market
price of produced goods. As a result it is not possible in most cases to take this loss into
account when calculating the changes in the package of goods. We still record in
national income today only an (unknown) part of the changes in the scarce goods that
we use. As a result, recording the change in the package of goods has lost its value as
an indicator of welfare. In the Thirties, when National Accounts were introduced and
environmental deterioration had not yet assumed such proportions, this may have been
permissible, but today it certainly is no longer feasible. From now on – and in this
volume too – we shall no longer be able to rely on the figures of national income for
assessing the results of growth and we may no longer automatically extrapolate these
figures with respect to prospects of economic growth on the strength of expectations
regarding the development of productivity.

2. The environment: a collection of new scarce goods

Our environment may be interpreted as a collection of functions (possible uses
possessing usefulness), on which man is entirely dependent in his doings. Owing to our
greatly increased level of activities the functions have entered into competition with one
another: the extent to which a human activity appropriates a given function of an environmental component (water, soil, air) is at the expense of another function. As soon
as that is the case, loss of function evidently appears. The environmental functions are
then no longer able to satisfy the wants for them. In other words, they have become
scarce and may therefore be regarded as economic goods, just like produced goods and
services. Use of environmental functions for a given purpose that excludes use for
another purpose forms costs.

    An example may illustrate this. For ages we have been disposing of our waste in our en-
vironment. We then use the function dumping ground for waste. After certain limits have
been exceeded (e.g. that of the self-purification capacity of water) the use of this function
proceeds to disturb other functions (e.g. drinking water, water for swimming in, air for
physiological functioning, natural environment). In this example the quality of the environmental component is the issue and we may therefore speak here of qualitative competition of functions, or simply pollution.

    But in the quantitative (amount of matter) and spatial (amount of room) senses too
environmental components are increasingly failing to meet the wants for them. The
resultant quantitative and spatial competition of functions is certainly as important as
the problem of pollution. Moreover, technical solutions are not possible here, because
the use of a quantity of matter (ground water, for instance) or of the space of an environmental component entirely excludes another use, and technology is unable to

create more matter and space than are present on earth. In particular the spatial competition of functions is becoming increasingly fierce. For example, urban space is less and less able to meet the existing demand for walking, cycling, driving, public transport and children's play. In most countries there is severe competition regarding the use of space for suburbanization, road-building, recreation, agriculture and natural environment.

We have now broadly reached a situation in which the use of an environmental function is always at the expense of one or more other functions (often the effect is passed on to the function natural environment via a number of functions). Our environment is of course a material one, like the things that we produce and consume with its assistance, whether these are wheat, music, medical aid or books. In this situation the subject-matter of economics may be described as the study of the problems of choice that occur when organizing the dead and living matter of our environment in accordance with man's wishes.

3. Economic growth: the unknown balance of production profit and environment loss

The reason why the uses to which our environment can be put are becoming scarce is the steadily growing production for and consumption by more and more people in a world in which space, the amount of matter and the carrying capacity of water, soil and air and of the natural ecosystems are limited. We have now reached a situation in which the growth of production not only reduces a shortage of desired goods but simultaneously creates new scarce goods as well. The increase in production, as measured in national income, can therefore, as we have already seen, no longer fulfil its traditional role of indicator of the extent to which society has succeeded in increasing the availability of economic goods (in the broad sense) desired by the public. On the one hand we are concerned with a loss of environmental functions (see above); on the other a growing part of production goes to compensating for these losses of function (e.g. the construction of swimming pools or of desalination of canals as a result of water pollution, remedying the consequences of road accidents). This part of production may not be interpreted in a long-term time series such as that of national income as a net contribution to the package of economic goods.[3] The effect of an increase in production on our welfare now depends on the importance that we attach to, on the one hand, more produced goods and, on the other, the resultant loss of environmental goods. Depending on this weighting, an increase in production can lead on balance to economic progress, to a neutral effect, or to economic decline (loss of welfare).

[3] Of course restoration of environmental harm that has been done contributes to welfare and thus to economic growth, counting from that moment. The point is that the loss of environmental functions is not written off at the moment when it occurs. Nor could it be, because shadow prices cannot be calculated.

Various authors (including the present writer) have in recent years sought for a method of answering this important question. The result of this research is that in most cases the answer cannot be given, for the following reasons. In the first place it proves impossible in most cases to construct a shadow price for environmental goods which is comparable with the market price of produced goods (which is a condition for striking a balance). It is, however, possible in principle to construct an elimination curve that indicates what expenditure on treating measures goes with a given degree of restoration of function (from 1 to 100 percent), or how much potential production expressed in money has to be forgone to get back environmental functions. But a demand curve for these functions can be constructed only exceptionally, because in most cases it is not possible to derive preferences for environmental goods from market data (e.g. expenditure on measures compensating for loss of environmental functions) or from market behaviour.

In the second place it is equally impossible in many cases to cause production to increase by the application of eliminatory measures (such as treating plants) without loss of environmental goods. This is, inter alia, the case when the production of goods and their consumption are accompanied by increasing use of space (as in the oil and petrochemical industries, road-building, suburbanization) or by the intensification of the use of land (as in agriculture). Fragmentation of the countryside and intensification of farming probably form the biggest threat to the survival of plant and animal species. In these cases it is therefore also not possible to estimate whether a gain in consumer goods still remains after total elimination of the environmental effects; the only possible eliminatory measure here is after all not to increase production. In other words, it is frequently impossible to set a tentative upper limit to the intensity of the wants for environmental goods in order to find out whether an increase in production could in principle cause the availability of scarce goods (in the broad sense) to grow.

In the third place we must allow for the need for a safe future, the intensity of which, in respect of the demand for more goods, cannot be quantified. In the problem of the environment we are concerned in a number of cases with future effects which may manifest themselves quite unexpectedly or be expected on the basis of data already known, but which can never be predicted for certain. An example of effects not expected in advance is the discharge of mercury into the water by factories along Minamata Bay in Japan, which led to symptoms of paralysis and to mortality among the predominantly fish-eating population; the cause (accumulation via the food chain with a strong increase in the mercury concentration) could not be established until after the event. Also, when chlorinated hydrocarbons like DDT, dieldrin and aldrin were introduced, their accumulation in food chains was not realized. The climatic consequences of the emission of carbon dioxide have only come to be realized in recent years. Probably many forms of production and consumption will have effects on the environment that are not yet or not sufficiently known today. Below we attempt to work out somewhat further a few of the effects that are expected and the occurrence of which is considered more probable if production continues to grow than in the case of stabilized production.

4. Future risks with continuing growth of production

The future is unpredictable. And yet we must try to form a picture of it, since decisions taken today will have later effects with which we ourselves or our children will be confronted. This applies above all to the environmental effects as a result of increasing production. We therefore state below a number of effects whose occurrence is in any case more probable if the growth of production continues than with stabilized production (and population).

In the first place, in all probability plant and animal species will proceed to die out even more quickly if production keeps on growing. For a long time the misunderstanding prevailed in some circles that deterioration of the environment is a matter of clearing the refuse away, whereupon everything will carry on growing again. Unfortunately that is not so. The effect on the decline of flora and fauna of an increasing use of space for all kinds of activities, the intersection of the countryside by roads and the intensification of use of land by agriculture, is at least as great as the influence of pollution. And it is difficult to see how this effect can be avoided if production for and consumption by a growing number of people carry on increasing. After all, as already mentioned, technology cannot make space larger than it is.

Quantitative data on the decline of the natural environment are difficult to obtain, because the numbers occurring in free nature per plant or animal species are more difficult to count than the number of cars or toothbrushes produced. However, some data follow on the Netherlands, as an instance of a highly industrialized region with a large car population, a dense road system and intensive agriculture, together with some worldwide data.

To record the decline of Dutch flora use is made of a classification by rarity categories in accordance with Van der Maarel (1971). The species are recorded by means of the number of "plots" (5 × 5 sq km) in which they occur in "plot" frequency classes (PFCs). These vary from 1 to 9, the extremely rare species being placed in PFC 1 and the very general ones in PFC 9 (0 = extinct). The shift of the solid line to the left in fig. 10.1 clearly shows the decline in Dutch flora (recording period of solid line: approx. 1930–1949, dotted line: approx. 1950–1975).

In the Netherlands between 1900 and 1975 5.5 percent of the vascular plants (1553 species) became extinct, while the number of extremely and very rare species increased from 16 to 22 percent; in the period 1950–1970 60 percent of the mammal species decreased in number; between 1960 and 1970 over 35 percent of the number of species

Vascular plants by class of rarity

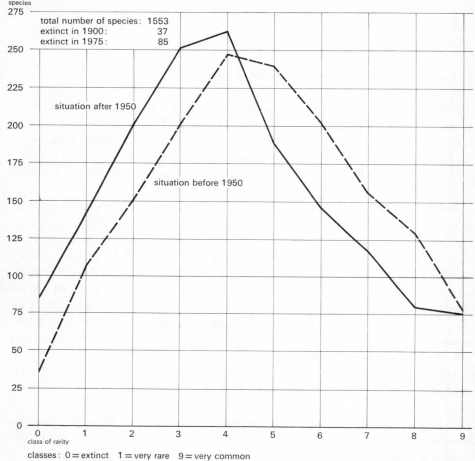

```
species
275

        total number of species: 1553
        extinct in 1900:            37
        extinct in 1975:            85
250



225


        situation after 1950
200


175


150


                        situation before 1950
125


100


 75


 50


 25


  0
        0       1       2       3       4       5       6       7       8       9
   class of rarity
        classes: 0 = extinct  1 = very rare  9 = very common
```

Source: C.B.S. Statistical Essays, The Hague, 1978

Figure 10.1. Vascular plants by class of rarity: 0 = extinct; 1 = very rare; 9 = very common.

of birds hatching in the Netherlands decreased; the same applied between 1940 and 1970 to 95 percent of the species of reptiles and amphibians; in the period 1920–1970 12.5 percent of the fish species died out and 19 percent became very rare; of the species of diurnal butterflies, 6 percent became extinct and 27 percent decreased between approx. 1930/40 and 1970.[4]

⁴ CBS (1974).

Between 1600 and 1980, 112 species of mammals have become extinct, of which 67 in the first 70 years of the twentieth century. Throughout the world the survival is now threatened of 291 mammal species, 402 bird species, 86 species of reptiles, 27 species of amphibians, and 79 fish species.[5] According to a study in preparation for the European Convention on the Preservation of Nature, of all the European species of amphibians (13) 30 percent are in immediate danger of dying out, and of all European species of reptiles (47) 45 percent. This situation is probably caused more by biotope destruction as a result of bringing land into cultivation (farming in large monocultures, deforestation, road construction and building), overhunting and overfishing and the closure of estuaries, than by pollution. Development is going on at breathtaking speed when considered against a geological (evolutionary) time scale.

Since the future is, after all, unpredictable, we shall have to make do with probabilities, also as regards biological stability on which all human life depends. Biologists say that they will not be able to establish in time that an irreversible situation is about to occur. Leading authors like Odum (1971) represent to us that natural ecosystems undergo a development from simple, rather unstructured systems with a small number of species and large production in respect of the biomass present, to complex, richly structured, mature systems with a great diversity of species and small production in respect of the biomass present. The young, rather unstructured systems are unstable. The mature, richly structured systems possess great internal stability. Through human activities a development is increasingly taking place which is resulting in mature, stable systems being replaced by younger, less stable stages. Accordingly, as fewer stable systems remain, restoration of impaired systems becomes increasingly difficult and lengthy, and a steadily decreasing number of possible uses remain. An irreversible situation will most probably occur when harm is done on a large scale to predators, if substantial numbers of species are lost, or general biological activity is suppressed. The chance of catastrophes can be minimized when human activities (again) become part of the biological cycle through the use of recycling processes, the upper limit of the level of activities being restricted by the condition that the degree of stability of this cycle does not decrease. This will amount in practice to recycling of raw materials, changing to nonpolluting, renewable sources of energy, and use of land leaving sufficient space for the functioning of natural ecosystems. It does not require much imagination to see that, in order to satisfy this condition, we shall have to drastically lower our level of production (and our population numbers).

In the second place the large-scale introduction of nuclear energy is almost inevitable if production continues to grow.[6] At the increase of production by 3–4 percent a year advocated by governments and business the supply of oil and gas will no longer be able to meet the demand within the foreseeable future. If no measures are taken now, this

---

[5] Survival Service Commission of the IUCN (1978).
[6] For a further elaboration of this point see Hueting (1978).

may lead to an energy crisis that will halt growth. For there is a positive relation between the growth of production and increase in energy consumption. Very broadly speaking a 1 percent growth in production is accompanied by a 1.5 percent growth in the consumption of energy.[7] True, this ratio can be improved by energy-saving measures, but owing to the cumulative nature of the growth this gives only temporary relief. There is a limit to the possibilities of energy-saving,[8] and as soon as this has been reached (or even before) continuing growth of production pulls energy consumption up again along with itself. In a cumulative growth process more is used in each last doubling time than in all the preceding periods together. As a result the depletion of fuel reserves is greatly accelerated. This acceleration can be somewhat mitigated by fuel saving, but not eliminated.

Switching to coal, the reserves of which are still sufficient for another 100 years or so with growing production,[9] likewise has great drawbacks. The enormous quantities that will have to be burnt if growth continues will probably have disastrous climatic effects through an accelerated further rise in the carbon dioxide content of the atmosphere. In addition, strip mining will severely impair the landscape. It is uncertain whether it will ever become feasible to supply energy via nuclear fusion. Moreover, it is generally assumed that solar energy will be able to meet only a small part of the energy requirement, and not before the year 2000, if production carries on growing. The development and penetration of this environmentally acceptable source of energy further requires very great investments, which in itself would already mean a considerable brake on growth.

For these reasons advocates of the growth of production consider quick introduction of fast breeder reactors necessary. These are expected to extract from a given quantity of uranium over 40 to 50 times as much energy as conventional reactors.[10] In this way the uranium reserves would be able to supply the energy requirement for several hundred years. There are, however, theoretical indications that the chance of accidents and the consequences thereof are considerably greater with a fast breeder reactor than with a light water reactor.[11] In principle the extent of the chance of a serious accident cannot be calculated, but it is in any case greater than zero and in-

---

[7] A discussion is going on about the form of this relation. See, among others, Smil and Kuz (1976). For a critique see Brooks (1977) and for a reply Smil and Kuz (1977). The form of the relation in time is of course important. However, all that matters here is that the relation is positive: an increase in production leads to an increase in energy consumption. This point is not disputed in the discussion.

[8] There is a (highly) theoretical possibility in which growth of production is not accompanied by an increase in energy consumption. This would be the case if a contest between finds for new energy-saving technologies plus sufficiently swift application of the latter and growth of production were constantly won by the first factor. It seems highly improbable to the present author that this as yet improbable situation will ever occur continuously. Moreover, it seems more sensible first to bring about this situation than to anticipate it.

[9] De Jong and Rathenau (1976) give a survey and an evaluation of the estimates of the periods of depletion of oil, gas, coal, and uranium.

[10] Penner and Icerman (1974).

[11] See, among others, Hayes (1976).

creases along with the number of nuclear reactors.

The point is that the calculations of the chance of accidents published so far relate to only one part of the fissile material cycle – the reactor – and even then are only highly theoretical in nature because they are built up from calculations for parts of the reactor. In this approach the chance of human error that may occur with a reactor in full operation can never be determined exactly.[12] But, supposing that the chance of a serious accident in the power plant now calculated as 1 in every 1 million light water reactor years,[13] which advocates of nuclear energy assume, is correct, then, with the 200 nuclear power plants now in operation 1 accident per 5000 years may be expected somewhere in the world. With the 5000 plants required to meet only 50 percent of the present world energy requirement, an accident may be expected once every 200 years. At the growth rate now advocated and maintaining the assumed (low) percentage of nuclear energy, 15 years afterwards a nuclear accident may be expected every 100 years, 15 years after that every 50 years, and so on.[14] And it should be borne in

[12] Attention is drawn to this point inter alia in Union of Concerned Scientists (1977), in which a large number of points of criticism of the draft and final Rasmussen Report are listed, such as errors, limitations and incorrect assumptions in the calculations of both the chances and the consequences. A concise version and a discussion of this may be found in Nash (1978).

[13] What is meant is melting of the reactor core, resulting in the release of a large amount of radio-activity (loss-of-coolant accident). The best known study of risks of such a serious accident is the Rasmussen Report, WASH 1400, of the US Nuclear Regulatory Commission (the draft report was published in August 1974, the final report in October 1975). In this report the chances and consequences have been calculated for a major accident with a light water reactor without signs of ageing. The draft of the Rasmussen Report contains a graph from which the chance of fatalities in a serious reactor accident can be read off. Because it was desired to compare the risk of road accidents, etc. only the numbers of immediate deaths were plotted in the graph. To illustrate the increase in the chance of an accident in a growth situation a point in the graph at which there are 100 or more deaths has been proceeded from below. According to the Rasmussen Report this occurrence has a chance of once per million light water reactor years. A discussion of the Rasmussen Report may be found inter alia in Eichholz (1976, p. 646 et seq.), Hayes (1976) and Gilette (1974). The consequences depend on the weather, the wind direction, population density and evacuation facilities. In the worst case, with a calculated chance of once in a thousand million light water reactor years, according to the final Rasmussen Report for the American situation the short-term consequences would be 3300 deaths and 45 000 cases of illness. The long-term consequences are stated as follows. In a period of 10–40 years after the reactor accident: 1500 fatal cases of cancer and 8000 cases of thyroid diseases per year. The calculated genetic effects in the first generation after the accident are 170 per year. In following generations this number slowly decreases.

For a nuclear reactor in a densely populated area like the western part of the Netherlands, Van Dijk and Smit (1976) arrive at higher figures. In the worst case a million casualties are to be expected there, of whom 140 000 to 350 000 would be killed at once, depending on the evacuation and shielding facilities. The most characteristic aspect of a major reactor accident is the long-term effect as a result of contamination of the ground. Irrespective of weather conditions, existing norms mean that a stretch of land 20 km wide and several hundred kilometres long becomes unusable for human occupation and industrial and agricultural purposes for years.

[14] Of course, the development described above is only hypothetical. Reserves of uranium are too limited to allow such growth for the system of light water reactors. Continuing with nuclear energy calls for a switch to the fast breeder reactor. For this type such detailed estimates of the chance of accidents have not been made. There are, however, theoretical indications that the chance of accidents and the consequences thereof are considerably greater. See, inter alia, Hayes (1976).

mind that when there is the chance of an accident once in so many years, that accident can occur tomorrow. In view of the serious nature of a nuclear accident large groups of the population will have to live in constant fear if this development takes place. That fear can already be found among the population in areas with considerable chemical industry (such as Holland's Rijnmond).

For the rest of the fissile material cycle – the enrichment, transport, regeneration and storage of radio-active fission products – no risk calculations have been made. Nor is that possible as regards happenings in society. This is because calculations of chances are based on extrapolation of the past, it being assumed that the events of the past will repeat themselves in the same way in the future. Now in this case there is as yet no past that could be used as "sample", while the future of society is anything but an identical repetition of the past. The impossibility of calculating chances presents many people with ethical problems, especially with regard to storage of the radio-active fission products which, depending on the radio-active isotope, have to be kept for hundreds to hundreds of thousands of years in a turbulent world full of incalculable people.[15]

In the third place there is, of course, also the problem of pollution.[16] The discharges of heavy metals and persistent compounds will lead, if growth of production continues, to intensified accumulation of these substances in natural organisms and food chains, because complete treatment at source is not possible; stopping the activities of the concerns in question would act as a brake on the growth of production. The same applies to phosphates, for which the expensive eliminatory measures have hardly begun. Phosphates adhere to silt at the bottom of rivers and the like and remain active for a long time owing to the silt being stirred up. As is known, this leads to eutrophication and oxygen deficiency in the water. Pollution of the oceans will increase through dumping, oil discharges and accidents. A growing mountain of sludge (from, among other places, treating plants) and chemicals has to be stored: the familiar shifting of the problem that occurs with everything falling outside the biological cycle.

Air pollution too is expected to increase. Treating efficiencies here lie between 20 and 95 percent (e.g. nitrogen oxides 20 percent, carbon monoxide 80 percent, hydrocarbons 50 percent, sulphur dioxide 75 percent). It is improbable that treating technology will be able to keep up with the rapid increase in emission that occurs with cumulative growth of production. Exceeding of the limiting values and smog situations will then occur much more frequently than now. Furthermore, climatic effects must be feared owing to the increase in the carbon dioxide content of the atmosphere. The chance of explosive developments of those bacteria that cause botulism will greatly increase as a

[15] No solution has been found as yet for this problem. Underground storage, for instance in salt domes, is one possibility envisaged. But according to some geologists, in view of our inadequate knowledge of geological mechanisms, the stability of an area in the past is not enough to establish the future stability of that area. Making galleries and shafts and depositing heat-emitting radio-active material may have unexpected effects. Cf. De Marsily et al. (1977, p. 519 et seq.).

[16] With reference to this point, see Scientific Council for Government Policy (1977).

result of heating of the water through greater discharges of cooling water. This applies not only to the bacterium that has caused massive mortality among birds in recent years, but also to other strains that may be fatal to man.

5. Expectations or scenarios; selective growth or selective economic development

With regard to the prospects of economic growth, interpreted as the extent to which society succeeds in increasing the availability of economic goods (in the broad sense) desired by the public, the following may be remarked. Continuing to step up the now desired package of produced goods will in all probability be accompanied by a reduction in the package of environmental goods. As for the effect on welfare of further increasing production, as advocated by the governments of all countries of the world and by the whole of business, nothing can be said for certain since, as we have seen, the intensity of the wants for on the one hand more produced goods and on the other the conservation of environmental goods cannot be measured. This applies in particular to the extent to which the occurrence of future adverse effects makes itself felt in people's present appraisals. These appraisals cannot express themselves in individual behaviour and are consequently not measurable in economic terms. For that reason the authorities cannot base themselves on the behaviour of the public when weighing one category of goods against another. Thus, the increase in car sales says nothing about our preferences for a clean environment. That would only be so if it were possible to market such an environment, backed by commercials showing a happy cycling family romping in its section of clean sea and fresh air purchased from the X concern, contrasted with a motoring family peevishly affected by the heat and wading in turbid, smelly sea water overhung by smog. Our normal inclination towards maximization of welfare makes us realize that individual action supplies us personally with a negligible gain in environmental goods and a great loss in pleasure of market goods. Most of us doubt the participation of others (the Prisoner's Dilemma from game theory) or prefer to wait and see (the Free Rider Principle from the theory of collective goods).

Two things are quite certain. Firstly, with an unlimited freedom of production and consumption, environment and nature will continue to deteriorate, even if this is against our will or, in other words, even if this leads to a loss of welfare, i.e. economic decline ("negative growth"). Secondly, the price of preserving desired environmental goods also includes a portion of – voluntarily accepted – coercion. It is as well to realize this, if we do not want the future to bear down on us as an uncontrolled process of individual decisions with an end-result that we shall presently regret.

In view of all these uncertainties, in my opinion no expectation can be voiced on the strength of economic data about the prospects of the future size of the available package of produced and environmental goods. However, information can be supplied to the public and the authorities in the form of scenarios in which the (interrelated) consequences of different degrees of growth of production for nature and environment, energy and natural resources are explored. An example of such an exploration may be found in Scientific Council for Government Policy (1977). What I consider to be the most important conclusion from this report is that continuation of the growth of production by 3 percent per annum up to the year 2000 will mean that harm to the natural environment by air and water pollution will continue to increase, that in spite of protective measures nature areas will continue to decline, and that cultivable land (over 90 percent of the rural regions) will display a complete impoverishment of nature and landscape. The fragmentation of space and the intensification of agriculture, which accompany the growth of production or are necessary to attain that growth, are regarded as the principal factors. With a production whose growth gradually decreases to zero, some restoration of the natural environment is not expected until after the year 2000. But a return to the present situation is considered out of the question, because in the interim too much irreversible interference has occurred, while the present situation itself is unstable. According to the report a great effort is already required to maintain the present importance of the natural environment assuming that external pressure remains the same.

When using this kind of information, the expected positive utility of the increase in production will have to be weighed against the negative utility of the loss of environmental goods that it causes. For prices give only an indication of the marginal utility of market goods in respect of one another, not in respect of environmental functions, and shadow prices for environmental functions cannot usually be calculated.

Recently much has been said about "selective growth". By this is meant an increase in national income – i.e. in volume of production – in which inter alia those goods are selected whose production and consumption are environmentally acceptable, require little energy, and benefit employment. But growth is obtaining more goods that one wants to have and, to judge by human behaviour, these doubtless include highly polluting and energy-devouring wishes such as holiday flights, summer vegetables in the depth of winter, a heated hallway, dish washers, and unrestricted use of the family car. "Selective growth" evidently amounts to reducing the supply of goods and services by which the consumer sets great store and is thus a misleading term (the gain obtained in environmental goods and safety does not enter into consideration in the growth figures and the traditional judgement of the results of growth). In all probability substantial application of such a policy will lead to a considerable restraint of production as the latter is traditionally measured in a country's national income. Economically trained advisers should advise against the use of terms from which a suggestion emanates which quite probably cannot be substantiated. A term like "selective economic development" would be nearer to "truth in advertising", which is also required of business.

Of course, it is possible to follow a narrow national policy that endeavours to mitigate the immediate environmental burden on the production side by steering highly polluting and energy-devouring firms abroad and replacing them by ones with a lower pollution level and less energy consumption. But, needless to say, this makes no contribution to the world energy and environmental problem, because the cumulative pollution and the cumulative consumption of energy are not reduced as a result. In such application of a selective growth policy it must above all be feared that the environmental burden will be passed on to the developing countries, where in general nature is even more vulnerable than in developed countries, and where the means and the political readiness to reduce that burden are considerably less.

The employment aspect of selective growth policy is regarded by many as conflicting with the energy and environmental aspect. They lose sight of the simple truth that environment and energy are scarce goods whose obtaining or conservation requires the use of factors of production, just as in the case of all scarce goods. In the industrialized countries 80–95 percent of national income goes to the labour factor. If a lower wage rate is accepted, a policy aimed at conservation of the environment (and energy-saving) will result in more work. In other words, a certain level of satisfaction of wants by produced goods demands more labour *with* conservation of the environment (and energy-saving) than without conservation.[17]

The reason why more is not done about conservation of the environment and energy-saving is, in my opinion, not the fear of loss of employment, but the reluctance to change to a production structure and consumption pattern in which relatively more labour must be utilized and which therefore requires the sacrifice of a piece of potential growth of production. The utilization of labour and capital on behalf of the environment and energy-saving pays off in the form of conservation of environmental functions and not in the form of an increased package of produced consumer goods. These are investments on behalf of nonmarket goods, which by definition cannot pay off in market terms but which are quite definitely sound from the economic point of view if we give a high ranking on our scale of preferences to a stable, safe environment and to the avoidance of the chance of sudden severe energy shortages. The crux of the matter is in the reduction of the (growth of the) wage rate (wage is after all a claim to produced goods; it does not cover nonmarket goods).

In general the pretence of the opposite is maintained because with existing market relations and wage rates businesses can be priced out of the market by (international) competition if they take environmental measures, or may have to contract if their products have a high price elasticity, while it is difficult to absorb the labour elsewhere in the machinery of production. Here the desires for optimal allocation ("the polluter

---

[17] Examples are: insulation of houses, a method of farming that offers less of a threat to plant and animal species, all kinds of treating equipment, recycling and more lasting products geared to repair. For an elaboration of this see Hueting (1975, 1977).

must pay" and may not be subsidized from public funds because in that case others than the producers and consumers of the product also pay), for equal pay for equal work (no lower wages in firms which are obliged by law to apply energy-saving and clean processes), for the conservation of collective goods (environment, safe future) and for the growth of production, all collide. I do not in any way wish to suggest that practical solutions are simple. The intention is to emphasize that beneath these problems there is a current that may not be ignored: the conflict between environment and growth of production and the division of welfare between the present and coming generations. Growth of production creates employment only in so far as suitable jobs in the production of desired goods can again be found for the labour shaken out by the increased productivity, while many increases of productivity and the resultant consumption are accompanied by environmental loss and the substitution of energy for labour.[18] Environmental conservation and energy-saving call at once for considerable labour. In so far as unpleasant work is involved, this would have to be fairly shared as part-time work: a considerable intervention in the labour market, but a logical consequence of the management of a collective good and not an insurmountable objection for anyone who, on the strength of the available information, is worried about the welfare of the generations after ours.

References

Brooks, L. G., 1977, Energy/GDP relationships – the elastic snaps, Energy Policy 5, 162–164.
CBS, 1974, Algemene Milieustatistiek 1973 (Staatsuitgeverij, The Hague).
Dijk, G. van and W. Smit, 1976, Kleine kansen, grote gevolgen (T. H. Twente, Enschede).
Eichholz, G. G., 1976, Environmental aspects of nuclear power (Ann Arbor Science Publishers Inc., Ann Arbor, Mich.).
Gilette, R., 1974, Nuclear power: Calculating the odds of disaster, Science 185, 838–839.
Hayes, D., 1976, Nuclear power: The fifth horseman, Worldwatch Paper 6 (Worldwatch Institute, Washington, DC).
Hueting, R., 1975, Milieu en werkgelegenheid, Economisch-Statistische Berichten 60, 216–220.
Hueting, R., 1977, Socio-economic effects of environmental policy (Paper presented at the Symposium on Quality of Life, Universidad de Deusto, Bilbao, 21–23 September 1977).
Hueting, R., 1978, Kernenergie en produktiegroei, Economisch-Statistische Berichten 63, 292–298.
Jong, W. M. de and G. W. Rathenau, 1976, The future availability of energy to the Netherlands (Working

[18] In agriculture, which is closely controlled by the authorities, plans are ready for considerably increasing production on a contracting area with the elimination of 80 000 of the 200 000 people employed in farming [see Ministry of Agriculture and Fisheries (1977a, b)]. It is uncertain whether it will be possible to find buyers for the increased production of agriculture. It is also uncertain whether 80 000 people can find work elsewhere in the machinery of production. Which products these people would have to make is unknown. And yet, if we are to look after our scarce resources properly, the positive utility of these products will have to be weighed against the negative utility as a result of the serious effects on nature and landscape that will almost certainly occur if these plans are put into effect [see Scientific Council for Government Policy (1977) and also, among others, Timmerman (1973)]. We are still far from making environmental impact statements for such government plans.

paper for the Scientific Council for Government Policy).

Maarel, E. van der, 1971, Florastatistieken als bijdrage tot de evaluatie van natuurgebieden, Gorteria 5, 176–188.

Marsily, G. de, E. Ledoux, A. Barbreau and J. Margat, 1977, Nuclear waste disposal: Can the geologist guarantee isolation? Science 197, 519–527.

Ministry of Agriculture and Fisheries, 1977a, Structuurvisie landbouw (Staatsuitgeverij, The Hague).

Ministry of Agriculture and Fisheries, 1977b, Landbouwverkenningen (Staatsuitgeverij, The Hague).

Nash, H., 1978, Rasmussen Report is demolished by Union of Concerned Scientists, Not Man Apart 8 (3), 5–20.

Odum, E. P., 1971, Fundamentals of ecology (W. B. Saunders Company, Philadelphia).

Penner, S. S. and L. Icerman, 1974, Energy, vol. 1, Demands, resources, impact, technology and policy (Addison-Wesley, Reading, Mass.).

Scientific Council for Government Policy, 1977, De komende vijfentwintig jaar; een toekomstverkenning voor Nederland (Staatsuitgeverij, The Hague).

Smil, V. and T. Kuz, 1976, European energy elasticities, Energy Policy 4, 171–175.

Smil, V. and T. Kuz, 1977, Reply, Energy Policy 5, 164–165.

Survival Service Commission of the International Union for the Conservation of Nature (IUCN), 1978, Red Data Books (IUCN, Morges, Switzerland).

Timmerman, A., 1973, Weidevogelgebieden, ontstaan en toekomst; biotoopeisen van weidevogels, veranderende landbouwmethoden en weidevogelstanden; weidevogelreservaten (Nature Conservation Division of the State Forestry Service, Leeuwarden).

Union of Concerned Scientists, 1977, The risks of nuclear power reactors (Union of Concerned Scientists, Cambridge, Mass.).

Chapter 11

p. 87 =

COMMENT ON HUETING'S PAPER

P. NIJKAMP

Free University, Amsterdam

105 - 08

Environmental economics has received a great deal of attention during the last decade from the point of view of both applied welfare theory and socio-ecological sciences. Hueting's paper is a welcome contribution to the rising tide of scientific concern about environmental deterioration. After a brief survey of traditional economic thinking, he introduces the concept of environmental decay via the loss of environmental functions. Any growth in production runs the risk of affecting these environmental functions. In addition, owing to the variety of economic activities, serious competition between functions may emerge. An economic or monetary computation of these losses is hampered by the non-market character of these functions as well as by the long-term risks of environmental deterioration. In his opinion, a set of scenarios may provide more insight into the directions to be chosen in order to attain a balanced economic growth.

Hueting's approach is a brief systematic survey of problems inherent in the intricate relationship between environmental conditions and economic growth. His paper does not provide new arguments for the economic growth – environmental quality debate, but presents elements for a further discussion.

His analysis is a traditional neoclassical approach in which marginality conditions in a market system play a crucial role. It is clear that this approach leads inevitably to the negative conclusions inferred by Hueting. In this respect it would have been advisable to pay more attention to alternative approaches in which environmental problems are placed in the framework of paradigm shifts in political economics. It seems that, in spite of the severe criticism of the validity of the traditional growth paradigm in neoclassical economics, Hueting only maintains the traditional lines of thought, so that an innovation of environmental economics is hampered. For example, Daly's exposition about a steady-state economy would certainly have deserved more attention in a discussion on economic growth and environmental quality [Daly (1973)]. The same holds true for Georgescu-Roegen's entropy approach [Georgescu-Roegen (1971)].

Prospects of Economic Growth, edited by S. K. Kuipers and G. J. Lanjouw
© *North-Holland Publishing Company*

It should be noted that even the meaning of the word "stagnation" is codetermined by the paradigms presupposed in economic thinking, so that it may be meaningful to broaden our views by considering alternative approaches. In the discussion about economic growth and environmental quality it may be worthwhile paying some attention to certain principles from other disciplines which may help us to formulate new ways of thinking.

1. Physical principles accruing from the materials balance model. Here especially the first law of thermodynamics (the law of conservation of matter and energy) and the second law of thermodynamics (the scarcity of low entropy) are extremely useful for indicating that a minimization of throughput (rather than a maximization) is a meaningful paradigm.

2. Ecological principles accruing from a systems approach. In this respect the energy basis of ecosystems and the equilibrium trends of dynamic ecological systems deserve more attention because these principles determine the stability of ecosystems.

3. Legal principles associated with the property of goods. Here the notion of common and nonappropriate goods is important in order to analyse the economic and distributive impacts of the "polluter pays" and "pollutee pays" principles.

4. Socio-psychological principles emerging from social choice theory. Contrary to Hueting's opinion, human priorities are quite well measurable, even for unpriced environmental goods. The derivation of a demand-price function is, of course, more complicated, but such a function is not necessary for arriving at satisfactory choices for environmental goods. The modern psychometric scaling methods offer great prospects for a non-traditional approach [see Nijkamp (1979)].

5. Social principles related to the social carrying capacity of our society. It seems that the social tolerance principle formulated by among others Hirsch (1976) is an even more important phenomenon in social decision-making than the ecological tolerance principle stemming from biology.

6. Operational research principles emerging from mathematical decision theory. The recently developed multicriteria principles for a balanced behaviour offer greater prospects for Hueting's plea for a balanced economic growth than his one-dimensional approach via loss of functions – although this approach is completely consistent with his neoclassical approach [see Nijkamp (1977)].

7. Spatial-geographical principles resulting from the existence of physical space. Space is a medium through which actions and externalities can be transferred, while it is at the same time a constraint for a further growth of many activities. Many environmental deteriorations stem essentially from the lack of space. Lack of space is, however, a relative problem, because technological innovations may lead to an increase in the efficiency of the use of space (cf. Hong Kong's residential solutions and also "multilevel" agriculture).

In view of the above principles it may be worthwhile making some additional comments on Hueting's paper.

(1) There is no empirical evidence that human needs grow less than proportionately with respect to the increase of commodities; the socio-psychological experiments reported by Scitovsky (1976) among others show that Western society has already passed a saturation level of welfare, so that the perceived welfare is even declining. According to Maslow's principle, the loss of socio-psychological functions may have even more serious welfare impacts than the loss of environmental functions. It is clear that this observation has extremely important consequences for current attempts to tackle unemployment by means of growth in traditional economic sectors.

(2) The utility of environmental goods means an increase in welfare, so that a decline in production growth does not necessarily imply a decline in welfare. The basic question is how to use our efforts so as to increase environmental quality without affecting employment; in other words, how to employ the spatial-environmental constraints as a tool to improve the employment situation.

(3) A further growth in traditional production sectors is hardly reconcilable with the materials balance principle, but on the other hand any abatement investment needs a certain amount of financial resources. Hueting has not answered the question whether the latter economic principle does not affect his plea for balanced economic growth.

(4) The analysis of risk situations and long-term disequilibria might perhaps be studied in a more satisfactory manner by means of catastrophe theory, in which the transition process after sudden perturbations is spelt out in more detail. In this respect the policy implications of nuclear energy might also be clarified within a more general framework.

(5) Hueting seems to take a rather pessimistic view of our future, but one may doubt whether a shift of tasks to public decision-makers can provide a better guarantee of balanced development. As long as the government is an institution with its own preferences, there is no reason to rely on public policy (cf. the replacement of trams by buses). Here again a more critical approach to the paradigm of infinite wants is an important condition. This is also in agreement with the author's opinion that the wage rate plays a crucial role. The consequence of this statement may, however, be that the unions are the institutions that implicitly bear the main responsibility for effective environmental management.

(6) The notion of selective growth is just as fuzzy and vague as the notion of balanced economic growth. Both notions, however, aim at emphasizing that economic decisions have to be placed in a broader framework of social, spatial and environmental variables. Recent calculations carried out by us for the Netherlands by means of integrated pollution-production models have shown that the range of variation of extreme options (maximum growth versus pollution, for instance,) is relatively low owing to the wide variety of constraints imposed by our economic-technological system.

Hueting's paper shows that traditional economic thinking provides a logical frame of analysis for studying environmental problems. Its operational validity for the stagnating growth-environmental quality dilemma is, however, very limited. In this respect, the use of more advanced holistic-action-orientated theories and methods based on multidimensional principles appears to offer more prospects.

References

Daly, H. E., ed., 1973, Toward a steady-state economy (Freeman, San Fransisco).

Georgescu-Roegen, N., 1976, The entropy law and the economic process (Harvard University Press, Cambridge, Mass.

Hirsch, F., 1976, Social limits to growth (Harvard University Press, Cambridge, Mass).

Nijkamp, P., 1977, Theory and application of environmental economics (North-Holland, Amsterdam).

Nijkamp, P., 1979, Multidimensional spatial data and decision analysis (Wiley, New York).

Scitovsky, T., 1976, The joyless economy (Oxford University Press, New York).

Chapter 12

p. 87:

COMMENT ON HUETING'S PAPER

J. B. OPSCHOOR

Free University, Amsterdam

109 -15

1. Introduction

It is not possible to comment on all the elements present in Hueting's paper within the space allowed. I therefore restrict myself mainly to some comments on "selective growth".

Societal activities take place in relation to a physical environment; they have an environmental impact in terms of resource use, pollution, etc. As such, these impacts may trigger off processes "within the environment" that may affect conditions relevant to society. Such changes in condition, and processes endogenous to the societal sub-system, may affect subsequent activities and their environmental impacts. Hueting presents information on floral and faunal developments, and associates indications of environmental deterioration with increased production and space and soil utilization. He points out that increasing future production necessitates the large-scale introduction of nuclear energy, thereby inducing various new types of risks. Although among ecologists there is, as yet, no full agreement on the interpretation of data of the type given by Hueting, the probability of increased future environmental degradation is greater than zero, and I do not hesitate to count myself among the risk-averters in this respect. However, changes in environmental conditions may have feedbacks in terms of societal adaptations (e.g. an environmental policy). We must look into the possibilities of such adaptations in relation to the dynamics "behind" the activities that, even now, are making an environmental impact that worries both Hueting and myself.

It seems unlikely that the economic processes in the industrialized countries are characterized by feedback mechanisms sufficient to keep them "automatically" within limits that can be sustained in the long run by ecosystems. In the "Western" part of the world this is due to the facts that the propensity to grow is in operation at all levels in the economic system, and that the direction of growth is hardly (if at all) influenced by

Prospects of Economic Growth, edited by S. K. Kuipers and G. J. Lanjouw
© North-Holland Publishing Company

motives other than financial return (and employment). In addition to these elements, attempts to bridge the welfare gap between "the North" and "the South" will add to rather than reduce the global environmental impact. At the global level (e.g. at UN conferences) there has been much discussion about a "New International Economic Order". At the regional level, even in the industrialized Western countries, at present one seems to think only in terms of increasing welfare ("economic growth") – as is evident in statements by OECD, EEC, and similar international bodies.

In such a situation the only hope – in my view – of a timely change in the direction and rate of economic developments is to emphasize the need for *selectivity* of such developments. This is not meant as an alternative to stopping the growth of material production, but as a process that might – through increasing environmental awareness at the individual and public level – prepare society to take measures sufficient to maintain socio-economic activities at sustainable levels, when the need for such measures is manifest even more clearly than today (see my concluding comments), and when the environmental "limits" to growth can be more precisely determined.

2. Selective growth and the environment: considerations and calculations

Hueting rightly points out that, for a variety of reasons, direct comparisons of the welfare or utility effects of increases in production and deterioration of the environment are impossible. Policy aims have to be formulated in terms of priorities and/or target-values with respect to various entities that are relevant from a societal point of view (such as employment, income, and environmental quality). Furthermore, one can defend the thesis that the invisible hand may not satisfactorily operate in an intertemporal or even intergenerational context – a context that is characteristic of many environmental problems. From the point of view of "sustainability", governments might feel pressed to set their target-values and/or priorities for environmental quality as high as their constituency would allow (assuming a conflict between the environmental impact of actual socio-economic activities and the concept of sustainability). In the medium and long run, these political margins must be seen as flexible ones; society can at least to some extent be influenced by education and information, thereby increasing for instance the value attached to environmental considerations relative to traditional components of economic welfare.

For various reasons, scenario approaches to possible future developments of environmental-economic processes are relevant and potentially useful:

(i) they may show the policy-maker how small or large the (technically and politically) feasible area is within which decisions should remain; one may expect that guesses and surmises – or even prejudices – rather than knowledge have often determined the area *perceived* as being feasible by policy-makers;

(ii) they may be used to demonstrate the trade-offs associated with relaxing or tightening certain restrictions (especially of a political nature, e.g. the desired level of material production) on the other variables considered;

(iii) their outcomes might be used as a basis for public action aimed at increasing societal awareness of certain problems, and at changing individual (and hence societal) preferences.

The official Dutch policy of "selective growth" aims at increasing production and employment within margins set by (among others) environmental considerations. In line with the feelings that seem to dominate present-day public opinion (both in the Netherlands and in other industrialized nations) as well as international economic policy (e.g. EEC, OECD) production and employment aims are given priority over environmental considerations. As Hueting points out, this (i) may be detrimental from a long-term point of view, and (ii) may reflect incorrectly postulated conflicts, such as between "environment" and "employment". Selective growth – from an environmental perspective – would imply increasing the levels of "low-environmental-impact" activities and decreasing the high-impact activities. Thus, lower levels of environmental impacts would result than with nonselective ("chaotic") growth. It is even conceivable that, up to some future point in time, overall production could grow and environmental impacts (at least some) decrease, compared with *present* levels. Again, it seems that present-day opinion would not accept lower levels of production and income, even if that were the only way to arrive at "safe", sustainable levels of environmental impacts (and I fear that environmental education and official propaganda might not even adequately change that).

Selective "developments" in production may or may not be accompanied by corresponding changes in consumption patterns. If not, the environmental burden may be passed on to the rest of the world, through foreign trade (assuming possibilities of market-clearing). Whether or not this is acceptable is perhaps a noneconomic question, but one element of the answer may be the extent to which a country at present suffers environmental impacts related to the production of export goods or on balance "exports" such impacts by its foreign trade. In view of the fact that many developing countries in particular claim increasing shares in global industrial activities over the coming decades (reflecting an understandable and "legitimate" priority of material welfare over environmental concern, in an environmental situation that is not more vulnerable in *all* circumstances), one might hesitate to adopt Hueting's approach toward "exporting" polluting, etc. activities in a transitional period. In Institute for Environmental Problems (1978) some of the questions raised above have been commented upon, on the basis of a 60×60 input–output model of the Dutch economy, augmented by a 60×74 sector of emissions of chemical pollutants (air, water, wastes) and fuel uses, reflecting the 1973 situation. This model has been applied to a number of hypothetical production patterns in 1985: a "trend scenario" based on official documents from the Central Planning Bureau and the Ministry of Economic Affairs, and eight "contrasting scenarios" reflecting various policy options. In these contrasting scenarios production levels per sector in 1985 were allowed to deviate by a maximum of 25 percent from the corresponding levels in the trend scenario. The results are summarized in table 12.1.

As can be seen, these theoretical calculations indicate the possibility of reducing environmental impacts in terms of pollution and energy use by "selective growth" to roughly three-quarters to four-fifths of the values corresponding to "non-selective growth", without negative effects on employment and income. (Assuming foreign trade to absorb or provide supluses and deficits between production and consumption, and production levels to be flexible upward and downward, to the extent indicated.)

Finally, some data on the Dutch "balance of pollution" are presented in table 12.2, where for some pollutants and for total energy use the balance of pollution in the Netherlands, related to production of export goods, and pollution abroad, related to production for goods imported into the Dutch economy, is given, as well as the contribution of the most important sector, that of base chemical products (including fertilizers).

It proves that the Netherlands bears a relatively high environmental burden as the price of having some (heavily polluting) sectors that yield considerable exports and income. This might provide a rationale for "selective growth" based on environmental concerns, in the form of a more even spreading of polluting and energy-absorbing activities.

Additional reductions (even without passing on environmental pollution elsewhere) could be found in stricter pollution abatement, energy conservation, and similar activities.

If Hueting is correct in suggesting that the combined effect of those measures will not be to bring environmental impacts within long-term sustainable limits (and, although this is not perhaps fully accepted, even by ecologists, I would prefer to avert the risks of being overoptimistic in this respect), then more drastic changes are furthermore in order:

(a) changes in consumption patterns and life styles in this part of the world; and

(b) changes in the decision structure with respect to production levels, energy use, research and development, product innovation, etc.

Recent experiences (the discussion on civil service income policy) have, to my mind, shown that such restrictive policies will have to be accompanied by an effective and egalitarian overall income policy, and to this I must add that the acceptability of such policies would – I expect – greatly depend on other countries (and "blocs") taking similar steps.

Table 12.1

Effects (expressed in percentages of the trend scenario) of nine scenarios for 1985 on seven criteria.

Scenarios Criterion	Trend A	Air pollution B	Energy C	Organic waste D	Heavy metals E	Chemical wastes F	Income G	Employment H	Iterative I
Air pollution	100	79	88	91	89	83	100	100	84
Energy input	100	78	77	79	82	78	90	88	79
Organic wastes	100	83	77	75	86	79	100	100	81
Heavy metals	100	75	100	100	75	75	100	100	76
Chemical wastes	100	76	87	90	78	74	95	95	76
Income	100	100	100	110	111	103	120	120	108
Employment	100	101	100	113	113	105	122	122	111

Table 12.2

Dutch balance of pollution (1973) for four pollutants and for energy input

	Units	Balance	Balance as % of total Dutch emission/consumption	Balance, base chemical products (incl. fertilizers) only
Air pollution (combustion)	(weighted) tonnes	2 716	25	1 456
Air pollution (process)	(weighted) tonnes	4 146	15	6 876
Organic wastes (excl. sewage)	1000 p.e.	2 583	14	2 890
Heavy metals	(weighted) tonnes	1	1	43
Chemical wastes	(weighted) tonnes	125 910	14	282 400
Energy (excl. transport)	Tj	320 420	14	482 280

References

Institute for Environmental Problems, 1978, Milieuverontreiniging en produktiestructuur in Nederland, parts I and II (Free University, Amsterdam).

Chapter 13

PROSPECTS OF EMPLOYMENT GROWTH IN THE NETHERLANDS: A CRITICAL SURVEY OF PREVAILING VIEWS

117-30

S. K. KUIPERS

University of Groningen

Since the early Seventies a vigorous debate on the nature and the causes of the slowdown of employment growth since the late Sixties has been conducted in the Netherlands. The aim of this paper is to survey this debate critically. Four lines of thought can be distinguished: the vintage approach, the spending approach, the system approach, and the long-wave approach. Discussion of these approaches yields two important conclusions. First, all branches of industry and services show the same tendencies, i.e. falling profit margins, a slowdown of employment growth, and a rise in real labour costs. This indicates that the causes of the stagnation of employment growth may be macroeconomic in character. Secondly, it is doubtful that the slowdown of employment growth is caused only by a deficiency of aggregate demand. The changes in real wages also have something to do with it. Hence, in order to improve employment prospects in the intermediate future, a combined policy of limiting the rise in real wages and stimulating aggregate demand is called for.

1. Introduction

In the Seventies unemployment in the Western countries has risen to a height unprecedented in the postwar period. While in the Netherlands, for instance, the average rate of unemployment was 2.1 percent in the Fifties and 1.1 percent in the Sixties, in the Seventies it was 3.0 percent. Moreover, the latter figure probably strongly underestimates the gravity of the unemployment situation. There is ample evidence that registered unemployment is only the tip of the iceberg. For instance, there is reason to believe that a substantial part of the rise in the number of people entitled to benefits under the Working Disablement Act since this Act became operative in 1967 has to be considered as representing the unemployed. Between 1967 and 1977 this number rose by about 240 000 persons [Den Hartog and Tjan (1976, pp. 32–33), *Wetenschappelijke Raad voor het Regeringsbeleid* (1977, p. 29)]. It is not out of the

Prospects of Economic Growth, edited by S. K. Kuipers and G. J. Lanjouw
© *North-Holland Publishing Company*

question that part of it should be conceived of as (voluntary) unemployment.[1] Further-more, sickness absenteeism rose considerably: from about 4.5 percent of the number of working days in 1955 to about 10 percent in 1975 [*Wetenschappelijke Raad voor het Regeringsbeleid* (1977, p. 43)]. In general this will mean an additional demand for labour and hence a relatively low rate of unemployment. Finally, some employment studies point out that a considerable part of the employment of personnel by firms is not profitable and should therefore be considered as hidden unemployment. These es-timates amount to about 150 000–200 000 man-years in 1976 [Kuipers et al. (1979)]. If all these developments are taken into consideration, it is hard to conclude that the rise of unemployment differs strongly from that in the Thirties, when about 15 percent of the working population in the Netherlands was unemployed. The great difference between these two periods is, however, that social security legislation makes present unemployment hurt much less than that of the Thirties did. From an economic point of view, however, it remains a waste of scarce resources. Moreover, social security laws do not prevent psychic damage being done to people who become unemployed.

For these reasons the great concern about the unemployment problem in the Netherlands can easily be understood. The discussion that started in the early Seventies is especially concerned with the slowdown of employment growth. In the Fifties and in the early Sixties employment in firms rose on the average by 1.2 percent a year, whereas in the second half of the Sixties this rise was 0.7 percent a year. The average growth rates of the output of firms in those two periods were 5.1 and 5.8 percent, respectively. These figures show that, although output growth has accelerated since the mid-Sixties, employment growth has decelerated. In the early Seventies the downward trend in employment growth showed up still more clearly: from 1971 onwards employ-ment even displayed a steady decline in absolute terms. However, up to 1974 the out-put of firms continued to expand at high rates of growth. It is this phenomenon in par-ticular that led the Central Planning Bureau to question the effective demand theory of employment prevailing until then and to formulate its labour cost theory [Den Hartog and Tjan (1974)].

Den Hartog's and Tjan's (1974) publication was the start of a vigorous debate on the nature and the causes of the decline of employment in the Seventies.[2] The aim of this paper is to survey this debate critically in order to establish what the prospects of employment growth are. Four lines of thought can be distinguished:

(1) the vintage approach:
(2) the spending approach;

[1] According to the *Interim-nota inzake de bestrijding van de werkloosheid* (1974, p. 10), every year 30 000 persons will leave the working population on the strength of the Working Disablement Act in the near future. This number would be considerably smaller if this act did not exist.

[2] Most of the papers appeared in Dutch periodicals, although not only in the Dutch language. An example of a collection of essays written fully in English in this area is the Employment Issue of *De Economist* (1976). Papers published in foreign books or journals are: Ellman (1977), De Klerk et al. (1977) and Pen (1978).

(3) the system approach; and
(4) the long-wave approach.
These four approaches will be discussed in sections 2–4. Some concluding remarks will be then made in section 5.

2. The vintage approach

The origin of this approach lies in Den Hartog's and Tjan's (1974) paper in which the authors investigated the relation between real wages and employment in a way which, although already wellknown in theory,[3] had not yet been applied in empirical work on employment theory. Their main analytical tool is the vintage model, in which capital goods of different vintages may differ with respect to the state of the art incorporated in them, as well as with respect to the labour intensity for which the capital goods are constructed. Of the various possible types of vintage models, Den Hartog and Tjan utilize the clay–clay model, in which substitutability exists neither ex ante nor ex post, probably mainly for reasons of estimation technique.[4] Technical progress is assumed to be only embodied and labour-augmenting. Capital goods are scrapped if they no longer yield a rent.

The strength of this model is that it gives a much more realistic description of the way in which substitution occurs than putty–putty models do. In reality machines cannot be adjusted to changing situations without costs and delay. If technical progress is only embodied and labour-augmenting, as Den Hartog and Tjan assume, then rising real wages will ultimately make the machines of a certain vintage obsolete, so that they will be scrapped. Owing to the higher average labour productivity in the younger vintages, the scrapped machines are replaced by those that are less labour-intensive. Hence, capital has indirectly been substituted for labour.

Just like everything else, this way of describing the substitution process has its price for, in contrast with aggregated production functions, vintage models are extremely difficult to estimate. The main reason is the lack of data, for instance on output and labour in the different vintages. This makes acceptance of non-testable assumptions inevitable and it is not surprising that much of the criticism is levelled at these assumptions.[5]

The Den Hartog–Tjan study of 1974 led to the following conclusions. The period 1959–1973 can be divided into two subperiods: a period of labour shortage

---

[3] The clay–clay vintage model was developed for the first time by Salter (1960) and Bergström (1962).

[4] A putty–clay model has been developed by Sandee (1976), but this model has not entered the employment growth discussion.

[5] See, for instance, Driehuis (1976, 1977), Driehuis and Van der Zwan (1977, pp. 857–859), Den Hartog and Weitenberg (1977, pp. 1236–1241) and Driehuis and Van der Zwan (1978, pp. 348–353). A somewhat revised version of Driehuis (1976) is Driehuis (1979).

(1959–1970) and a period of capital shortage (1970–1973). Owing to an accelerated rise in real wages since 1964, excess capacity has tended to disappear since that year. As strong real wage increases were going on in the early Seventies, this decade has been characterized by a shortage of jobs. Other important characteristics of the period 1959–1973 were: (a) a fall in the life span of the oldest equipment from 45 years in 1959 to 17 years in 1973; (b) a fall in the profit rate on newest equipment from 39 percent in 1959 to 28 percent in 1973; and (c) a strong rise in replacement investment as a proportion of gross investment in equipment [Den Hartog and Tjan (1974), Kuipers (1977, pp. 14–15)].

In the discussion which followed Den Hartog's and Tjan's seminal article, two main trends can be distinguished. In the first Den Hartog's and Tjan's basic approach was accepted, but criticism was levelled at some specific points,[6] mostly technical ones. Some of the criticism was accepted, some was not. This led to a revised version which was published in 1976 [Den Hartog and Tjan (1976)]. The main difference between this version and the original one is that in the revised version a distinction was explicitly made between capacity output and capacity labour demand on the one hand, and actual output and actual employment on the other. This was done by formulating two employment equations: one for a period of labour shortage, the other for a period of capital shortage. In the former actual employment depends on capacity labour demand and the available labour force, in the latter on capacity labour demand and the degree of capacity utilization.[7]

Two points are worth mentioning.

(1) As has been argued by Van Schaik (1978), the employment theory is not only a supply-orientated one. In particular, in the capital shortage situation the employment equation also contains a spending variable. Hence, the theory allows in principle a testing of the hypotheses that the slowdown in employment growth is due to a shortage of jobs, a deficiency of aggregate demand, or both. The theory could be further elaborated, however, by also including a spending variable in the employment equation in a situation of labour shortage.[8]

(2) The theory was built on modern disequilibrium theory according to which employment is determined either by supply factors or by demand factors, depending on which of the two sets of factors determines the minimum amount of employment.[9] The

[6] These points are surveyed in Driehuis and Van der Zwan (1977). For an answer see Den Hartog and Weitenberg (1977). The criticism concerns among others the estimation method, the survival fractions assumed, the bias in technical progress, and the sensitivity of the model to changes in the parameter values and the scrapping condition.
[7] As has been argued by Kuipers et al. (1979), the capital shortage equation is highly sensitive to the length of the estimation period. More satisfying estimation results were obtained by including a distributed lag in this equation. See also: Kuipers et al. (1978).
[8] This has been done in Kuipers et al. (1978, 1979). See also Kloek (1977, p. 1043).
[9] See, for instance, Solow and Stiglitz (1968), Barro and Grossman (1976) and Malinvaud (1977).

Den Hartog–Tjan employment theory therefore contains a choice-theoretical basis.

The 1976 version of the Den Hartog–Tjan model is the structural basis for medium-term planning in the Netherlands. It is included in both the Vintaf I model [Den Hartog et al. (1975)] and the Vintaf II model [Central Planning Bureau (1977)]. Hence, official forecasts by the Dutch Government with respect to output and employment growth crucially depend on the philosophy underlying the vintage approach.

It is against this philosophy that the second trend of criticism is directed. Instead of emphasizing the rapid growth of real wages as the main source of the unemployment problem, Driehuis (1976) argues that much more attention should be paid to the slow-down in the growth of aggregate demand and the changing composition of its components. Van der Zwan is even more fundamental. He denies that the development of mature capitalist economies can be described in terms of production costs and aggregated demand. According to him this development is inherent in tendencies in the market economies themselves [Van der Zwan (1975, 1976, 1977)]. Both the Driehuis and the Van der Zwan view will be discussed in the next sections.

3. The spending approach

Driehuis' criticism of the Den Hartog–Tjan model is partly based on the technical problems which exist in estimating the vintage model. He thinks that the number of non-testable assumptions which are necessary because of the problem of non-observable variables is too great for the estimation results to be sufficiently reliable [Driehuis (1976, p. 14)].

In addition to this he criticizes the model on three more fundamental points [Driehuis (1976, pp. 3–14)]:

(1) capital goods are not scrapped at the moment that they no longer yield a rent, but at the moment that capital goods become available which yield a higher rate of return;

(2) the analysis is too aggregative: more attention should be paid to the changes in the structure of aggregate demand and aggregate supply; and

(3) the analysis is rather sensitive to the changes in the values of the parameters and the coefficients.

In order to evade the technical estimation problems and some of the more fundamental difficulties, he investigates in his 1976 paper the possibility of going back to a good old Keynesian demand equation in which actual employment growth is related to the growth in aggregate demand,[10] the utilization rate of capital, the relative changes in

---

[10] Reweighted according to the labour intensity of its components [Driehuis (1976, pp. 15–16)].

the utilization rate of capital, the rate of return on capital after taxation, and a geometrically distributed lag of past gross investments in equipment and in transportation. Although he admits that this analysis has its weaknesses as well, in his 1977 publication he states that the slowdown of employment growth can be explained in terms of this analysis as well as in terms of the vintage analysis [Driehuis (1977, p. 6)].

This attempt to rehabilitate demand theory cannot, however, be considered very successful. In the first place Driehuis encounters the same kind of problems with non-observable variables as do Den Hartog and Tjan. In order to be able to construct a time series of the utilization rate of capital, one has to know the capacity output series. Driehuis tries to evade that problem by using instead the rate of unemployment, but this procedure is hardly convincing since it implies that changes in capital utilization do not have any consequence for the average productivity of labour [Kuipers (1974, pp. 13–14)]. This property is completely in contradiction with reality, in which average labour productivity increases as underutilization of capital decreases, and vice versa. A further complication of this procedure is that, owing to the fact that the labour force is relatively stable, employment growth is used to explain itself. It is therefore not surprising that this very variable is the most significant determinant of employment growth.

Secondly, the estimation results are rather bad. Only the coefficient of the unemployment rate turns out to be significantly different from zero. Owing to multicollinearity the coefficient of the aggregate demand variable could not be estimated independently: the estimations were performed for given values of this coefficient.

Thirdly, changes in (reweighted) aggregate demand are hardly able to explain changes in employment in two of the three subperiods 1956–1963, 1963–1970 and 1970–1974 [Hoekstra (1976, pp. 40–42)]. The actual annual growth rates of employment in these three periods were 1.15, 0.9 and −0.35 percent, respectively. If one follows Driehuis in assuming that a change of 1 percent in the growth rate of aggregate demand leads to a change of 0.25 percent in the growth rate of employment, then the predicted annual growth rates of employment on the basis of the output growth rates in these three periods are 1.35, 2.0 and 0.9 percent [Hoekstra (1976, p. 41)]. Hence, only in the first period does aggregate demand explain employment satisfactorily. In the Sixties the actual employment growth rate is much lower than that predicted on the basis of the growth rate of output; in the Seventies the predicted growth rate even has the wrong sign. Hence, there is ample reason to doubt whether Keynesian demand theory is able to explain the slowdown of employment growth since 1963.

On the strength of the above it is not surprising that Driehuis himself is not content with the demand analysis. This makes him adopt a different approach. Instead of formulating a theory according to which unemployment is due to a limited number of variables which can be falsified or not, Driehuis develops what he calls a synthetic view in which he describes in a rather impressionistic way the factors which might have influenced employment growth [Driehuis (1976, pp. 20–27)].[11] It will be obvious that in this description the distinction between sectors is considered extremely significant.

The synthetic approach does not seem very promising from a theoretical point of view. The main reason is the highly descriptive nature of the analysis, which makes it impossible to discriminate between the different hypotheses and hence does not yield a deeper insight into the very reason(s) for the slowdown of employment growth. In order to enlarge upon that insight, economists should formulate alternative, conflicting hypotheses and try to reject them. Only in this way will a better explanation of the current unemployment problem be forthcoming.

Before finishing this section, one more remark will be made; it concerns the question of whether the macroeconomic approach is a useful one. As has already been mentioned, Driehuis is rather negative in this respect. Whether this is justified is doubtful, however.

In the past, the trade cycle has almost always been approached in a macroeconomic way. Upswing and downswing can be observed more or less in all sectors. If one compares the growth rates of the effective demand components between the periods 1964–1970 and 1970–1974, one will see that all growth rates were highest in the former period [Hoekstra (1976, p. 41)]. There are differences, though. Growth rates of investments of firms and government fell very sharply, whereas the growth rate of exports of goods remained at a relatively high level. Calculations by Den Hartog and Weitenberg show, however, that these differences were not so large as to cause major deviations between growth rates of weighted and unweighted effective demand [Den Hartog and Weitenberg (1977, pp. 1239–1240)].

If one considers the stagnation of employment growth to be a supply phenomenon, there is no reason either to expect strong deviations between a sectoral and a macroeconomic approach.[12] The reason is that if one compares the periods 1953–1963 and 1964–1973, then the main trends, such as a fall in rates of return, a rise in the labour share in output and a fall in employment growth, can be observed in almost all sectors, including the service sector [Central Planning Bureau (1976, pp. 143–153)].[13] Moreover, the macroeconomically estimated relation between employment growth and the growth of real wages can also be derived intersectorally.[14] Hence, from this point of view the necessity of a sectoral approach has not been sufficiently established either.

[11] In his 1977 paper he employs the same method to conclude that structural unemployment is due to changes in the structure of aggregate demand, market imperfection and the rise in labour costs relative to capital costs.

[12] The postwar recovery period may be an exception. See, for instance, Den Hartog and Tjan (1975, pp. 487–488).

[13] In Ministry of Social Affairs (1975, pp. 106–107) it has been established that there is indeed a very strong relation between the acceleration of the rise in real labour costs between these two periods on the one hand, and the deceleration of employment rise between the same periods on the other, in the different sectors.

[14] According to the Den Hartog–Tjan vintage model a rise in real wages by 1 percent will lead to a fall in employment of 35 000 man-years, i.e. 0.8 percent of the working population of firms [Ministry of Social

4. The system approach

As already mentioned at the end of section 2, in his explanation of stagnation and unemployment Van der Zwan refers to tendencies which are inherent in a market
economy itself. In particular, the relative strength of the manufacturing and the service
sector is considered to be essential. The Fifties were characterized above all by concentration and market control within manufacturing. In many branches of industry
oligopoly became the ruling market form. The implication is that the market position of
producers was a very strong one.

In the Sixties things began to change. First, a concentration in the service sector too
could be observed. Furthermore, technological changes led to a strong increase in the
scale of operation within the manufacturing sector, while at the same time the economy
became more and more internationalized. These two tendencies necessarily led to an
uncontrolled expansion of the productive capacity in many branches of industry.
Hence, there was a structural tendency towards the creation of excess capacity which
weakened the market position of these industries. In particular, their position vis-à-vis
the service sector was fundamentally weakened. The concentration in the service sector
itself also tended to make the manufacturing position less strong. It made it possible to
shift cost increases to manufacturing and to take over activities which until then had
been performed by manufacturing. Van der Zwan therefore concludes that in the
Sixties there had been structural worsening of the terms of trade of the manufacturing
sector with respect to the service sector. This fact, together with the general tendency
towards the creation of excess capacity, should be considered the main cause of the
bad profit situation in manufacturing and hence of the employment situation. Improving the terms of trade and the degree of capacity utilization should be the main
goal of economic policy, not a slowdown of real wage growth. In order to achieve this,
planning and control of industrial investments are inevitable in his view.

Nobody will deny that excess capacity exists nowadays in some important industrial
sectors, such as steel, shipbuilding and chemicals. Nor will it be denied that part of the

---

Affairs (1975, p. 109)]. Hence, the demand-for-labour elasticity is 0.8. From a cross-section analysis of
employment growth in the Dutch branches of industry and services and the agricultural sector the following
regression equation can be derived:

$$\frac{\dot{a}_i}{a_i} = 0.586\frac{\dot{y}_i}{y_i} - 0.666\frac{\dot{w}_i}{l_i} + 0.431, \qquad R^2 = 0.7645,$$

$$(7.753) \quad (-4.022) \quad (0.366) \qquad DW = 1.335$$

$\dot{a}_i/a_i$ average growth rate of employment in sector i in the period 1963–1973; $\dot{w}_i/w_i$ average growth rate of real
labour costs in sector i in the period 1963–1973; and $\dot{y}_i/y_i$ average growth rate of output in sector i in the period
1963–1973. The terms in parentheses are t values; R^2 is the coefficient of determination; DW is the Durbin–Watson statistic. The data are derived from Central Planning Bureau (1976, p. 153).

The regression equation shows a demand elasticity of 0.7. Hence, the vintage approach and the sectoral
approach hardly yield different results.

problem is due to this fact. The question is, however, whether this is the dominating picture. Van der Zwan does not succeed in making this sufficiently clear. One has too strong a feeling that this picture is based mainly on casual observation (Enka synthetic fibres, Philips computers, Shell nuclear power stations) [Van der Zwan (1976, p. 117)].

Apart from this more general point of criticism, one can also question the postulated mechanisms, especially that which runs via the service sector. First, the deterioration of the terms of trade had already taken place in the period 1953–1963 and is not therefore a phenomenon which is characteristic of the period 1963–1973. In the former period domestic prices of manufacturing rose on average by 0.9 percent a year and domestic prices of services by 3.9 percent a year; in the latter period these figures were 3.7 and 7.6 percent, respectively.[15] Hence, it is doubtful whether the service sector's position did in fact become stronger.

This tendency cannot be derived from the demand figures either. Not only did domestic demand for manufacturing products display a slower growth, but the same holds for the service sector. In the period 1953–1963 these figures were 6.3 and 5.0 percent for manufacturing and services, respectively, and in the period 1963–1973 3.6 and 3.9 percent respectively. Export demand for manufacturing output between these two periods even showed a stronger rise than export demand for output of services: 3.4 and 0.5 percent, respectively.

A second comment concerns the relation between excess capacity and profitability. It is indeed true that excess capacity may very strongly influence profitability.[16] If Van der Zwan is right, then in particular manufacturing profits should have declined. However, profit margins in both sectors declined between the periods 1953–1963 and 1963–1973. In the first place this is shown by the labour share in output of firms. In manufacturing it rose from 69.5 to 77.0 percent, in services from 68.0 to 76.4 percent. [Central Planning Bureau (1976, p. 143)]. Hence, the fall in the profit margins of services was even stronger than that of manufacturing. The same tendency is shown by the ratio of profits[17] and gross investments: in manufacturing this ratio fell from 195 to 165, in services from 160 to 130 [Central Planning Bureau (1976, p. 160)].

Therefore, one may conclude that it is difficult to maintain that the development in the service sector has happened at the expense of the manufacturing sector. It is really surprising that the analysis clearly points in only one direction, namely that the sectors show the same tendencies. In this respect, this analysis leads to the same results as that in the previous section did. The dominating features are a deterioration of profitability and a slowdown of employment growth in all sectors.

---

[15] The rise in export prices between those two periods in the service sector was even less than that in the manufacturing sector [Central Planning Bureau (1976, p. 163)].

[16] According to Kuipers et al. (1978), almost half the deterioration of the profit margin between 1973 and 1975 of 11 percent may be due to a fall in the utilization rate of capital between these two years.

[17] Gross, before taxes and depreciation allowances.

5. The long-wave approach

Since the early Seventies more and more attention has been paid to the existence of a long wave in economic life.[18] The reason is that the slowdown of economic growth since the early Seventies might be interpreted as the downward movement of the economy after an upswing of about the first twenty-five years after the Second World War. In the past, several hypotheses have been formulated to explain such a long wave.[19] In his inaugural lecture Van Duyn tries to synthesize the main hypotheses:[20]

(1) Forrester's multiplier–accelerator two-sector model;[21]
(2) Schumpeter's innovations theory;[22] and
(3) the product life cycle theory.

By means of these theories it is not difficult to explain the upper turning point. The lower turning point gives more trouble, however. With respect to the latter, Van Duyn refers to Mensch (1975), according to whom clusters of innovations occur during the long-cyclical downswing. During this phase of the long wave new investment outlets are exhausted and the only possibility of escaping this technological stalemate is to introduce new products and production techniques, however risky these innovations are. In the stalemate the entrepreneurs do not have any choice.

The long-wave approach is not without problems. In the first place, owing to time series that are too short, the hypothesis of the existence of a long wave cannot directly be tested. Although computer simulation can help to some extent, this technique cannot be considered a perfect substitute. It is not too difficult to generate cycles with the desired periodicity. It all depends on the parameter values and the lag structure adopted.

From a theoretical point of view the greatest trouble appears in the field of innovations. As long as economic theory is not able to give a deeper insight into their origin, their appearance and their diffusion, it is very difficult to say anything definite about hypotheses as formulated by Schumpeter and Mensch.

With respect to the postwar period, there is some evidence that the postwar trend has to be considered the upswing of the Kondratieff cycle.[23] If this were true, Van Duyn's synthesis implies that the slowdown of employment growth is caused by excess capacity due to too strong an expansion of the capital goods sector and saturation of consumer demand owing to the fact that for some consumables the end of the life cycle

---

[18] In this country Van Duyn (1977b, 1978) and Broersma (1978) should be mentioned.

[19] For a survey of these theories see Broersma (1978, ch. 2 and 3) and Van Duyn (1977b, pp. 547–556).

[20] Van Duyn (1977b) is a translation of his inaugural lecture originally published in Dutch in Van Duyn (1977a).

[21] See, for instance, Forrester (1977).

[22] Schumpeter (1939).

[23] Broersma for the US economy and Van Duyn for the Dutch economy show that in some macroeconomic time series there has been a deceleration in economic growth since the mid-Sixties [Broersma (1978, ch. 4), Van Duyn (1978, p. 79)].

has been reached and new products have not been developed in the recent past.

If there is a long cycle then, owing to the internationalizing of the Western economies, this cycle is a world-wide one. It is quite possible that part of the slowdown of economic growth should be interpreted in terms of excess capacity and the lack of growth markets. However, it is doubtful whether the slowdown of employment growth can be explained solely in this way. The fact still remains that in almost all Western countries the early Seventies were characterized by high output growth rates and low or negative employment growth rates [e.g. Central Planning Bureau (1973, pp. 42–43)], a phenomenon which cannot be explained by the above-mentioned tendencies alone.[24]

6. Concluding remarks

The above discussion yields two important conclusions. First, all branches of industry and services show the same tendencies: falling profit margins, a slowdown of employment growth, and a rise in real labour costs. This indicates that the causes of the stagnation of employment growth may be macroeconomic in character. This is strengthened by the fact that macroeconomic and intersectoral calculations of the demand elasticity of labour yield about the same results. The same applies to the explanation of labour demand from the demand side, whether or not account is taken of intersectoral changes.

This conclusion implies that the slowdown of employment growth is due either to a slower growth of effective demand or to a rise in real labour costs, or to both. The above discussion makes it seem doubtful that the slowdown of employment growth is caused only by a deficiency of aggregate demand. Changes in aggregate demand in the period 1964–1970 explain only a relatively small part of the changes in employment in this period; in the early Seventies the change in aggregate demand even has the wrong sign. Hence, it is clear that changes in real wages also have something to do with it.

This implies that both real wages and capacity utilization rates should appear in the employment equation. The strength of the Den Hartog–Tjan employment theory is that they do indeed appear. As has been mentioned, however, the specification used gives some trouble [Kuipers et al. (1978)]. In particular, the equation is too static. A more dynamic specification is better able to explain employment growth in the Seventies. It then turns out that the adjustment is very slow. In one year only 20 percent of the gap between actual and desired employment is filled. The consequence of this is that, until the early Eighties, employment in the Netherlands will still be influenced by the bad experiences of the early Seventies.

[24] For the same argument, see Schouten (1977).

The Kuipers–Muysken–Van Sinderen study also yields another important result. It is that changes in the degree of capacity utilization hardly have any direct influence on employment in the Seventies.[25] Hence, the slowdown in employment growth is mainly due to a rise in real wages.

What are the prospects for employment growth in the intermediate future? In the Kuipers–Muysken–Van Sinderen study some predictions have been made on the assumption that real wages, output and investment in equipment grow with the growth rates projected by the Central Economic Commission, that is by 3, 3.5 and 5 percent a year, respectively, from 1979 onwards [Van Schaik (1978, p. 105)]. These projections demonstrate that employment in firms will go on falling until 1979. From 1979 onwards it shows a slight rise, which should mainly be attributed to the creation of new jobs and to the disappearance of the effects of the negative developments of the early Seventies. In 1981 predicted employment is 3947 million man-years which, with the labour supply constant since 1977, implies about 250 000 unemployed.

What may be still more important, however, is that a growth rate of output of 3.5 percent a year is not sufficient to maintain full capacity utilization. The utilization rate of capital falls from 0.987 in 1977 to 0.947 in 1981. This may have two different consequences. First, investment growth of 5 percent a year may prove to be too optimistic. Hence, fewer jobs may be created. Secondly, low utilization rates may also result ultimately in a direct adjustment of labour demand.

Intermediate prospects of employment growth are thus hardly favourable. The rise in real wages, although already considerably diminished, may still be too strong. However, the rather strong fall in the utilization rate may seem to be even more important. This has a negative effect on investment decisions. If in addition employment is not adjusted to capacity labour demand, this leads pari passu to lower profit margins which also tend to influence investment decisions negatively. Hence, there is ample reason to combine a policy of limiting the rise in real wages with one of stimulating aggregate demand.

References

Barro, R. and H. Grossman, 1976, Money, employment and inflation (Cambridge University Press, Cambridge).
Bergström, A. R., 1962, A model of technical progress, the production function and cyclical growth, Economica 29, 357–370.
Broersma, Tj. J., 1978, De lange golf in het economische leven, Doctoral dissertation (University of Groningen, Groningen).
Central Planning Bureau, 1973, Central economic plan 1973 (Staatsuitgeverij, The Hague).
Central Planning Bureau, 1976, De Nederlandse economie in 1980 (Staatsuitgeverij, The Hague).

[25] This does not mean that an indirect effect, via investment growth and hence via the creation of jobs, does not exist. The study mentioned above did not, however, investigate investment behaviour.

Central Planning Bureau, 1977, Een macro model voor de Nederlandse economie op middellange termijn, Occasional papers, no. 12 (The Hague).

Driehuis, W., 1976, An analysis of the impact of demand and cost factors on employment in the Netherlands, Mimeographed research memorandum, no. 7604 (University of Amsterdam, Amsterdam).

Driehuis, W., 1977, Capital–labour substitution and other potential determinants of structural employment and unemployment, Mimeographed research memorandum, no. 7708 (University of Amsterdam, Amsterdam).

Driehuis, W., 1979, An analysis of the impact of demand and cost factors on employment, De Economist 127, 255–286.

Driehuis, W. and A. van der Zwan, 1977, De voorbereiding van het economisch beleid kritisch bezien, Economisch-Statistische Berichten 62, 828–836 and 856–863.

Driehuis, W. and A. van der Zwan, 1978, De voorbereiding van het economisch beleid kritisch bezien, Economisch-Statistische Berichten 63, 316–319, 348–359 and 376–387.

Duyn, J. J. van, 1977a, Eb en vloed, De lange golf in het economische leven, Inaugural lecture (Graduate School of Management, Delft).

Duyn, J. J. van, 1977b, The long wave in economic life, De Economist 125, 544–576.

Duyn, J. J. van, 1978, Actualiteit en beleidsindicaties van de Kondratieff-cyclus, Economisch-Statistische Berichten 63, 76–82.

Ellman, M., 1977, Report from Holland: The economics of North Sea hydrocarbons, Cambridge Journal of Economics 1, 281–290.

Forrester, J. W., 1977, Growth cycles, De Economist 125, 525–543.

Hartog, H. den and H. S. Tjan, 1974, Investeringen, lonen, prijzen en arbeidsplaatsen, Occasional paper, no. 2 (Central Planning Bureau, The Hague).

Hartog, H. den and H. S. Tjan, 1975, Commentaar, Economisch-Statistische Berichten 60, 484–489.

Hartog, H. den and H. S. Tjan, 1976, Investments, wages, prices and demand for labour (A clay-clay vintage model for the Netherlands), De Economist 124, 32–55.

Hartog, H. den and J. Weitenberg, 1977, Econometrische modellen en economische politiek, Economisch-Statistische Berichten 62, 1236–1243 and 1269–1273.

Hartog, H. den, Th. C. M. J. van de Klundert and H. S. Tjan, 1975, De structurele ontwikkeling van de werkgelegenheid in macro-economisch perspectief, in: Werkloosheid, Aard, omvang, structurele oorzaken en beleidsalternatieven (Martinus Nijhoff, The Hague) pp. 49–110.

Hoekstra, Th., 1976, De werkgelegenheidsontwikkeling in Nederland, Doctoral paper (University of Groningen, Groningen).

Interim-nota inzake de bestrijding van de werkloosheid, 1974 (Staatsuitgeverij, The Hague).

Klerk, R. A. de, H. B. M. van der Laan and K. B. T. Thio, 1977, Unemployment in the Netherlands: A criticism of the Den Hartog–Tjan vintage model, Cambridge Journal of Economics 1, 291–306.

Kloek, T., 1977, Vintaf II bezien tegen de achtergrond van eerdere planbureaumodellen, Economisch-Statistische Berichten 62, 1040–1045.

Kuipers, S. K., 1974, On the estimation of capacity output, Mimeographed memorandum (Institute of Economic Research, Groningen).

Kuipers, S. K., 1977, Over structurele en conjuncturele ontwikkelingen binnen de Nederlandse economie sinds de eerste wereldoorlog, Inaugural lecture (North-Holland, Amsterdam).

Kuipers, S. K., J. Muysken and J. van Sinderen, 1978, De werkgelegenheidsontwikkeling in Nederland sinds 1970; een nadere analyse, Economisch-Statistische Berichten 63, 648–652.

Kuipers, S. K., J. Muysken and J. van Sinderen, 1979, The vintage approach to output and employment growth in the Netherlands, 1921–1976, Weltwirtschaftliches Archiv 115, 485–507.

Malinvaud, E., 1977, The theory of unemployment reconsidered (Basil Blackwell, Oxford).

Mensch, G., 1975, Das technologische Patt (Umschau Verlag, Frankfurt am Main).

Ministry of Social Affairs, 1975, Nota inzake de werkgelegenheid (Staatsuitgeverij, The Hague).

Pen, J., 1978, Wages, profits and employment in the mid-Seventies: The controversial case of the Netherlands, in: Pioneering economics (Cedam, Padova) pp. 781–799.

Salter, W. E. G., 1960, Productivity and technical change (Cambridge University Press, Cambridge).

Sandee, J., 1976, A putty–clay model for The Netherlands (Central Planning Bureau, The Hague).

130   S. K. Kuipers

Schaik, A. B. T. M. van, 1978, Neo-keynesiaans en neo-klassiek: Wel een onderscheid maar geen tegenstelling, Economisch-Statistische Berichten 63, 104–108.

Schouten, D. B. J., 1977, Hoe komen we eigenlijk aan meer winst, want meer winst is op den duur meer werk!, Economisch-Statistische Berichten 62, 1128–1131.

Schumpeter, J. A., 1939, Business cycles (McGraw-Hill, New York and London).

Solow, R. M. and J. B. Stiglitz, 1968, Output, employment and wages in the short run, Quarterly Journal of Economics 82, 537–560.

Wetenschappelijke Raad voor het Regeringsbeleid, 1977, Maken wij er werk van (Staatsuitgeverij, The Hague).

Zwan, A. van der, 1975, Dalend rendement op geïnvesteerd vermogen, Economisch-Statistische Berichten 60, 656–660 and 680–685.

Zwan, A. van der, 1976, Over de vergroting van de omweg in de produktie en de bekorting van de omlooptijd van het in bedrijven geïnvesteerde vermogen, Economisch-Statistische Berichten 61, 60–65, 80–83 and 117–122.

Zwan, A van der, 1977, Na de smalle marges van het beleid, nu de "dreigende" vervaging van de politieke keuzen, Economisch-Statistische Berichten 62, 244–248, 268–277 and 300–302.

Chapter 14

p. 117 :

COMMENT ON KUIPERS'S PAPER

W. DRIEHUIS

University of Amsterdam   131 - 36

1. Introduction

There is a saying that one can be "plus royaliste que le roi". This seems to hold for Kuipers when he concludes his paper with the statement that the causes of the stagnation of employment growth are mainly macroeconomic in character.

Recent debates and publications on the determinants of demand for labour by enterprises have at least shown one thing, namely that most economists (including those at the Central Planning Bureau), each with his own orientation in economic policy, agree as to the analysis of demand for labour. In a recently published book [Driehuis and Van der Zwan (1978)] which presents a lively debate on the preparation of economic policy in the Netherlands, it becomes clear that the study of aggregate demand for labour is not legitimate from an *analytical* point of view, not desirable from an *empirical* point of view and not fruitful from a *policy* point of view. Similar views are expressed in a recent report on the state of the economy by the Committee of Economic Experts of the Socio-Economic Council (1978).

Instead of continuing the attempts to integrate the ideas which have been put forward in the course of the employment debate, a way which, for example, Driehuis and Van der Zwan (1978) and the above-mentioned Committee of Economic Experts prefer to take, Kuipers's paper is back where Den Hartog and Tjan (1974) started in their admirable, but arguable, paper. I therefore judge Kuipers's study a disappointing one.

2. Are there four approaches to analysing demand for labour?

Kuipers's paper is not, as the title suggests, about the prospects of employment growth, but about the prevailing views as regards the determinants of demand for labour in enterprises in the past, particularly during the years 1953–1973. Only at the end of the study is Kuipers's view of the prospects of employment growth up to 1982 given.

Kuipers's distinction into four lines of thought, namely the *vintage* approach, the *spending* approach, the *system* approach, and the *long-wave* approach, does not seem an appropriate one. In fact, he is labelling fellow economists instead of distinguishing analytical directions. Den Hartog and Tjan are labelled with vintages, Driehuis with spending, Van der Zwan with institutions, and Van Duyn with long waves. In reality, the ideas of Den Hartog and Tjan also comprise demand elements in addition to real wage costs; Driehuis mentions the wage–capital cost ratio as well as demand and changes in its composition, but also changes in the organization of the production process and the role of innovations. The impact of the last variable is also investigated by Van der Zwan, who pays attention to wage and capital costs and demand factors as well, but in a sectorally differentiated way. Similarly, Van Duyn in fact looks also at all the factors mentioned.

What then are the differences in the work of the authors mentioned? Two broad groups can be distinguished: one consisting of CPB and former CPB members (Den Hartog, Tjan, Driehuis), who try to investigate employment in enterprises by econometric methods. This group hopes to find the "stylized facts" behind the development of employment and uses annual data. The other group (Van der Zwan and Van Duyn) has a much longer time perspective and aims at the description and analysis of *processes* in society, particularly as regards firms and groups of firms.

The latter approach therefore does not necessarily compete with the econometric one. The two are inseparable, both from the viewpoint of analysis and from the viewpoint of policy, and therefore complementary rather than substitutive. It is characteristic of the work by Van der Zwan and Van Duyn that it focuses on aspects of economic life which cannot be adequately criticized with the aid of aggregate or broad sectoral data, as Kuipers tries to do.[1] For instance, his conclusion about the stronger decline in the profit rate in the aggregate services sector as compared with the manufacturing sector from the period 1953–1963 to the period 1963–1974 cannot be considered as a conclusive test of the relevance of Van der Zwan's ideas.

3. Econometric work

It is remarkable that Kuipers approaches the vintage analysis rather uncritically. He mentions critiques raised, but largely fails to assess their relevance. His main attack is on previous preliminary work by this discussant, which was therefore published as a research memorandum. Careful reading of this memorandum shows that its author is

[1] See also Van der Zwan (1978).

critical of his own work. He mentions its pitfalls, which Kuipers partly repeats in his paper, and concludes that "this analysis, however, has its weaknesses as well, particularly in that it was not sufficiently able to include the effects of capacity utilization". The author furthermore mentions the fact that technical change was specified too simply and that the analysis was undertaken at too high a level of aggregation.[2] In addition he specifies a synthetic view at a sectoral level, which has since been elaborated in several other papers.[3] The core of his reasoning is:

(a) several specifications can be constructed and empirically estimated which "explain" aggregate employment in a way which does not differ very much in terms of R^2;

(b) these reduced-form specifications do not allow any conclusion about the correctness of the underlying basic theory, because a specific reduced form may result from different basic theories; and

(c) from the obvious differences in market structure, production structure and technical change it follows that one should not apply one specification to all industries.

As support for his view that it is sufficient to consider the negative relationship between the rate of change of employment and the rate of change of real wages, Kuipers presents the following equation:

$$\dot{a}_i = 0.586 \ \dot{y}_i - 0.666 \ (\dot{w}_i - \dot{p}_i) + 0.431 \tag{1}$$

where

$\dot{a}_i$ = average rate of change of employment in sector i during the period 1963–1973,

$\dot{y}_i$ = average rate of change of output in sector i during the period 1963–1973,

$\dot{w}_i$ = average rate of change of compensation per employee in sector i during the period 1963–1973,

$\dot{p}_i$ = average rate of change of output price of sector i during the period 1963–1973.

This equation can hardly be considered a satisfactory employment equation, for the following reasons. It is highly questionable that each sector would have the same real-wage and output elasticity of employment. This is all the more remarkable since some sectors, for instance the building and some service industries, are able to raise their prices because of rising wage costs much more easily than sectors which are under pressure from international competition. The "sheltered" sectors just mentioned also use a relatively low amount of equipment per worker, so that a reduction of employment due to economic obsolescence of equipment cannot take place there.

It seems to me that the equation which Kuipers presents is in fact a (mis-specified)

---

[2] The 1976 paper has been revised recently. It proves that an aggregate employment equation for the Netherlands can be estimated in which all variables are significant [Driehuis (1979a)].

[3] See Driehuis (1979a), Driehuis (1979b) and Driehuis and Van der Zwan (1978).

"reversed" price equation. The reason for this hypothesis is that nominal wage increases are fairly equal for different sectors, owing to "solidaristic wage formation". But changes in labour productivity deviate far more from each other, so that a spread in output price changes can be observed. It is not so difficult to write the following price equation, which can be transformed into Kuipers's specification:

$$\dot{p}_i = \dot{w}_i - \lambda(\dot{y}_i - \dot{a}_i) + \xi\,\dot{y}_i - \varepsilon \qquad (\lambda > \xi), \tag{2}$$

where average price changes per sector are a function of nominal wage increases, changes in labour productivity, and changes in output as an indicator of fluctuations in demand. The coefficients of the wage and labour productivity variable are supposed to differ according to the observation that some of the firms follow a standard cost price policy, in which the *trend* of labour productivity plays a part. This impact is then included in the constant term. It should be noted that the price equation above cannot be considered an adequate description of reality because it ignores the impact of foreign prices, but this is precisely why Kuipers explains "only" 75 percent of the variation.

4. An attempt at a synthetic approach

Let me, finally, summarize the employment analysis given by the Committee of Economic Experts in its June 1978 report in order to show that more adequate alternatives are available.

A distinction is made between:

(a) strongly internationally orientated industries, which have a capital-intensive character and use advanced technologies (type 1);

(b) industries which are orientated both to international and to domestic markets and which are rather labour-intensive and use rather traditional technologies (type 2a);

(c) ditto, which are not particularly labour-intensive and use advanced technologies (type 2b);

(d) industries which produce mainly for domestic markets, have a labour-intensive production structure and use mostly rather simple technologies (type 3).

Table 14.1 presents some data on these industries for the years 1963–1978.

The employment development of type 1 has, according to the Committee, less to do with relative factor prices than the considerable, international, underutilization of capacity. Employment in industries 2a and 2b is influenced by rationalization investments owing to the development of relative factor prices. Furthermore, the considerable slowing down of the volume growth of autonomous expenditure growth (government investment, government consumption and investment in dwellings) plays a part because of repercussive effects. Employment growth in industries of type 3 is mainly influenced by demand. The building industry lost 70 000 jobs between 1970

Table 14.1

Growth of output, employment and labour productivity per sector, 1953–1978.

Period[a]	Output volume		Employment		Labour productivity	
	I	II	I	II	I	II
	Average annual change in %					
Type 1	7.5	1.5	0.5	−2	7	3.5
Type 2a	2.5	−2	−4	−6.5	6.5	4.5
Type 2b	5.5	3	−1	−1	6.5	4
Type 3	5	3	2	0.5	3	2

Source: Committee of Economic Experts (1978, table 2.3).
[a] Period I: average 1953–1973;
   Period II: average 1974–1978.

and 1975, mainly because of the development of autonomous expenditure. Part of the services sector is related to manufacturing industries (commercial services) and so is its employment growth. The other part of employment in the services industries mainly depends on demand by the government, firms and consumers.

It follows from this short and incomplete sketch that all four approaches mentioned by Kuipers can easily be considered in an integrated way. The rate of capital accumulation, changes in the economic lifetime of equipment, relative factor costs, technical change of a different nature, development of demand and changes in its composition, the organization of the production and consumption process, innovations, product cycles, etc., can all be considered in an industrially differentiated way, without ignoring the macroeconomic aspects. Yet unpublished econometric work undertaken at the University of Amsterdam shows that it is in fact possible to incorporate a large number of the variables mentioned. Hence, it is not true, as Kuipers argues, that an initially impressionistic programme of research cannot serve later on as a basis for an alternative hypothesis which is open to testing procedures. It is my conviction that both economic analysis and economic policy will benefit from this type of work, which can simply be called the *economic* approach.

References

Committee of Economic Experts, 1978, Annual report (Socio-Economic Council, The Hague).
Driehuis, W., 1979a, An analysis of the impact of demand and cost factors on employment, De Economist 127 (forthcoming).
Driehuis, W., 1979b, Capital labour substitution and other potential determinants of structural employment and unemployment (forthcoming) in: Structural determinants of employment and unemployment, vol. II (OECD, Paris).

136   *W. Driehuis*

Driehuis, W. and A. van der Zwan, 1978, De voorbereiding van het economisch beleid kritisch bezien, ch. 2 and 9 in the book with the same title (Stenfert Kroese, Leiden).

Hartog, H. den and H. S. Tjan, 1974, Investeringen, lonen, prijzen en arbeidsplaatsen, Occasional Paper, no. 2 (Central Planning Bureau, The Hague).

Zwan, A. van der, 1978, On the assessment of the Kondratieff cycle and related issues, Chapter 19, this volume.

Chapter 15

COMMENT ON KUIPERS'S PAPER

H.-J. WAGENER and H. W. PLASMEIJER

137-40

University of Groningen

Professor Kuipers has presented a most valuable survey of recent discussions on the causes of unemployment in the Netherlands during the 1970s. We are not going to debate the surveyed arguments but will rather concentrate on Kuipers's view of the present state of affairs and on his conclusions.

In the introduction the prevailing situation is compared gloomily with unemployment during the Great Depression, thus suggesting that one could speak of a new great depression. Actually, we cannot follow the arithmetic and its underlying assumptions. Completely different social environments and completely different supply situations (think only of foreign and female labour supply) make off-hand comparisons a rather doubtful affair. It may certainly be true that a worker who became seriously ill had no opportunity in the Thirties to leave the labour force. But that does not make a worker who has to retire owing to ill health in the Seventies voluntarily unemployed. It would need further investigations to find out how the relative stress of work has changed in the course of time. Similarly, it may be perfectly correct that some employment is unproductive in the present depression. But there is no indication whatsoever that the same did not happen during the Great Depression.

On the other hand we would agree with Kuipers that labour supply is not independent of the state of the system. For the supply of foreign labour this is plainly visible. For the supply of female labour it seems to be the case too. Economic policy commands several instruments for manipulation, thus rendering the term "unemployment" rather elusive.

Although allowing for different explanations of the present situations of unemployment, Kuipers concludes: "the slowdown in employment is mainly due to a rise in real wages". This rise took place at an accelerated pace during the 1960s and was going on in the early 1970s. It reduced profitability and consequently the propensity of private business to invest, which ultimately led to a lack of jobs. The whole process was accompanied by a more or less stable development of output and demand.

This monocausal explanation has, as Kuipers reports, raised some doubts which presented themselves as monocausal explanations, too. By telling the same (or almost the same) story in somewhat different words we think we shall arrive at somewhat different conclusions. We concentrate on the business sector, since this is where the laws and mechanisms of capitalist market economies function. For the development of demand GNP growth is taken as a proxy. Propositions on capital are difficult and will remain vague, for reliable data on this key item of capitalism are not, as a rule, available. Thus, the statistical data given in table 15.1 must be taken rather as an illustration of our argument.

Table 15.1

Average rates of growth in percent (1970 prices)

Period	GNP	Business sector			
		Gross invest.	Employ- ment	Labour product.	Average labour cost
1951–1976	4.7	5.4	0.7	4.4	4.9
1951–1960	4.8	6.6	0.9	4.7	4.4
1961–1965	5.0	6.9	1.6	3.8	5.6
1966–1970	5.6	8.6	0.7	4.7	6.6
1971–1976	3.6	−0.6	−0.5	4.1	4.0

Sources: De Nederlandsche Bank N.V., Jaarverslagen; CBS, Nationale Rekeningen.

Taking the growth of labour productivity as given, the decline of demand during the 1970s would suffice to explain the negative employment growth. We do not think, however, that this could serve as a valid explanation. For then it is the decline of demand which has to be accounted for.

The first point to be made is that rises in real wages have to be related to the growth of labour productivity. Table 15.1 shows that, although real wages rose at an accelerated pace during the 1960s, the profit squeeze was more or less equal during the first and the second half of this decade. The immediate reaction of private business to the profit squeeze in the first half of the 1960s seems not to have been a reduction of investments, but rather the opposite. Investments were stepped up markedly, obviously substituting capital for labour and thus creating a very favourable demand situation. The profit squeeze continued during the second half of the 1960s but stopped entirely during the 1970s. Whether rising real wages can be held solely responsible for the declining employment during the latter period therefore seems doubtful in our eyes. We suggest that the mechanism of the economic crisis was somewhat more complicated and, most important, endogenous to the system.

The second point to be made has some connection with the argument of Van der Zwan. If we can take the growth of gross investment as a very rough indication of the development of capital stock, we find that a moderate deterioration of capital productivity in the 1950s and the early 1960s was followed by a more drastic decline in that variable accompanied by a rapid growth of the capital–labour ratio. This allows for the conclusion that even without any profit squeeze the rate of profit would have fallen.

According to standard Marxian theory it needs a crisis to stop the falling rate of profit and raise it to a newly acceptable level. What can prevent capital productivity from falling further? Besides simply reducing investment temporarily, the two most conspicuous measures are technical progress and social regress. The first is well described by the Den Hartog–Tjan model: while in 1959 the oldest equipment in use was from 1914, in 1973 it was from 1956. By social regress we mean among other things the possibility of stepping up labour discipline and work intensity in the face of unemployment. Both measures improve labour productivity without relying on an increasing capital–labour ratio, that is to say without net investment.

The crisis manifests itself in declining net investment, which may even lead to declining gross investment, as was the case during the 1970s. Capital stock does not only stop to grow but it even encounters destruction: insolvencies increase and excess capacities have to be removed from the production process. Both phenomena bring about an acceleration of the process of concentration, which has been dealt with in another contribution to the volume. It is obvious that the base materials and investment goods sectors will be hurt most by the crisis, i.e. steel, base chemicals and the like.

This brings us to the third point. The picture Kuipers gives us of the present economic situation is one of stable growth of demand, full capacity utilization, and unemployment: real capital shortage. This could be called a capitalist's dream of a crisis. The data show clearly, however, that the collapse of investment had its impact on total demand and, as we should like to suggest, in that way also on employment. Furthermore, it is unthinkable that the demand for investment goods declines drastically with full capacity utilization in this sector of the economy. Such a development would be possible only if export demand were to make up for the internal losses. But since the crisis described above is universal, at present, no such remedy can be expected. We know that utilization rates can be defined in different ways, but in any case a utilization rate of 0.987 in 1977 (with evidently 1.0 depicting full capacity utilization) raises our strongest doubts. It should be noticed, by the way, that while the capital–output ratio rose permanently during the 1950s and 1960s it declined during the crisis of the 1970s. At the same time labour productivity was growing unabated. The reason must be seen in a special form of "technical" progress: scrapping of less and less aged equipment (capital destruction), and the rejuvenating of capital stock which was accompanied by a concentration movement.

Drawing conclusions, we would argue that the employment crisis of the 1970s is a typical specimen of capitalism's recurring crises. It has been prompted by a falling rate of profit due to a profit squeeze and a declining capital productivity because of "overinvestment". What seems to be new is the relatively high rate of output growth, which could only have been brought about by a continuously growing demand for consumer goods. This is due to further rising real wages and social security measures.

Coming to the prospects for the future, it should be clear that negative investment growth rates will not go on for ever. It is the crisis which creates a real capital shortage in the end and at the same time improves on the conditions for its abolition; capital productivity will recover and the profit squeeze will be suspended. It is hard to tell at what exact point of time investment behaviour is going to change. We have no reasons whatsoever to dispute Kuipers's scepticism for the next two or three years to come. However, we are not of the opinion that the cure must be sought exclusively in a low rate of real wage increase and a high rate of output growth, although we know that this is the capitalist panacea.

The rejuventation of capital stock has its limits. Moreover, we think it was very functional with respect to the internationalization of the economy. (It even may have a completely neglected causal relation to growing international competition: in the 1960s and 1970s you would have fared poorly on the world market with equipment designed during the First World War.) But if technical progress should allow for smaller growth rates of investment and hence of total demand or if total demand should for some other reason remain lower in the long run, it could be labour supply that has to be adapted to the new situation. This runs contrary to the completely growth-orientated logic of capitalism and would entail some elements of investment and growth planning.

From this very logic the second proposition is derived: the necessary high rates of growth can be obtained only with high rates of profitability, it is argued. Given the decision and motivation structure of capitalist free enterprise, this seems rather obvious. But the experience of the present crisis may suggest that the trough of a depression will be less deep if consumer demand is held up by growing real wages and social security payments. A relative or even absolute wage deflation may prolong the depression.

A final remark: production is growing by some 3–4 percent; the necessary social labour input is decreasing slowly. Although goods and services produced are considered as utility and labour as disutility, people are not happy and content. For there are the unemployed who cannot get any work other than by the expansion of growth *and* labour demand. It seems to us that not only economic science but also the profession of economists exhibits a lack of imagination in this context.

Chapter 16

SECTORAL CHANGE AND ECONOMIC GROWTH
IN NINE DEVELOPED COUNTRIES

F. MULLER and W. J. ZWEZERIJNEN*

Erasmus University, Rotterdam

The problem of growth is studied from two sides: the level of expenditure and the availability of the production factors, labour and capital. Imports are also considered an important production factor; the contribution of this factor to gross domestic product seems to form a substitute for autonomous technical progress. Because the rate of growth and the level of gross domestic product influence the production of sectors to different degrees, a sectoral approach is followed. Special attention is paid to the importance of foreign trade and the share of each country in world production.

1. Introduction

During the last few years all Western economies have been confronted with a stagnation of economic growth and a decline in production in the major sectors of the economy. These problems have been examined for some individual countries, e.g. the study of France by Carré et al. (1976), of Germany by Schatz (1974) and Bombach et al. (1977), and the United Kingdom by Caves (1968) and Phillips and Maddock (1973). Studies of several countries have been undertaken by Denison (1967), and more recently by Bergson (1978) and Rostow (1978). All these studies come to the conclusion that it is not easy to study a country in isolation. All countries are bound together, particularly through international trade. Furthermore, a combination of time-series and cross-sectional analysis may reveal certain developments more rapidly than would otherwise be the case. It may also be illuminating to see that certain things are not specific to one country, but that analogous developments occur elsewhere.

It is the purpose of this study to analyse some common factors which are important to all developed countries. This comprises some major categories of expenditure (section 2) as well as the contribution of different sectors to gross domestic product (section

* The authors acknowledge the help of Niko Boxhoorn who gathered important data.

Prospects of Economic Growth, edited by S. K. Kuipers and G. J. Lanjouw
© *North-Holland Publishing Company*

5) and the share of a country in world production (section 6). The production factors, labour and capital, are also dealt with (sections 3 and 4). Apart from this, special attention is devoted to the importance of foreign trade (section 4).

The present study makes use of a great deal of data. The statistical sources that have been consulted are reported at the end of the study.

Unfortunately a satisfactory, all-embracing multisector model, explaining both the demand and the supply side of the economy, does not exist at the time of writing. Under these circumstances we have to confine ourselves to partial theories and data analysis. It is our conviction, however, that even in this way very valuable insight may be obtained.

2. The growth of expenditure

The growth of income can be studied from several sides. In this section we concentrate on the growth of broad categories of expenditure influencing the rate of growth of gross domestic product. Before discussing these categories it seems useful to pay some attention to the level and pattern of the growth of gross domestic product. Table 16.1 shows that there are considerable differences in magnitude and dispersion of the growth rate.

Table 16.1

Average yearly rate of growth of gross domestic product (constant prices).[a]

	$\bar{g}_y$	$\sigma_{\bar{g}_y}$	$\sigma_{\bar{g}_y}/\bar{g}_y$	Period
Belgium	4.0	2.3	0.6	1954–1975
France	4.9	1.6	0.3	1951–1975
GFR	5.5	3.4	0.6	1951–1975
Italy	4.9	2.4	0.5	1952–1975
Japan	8.9	4.0	0.4	1953–1975
The Netherlands	4.8	2.7	0.6	1952–1975
Sweden	3.6	1.5	0.4	1951–1975
UK	2.5	2.0	0.8	1952–1975
US	3.4	3.0	0.9	1951–1975

[a] $\bar{g}_y$, average yearly rate of growth;
$\sigma_{\bar{g}_y}$ standard deviation;
$\sigma_{\bar{g}_y}/\bar{g}_y$, coefficient of variation.

It is argued that a more or less frequent intervention of government in the economic process may result in a dangerous stop–go policy. The effect of this policy in this case is measured by the coefficient of variation [cf. Peaker (1974)]. To a certain degree a broad examination of table 16.1 might seem to confirm this conclusion. A regression analysis of $\bar{g}_y$ on $\sigma_{\bar{g}_y}$ (omitting the US from the sample) gives[1].

$$\bar{g}_y = \underset{(0.150)}{1.945} \; \sigma_{\bar{g}_y} \qquad R^2 = 0.652 \tag{1}$$

Our results suggest a positive influence of dispersion on the rate of growth in this respect. It is quite imaginable, however, that a successful economic policy, fostering economic growth, may be combined with fewer fluctuations in economic activity. Moreover, the coefficient of variation used by Peaker is not a very good statistic for measuring this effect; the correlation between $\bar{g}_y$ and $\sigma_{\bar{g}_y}/\bar{g}_y$ proved to be very weak.

It is quite common to explain the dispersion in yearly growth rates by changes in excess capacity. The OECD published a study containing degrees of utilization in 18 countries for the period 1955- 1972 [cf. Bolto and Keating (1973)]. The potential output of a country in a certain period is computed on the basis of an estimated Cobb–Douglas production function. Excess capacity is then defined as the difference between actual and potential output as a percentage of the latter. The OECD study suggests a reasonable correspondence between excess capacity in all countries in the course of time. High rates of utilization are realized in nearly all countries during the years 1955/56, 1960/61, 1965/66 and 1970/71, low rates in 1958/59 and 1971/72. Table 16.2 shows average idle capacity and its dispersion.

Table 16.2

Average idle capacity related to potential GDP. [a]

	$\bar{x}$	$\sigma_{\bar{x}}$
Belgium	1.4	1.5
France	0.6	1.1
GFR	1.1	1.9
Italy	2.0	1.8
Japan	2.8	2.7
The Netherlands	1.5	1.6
Sweden	0.8	1.3
UK	1.3	1.6
US	3.3	3.1

$$^a x_t = \frac{GDP_t^* - GDP}{GDP_t^*}; \qquad \bar{x}\frac{\Sigma_{t=1}^{T}x_t}{T}$$

GDP^* is potential gross domestic product.

---

[1] The coefficient in parentheses is the standard error.

Because of the upper level of the rate of utilization a close relationship between average idle capacity and its standard deviation can be expected. This hypothesis is confirmed by the regression analysis ($R_{\bar{x},\sigma_{\bar{x}}} = 0.95$).

Although in neoclassical theory the level of demand does not affect steady-state economic growth, there may be some influence in disequilibrium situations. To investigate this possibility we applied a regression of $\bar{g}_y$ on $\bar{x}$ and $\sigma_{\bar{x}}$, respectively, which produced as best results (again omitting the US from the sample):

$$\bar{g}_y = \underset{(0.781)}{1.882}\ \bar{x} + \underset{(1.234)}{2.182} \qquad R^2 = 0.492, \tag{2}$$

$$\bar{g}_y = \underset{(0.229)}{2.911}\ \sigma_{\bar{x}} \qquad\qquad R^2 = 0.638 \tag{3}$$

In this case too countries experiencing fluctuations in the level of economic activity reveal high growth rates, as is clear from eq. (3). Equation (2) shows a positive correlation between growth rate and idle capacity. A possible explanation of this fact is that countries facing a large idle capacity are in a good position to profit from a sudden rise in economic activity by increasing their exports. In one way it is disappointing that a certain degree of demand pressure does not lead to *higher* growth rates, e.g. by inducing additional investments. We now discuss the development of expenditure separately (see Appendix A).

2.1. Private consumption

In 1953 the share of private consumption in gross domestic product measured in current prices varied from 62 percent in Japan to 71 percent in Belgium. In the course of time this share gradually declined in all countries except the United States, where it remained remarkably stable. Measured in constant prices, the share of private consumption declined in Belgium and Japan, but remained more or less the same in all other countries. It may be useful to compare the rate of increase of the price of consumer goods with that of the general price level. In Germany, the Netherlands and the United Kingdom the price of consumer goods clearly increased at a lower rate than the price of gross domestic product. Only in Japan did the rate of increase in the price of consumer goods exceed that of the general price level, leading to a declining share of private consumption in the volume of gross domestic product.

2.2. Government expenditure

The share of government expenditure in the volume of gross domestic product exceeds 20 percent in Sweden, the United Kingdom and the United States. This share is traditionally low in Belgium, Germany and Italy (about 15 percent). Starting at a rather high level of 20 percent in 1951, the Netherlands too is approaching this low level.

Real government expenditure is an important autonomous term in nearly all short-term economic models. It may be helpful to divide the share of government expenditure in nominal terms between the change of the share in real terms and the change in prices; this can be done as follows:

$$\mathrm{d}\left(\frac{G}{p_q Q}\right) = \left(\frac{G}{p_q Q}\right)_0 (\dot{g} - \dot{q}) + \left(\frac{G}{p_q Q}\right)_0 (\dot{p}_g - \dot{p}_q), \tag{4}$$

where

G = nominal government expenditure,
Q = gross domestic product (constant prices),
$\dot{g}$ = rate of change of government expenditure (constant prices),
$\dot{q}$ = rate of change of gross domestic product (constant prices),
$\dot{p}_g$ = rate of change of the price of government expenditure,
$\dot{p}_q$ = rate of change of the price of gross domestic product.

If the share of government in real expenditure is considered to have a fixed desired level the change of this share in nominal terms depends only on the difference between the rate of change of the price of government expenditure and the general price level.

It has to be added that government expenditure is not the only influence the government can exercise on total expenditure. Apart from this tax and subsidy policies have their impact on private expenditure.

2.3. Investments

The investment ratio varies from 12 percent in the United Kingdom to as much as 27 percent in Japan. The rate has changed very little with time, but increased slightly in Belgium, France, Japan and the Netherlands. The price of investment goods more or less followed the general price level, except in Japan where investment goods did become somewhat cheaper compared to the general price level.

The sudden decline of the investment ratio in all countries when 1975 is compared with 1971 is very remarkable. This clearly demonstrates the worsening of the economic situation. Consumer demand turns out to be less vulnerable to the fluctuations of economic activity, which is shown by a small increase in the consumption ratio.

2.4. Foreign trade

The share of foreign trade reflects marked differences between the countries, as is shown in table 16.3. In 1951 the Netherlands already had an export share of about 50

Table 16.3

Foreign trade and gross domestic product.

	Export share				Import share			
	Current prices		Constant prices		Current prices		Constant prices	
	1951	1975	1951	1975	1951	1975	1951	1975
Belgium	0.28	0.46	0.22	0.47	0.29	0.46	0.22	0.46
France	0.15	0.21	0.15	0.21	0.15	0.20	0.09	0.20
GFR	0.16	0.25	0.13	0.31	0.14	0.22	0.08	0.28
Italy	0.12	0.25	0.06	0.27	0.13	0.25	0.07	0.22
Japan	0.12	0.13	0.07	0.16	0.11	0.13	0.05	0.12
The Netherlands	0.48	0.53	0.31	0.71	0.50	0.50	0.30	0.64
Sweden	0.30	0.29	0.17	0.28	0.28	0.30	0.17	0.28
UK	0.25	0.26	0.18	0.26	0.30	0.28	0.17	0.25
US	0.05	0.09	0.04	0.07	0.05	0.08	0.03	0.05

percent, this share being only 5 percent in the United States. The export share of Japan is much lower than generally thought (about 10 percent). In order to maintain its export ratio Japan has to offer lower and lower prices, as is shown by the big surplus on the balance of trade measured in constant prices, which disappears when measured in current prices. Italy too has to export increasing volumes of goods and services to maintain equilibrium in current values.

The export ratio increased greatly between 1951 and 1975 in almost every country, except Sweden and the United Kingdom. Owing to a concomitant increase in the import ratio, however, this has no *direct* influence on the level of gross domestic product. There may be large indirect effects, however, as we shall see in section 4.

3. The contribution of capital to gross domestic product

The relation between the inputs of production factors and the resultant gross domestic product is described by the production function. In a simple Harrod–Domar model production is completely determined by the stock of capital, so that the rate of growth of gross domestic product in this case equals

$$\dot{Q} = s/\kappa, \tag{5}$$

where

Q = rate of growth of gross domestic product,
s = savings (investment) ratio,
κ = capital–output ratio (capital coefficient).

In these circumstances, where eq. (5) gives a good description of reality, the capital–output ratio can be calculated from data on $\dot{Q}$ and s; this has been done in table 16.4. From this table the capital coefficient appears to be reasonably stable,

Table 16.4

Capital coefficients calculated from the Harrod–Domar model.

	Growth of GDP (%)		Investment ratio (%)		Capital coefficient	
	1951–63	1964–75	1951–63	1964–75	1951–63	1964–75
Belgium	3.7	4.4	19.5	22.1	5.3	5.0
France	4.7	4.6	19.5	22.1	4.1	4.8
GFR	7.5	3.9	24.5	24.6	3.3	6.3
Italy	5.8	4.0	19.4	19.0	3.3	4.8
Japan	8.9	8.7	18.7	27.7	2.1	3.2
The Netherlands	4.6	5.1	19.8	21.2	4.3	4.2
Sweden	4.5	3.5	15.2	16.3	3.4	4.7
UK	2.7	2.4	11.1	13.3	4.1	5.6
US	3.1	3.1	15.6	14.2	5.0	4.6

Table 16.5

Direct calculation of the capital coefficient.

	1955	1959	1963	1967	1970
France	1.6	1.5	1.5	1.5	1.6
GFR	–	3.1	3.2	3.4	3.5
Sweden	4.3	4.3	4.2	4.2	4.2
UK	3.8	3.7	3.7	3.9	4.0
US	2.1	2.1	2.1	2.1	2.1

although fluctuations also occur. One reason for this is that there may also be contributions from other production factors. The Harrod–Domar model holds only in the case of constant productivity of capital. Direct calculation of the capital coefficient from the stock of capital and the volume of gross domestic product gives the results shown in table 16.5.

In the calculations given above, the capital stock has been corrected by the rate of utilization. The capital coefficients obtained in this way turn out to be remarkably stable. Only in Germany is there a tendency towards a slow increase in the capital coefficient. Owing to the many uncertainties in collecting data, however, it would not be surprising if the stock of capital has been calculated exactly on the basis of a fixed capital coefficient; the figures for the United States are particularly suspect in this respect. Moreover, constancy of the capital coefficient does not prove the Harrod–Domar model to be correct. In the case too of a Cobb–Douglas production function, for example, it is possible that the rate of growth of capital equals the rate of growth of income. In section 4.3 the contribution of capital to gross domestic product is further analysed, but first we investigate the contribution of labour and foreign trade.

4. The importance of foreign trade

4.1. Introduction

The importance of exports as a category of expenditure was mentioned in section 2. According to many economists imports too make their contribution to gross domestic product. In this view imports are regarded as a production factor in themselves, together with labour and capital. An example of this can be found in the study by Gehrig and Kuhlo (1972), who propose the following production function:

$$Q = Q(a, Y, X, M, t) \tag{6}$$

where

Q = gross domestic product,
Y = labour employed,
M = volume of imports,
X = capital employed.

Trying to estimate the coefficients of a Cobb–Douglas production function, we obtained the following results:

France

$$\log Q = 0.545 \log Y + 0.620 \log M, \qquad\qquad R^2 = 0.985; \tag{7}$$
$$(0.017)\qquad\;\;(0.019)$$

German Federal Republic

$$\log Q = \underset{(0.053)}{0.574} \ \log X + \underset{(0.075)}{0.482} \ \log M - \underset{(0.004)}{0.034} \ t, \qquad R^2 = 0.995; \qquad (8)$$

Sweden

$$\log Q = \underset{(0.010)}{0.79^4} \ \log X + \underset{(0.013)}{0.108} \ \log M, \qquad R^2 = 0.995; \qquad (9)$$

United Kingdom

$$\log Q = \underset{(0.055)}{0.882} \ \log Y + \underset{(0.059)}{0.236} \ \log M + \underset{(0.002)}{0.015} \ t, \qquad R^2 = 0.995; \qquad (10)$$

United States

$$\log Q = \underset{(0.057)}{1.027} \ \log Y + \underset{(0.067)}{0.154} \ \log M + \underset{(0.004)}{0.010} \ t, \qquad R^2 = 0.992. \qquad (11)$$

Imports turn out to be a significant factor in all countries. The labour coefficient is significant for France, the United Kingdom and the United States, whereas the capital coefficient is significant in Germany and Sweden. The sum of the elasticities was not restricted to one, leaving open the possibility of economies of scale. These prove to be important in France, the United Kingdom and the United States, and to a lesser degree also in Germany. The Swedish economy, however, is characterized by diseconomies of scale.

A very important result is that the rate of exogenous technical change tends to disappear when imports are considered in the production function; economies of scale may also have led to this phenomenon. Technical change is even negative in Germany. It seems more satisfying, however, to look for factors which *explain* technical change than to consider technology to be entirely exogenous. In our opinion international specialization is one of the major factors explaining technological progress. This fact may be accounted for by the integration of imports into the production function.

4.2. Labour productivity and foreign trade

A thorough study of the role of imports has been made by P. Carré (1960). In his opinion the growth of imports greatly contributes to the efficiency of labour; the argument is also put forward by J.-J. Carré et al. (1976).

The original specification by P. Carré is

$$Q = k(y + y')^\gamma, \tag{12}$$

$$M = k(y')^\gamma, \tag{13}$$

where

$Q =$ production (value added).
$y =$ labour employed,
$M =$ volume of imports,
$y' =$ fictitious labour available through imports,
$\gamma =$ elasticity of production with respect to labour,
$k =$ constant factor; equal to average labour productivity for $\gamma = 1$.

Carré obtained encouraging results for the US (1869–1955) and eight European countries (1952–1955). His estimation (by graphic adaptation) suggests that $\gamma = 2.2$. We think his analysis interesting enough to pursue the study for 1951–1975. First, however, some additions have to be made.

Carré's reasoning is that the economy is able to have at its disposal additional labour by importing products. In our opinion a correct interpretation of the argument, however, proceeds as follows. Foreign trade makes it possible for each country to specialize in those products for which it has the greatest advantages. Because it is not necessary to produce imported products oneself, labour becomes available, which offers gains from specialization and economies of scale. The extra amount of labour in this case does not originate from *imports*, but from allocating labour to the export industry and thereby increasing its productivity by giving up less productive activities. The amount of labour becoming free in this way is obtained by inverting eq. (13):

$$y' = \left(\frac{M}{k}\right)^{1/\gamma}. \tag{14}$$

Total labour expressed in efficiency units (Y) would then become

$$Y = y + y' = y - y' + 2y'. \tag{15}$$

It is not clear, however, why the amount of labour becoming available becomes exactly *twice* as productive as the remaining labour, as is implicitly assumed in eq. (15). For this reason we allow for different increases in labour productivity by rewriting eq. (12) as

$$Q = k(y + \pi y')^\gamma. \tag{16}$$

In this equation π indicates the increase in productivity of the amount of labour becoming free by foregoing less-efficient operations, the gains of foreign trade being zero if $\pi = 0$. Substituting eq. (14) into (16), we get

$$Q = (k^{1/\gamma}y + \pi M^{1-\gamma})^\gamma. \tag{17}$$

This equation reminds us of the CES production function, although it is not exactly the same. Furthermore, we allow for (neutral) technical progress by substituting

$$k = k_0(1 + \rho)^t. \tag{18}$$

It is clear that eq. (17) does not lend itself to direct estimation of the parameters; this is why Carré adapted a graphic estimation procedure. Another possibility would be linearization by Taylor expansion. Applying the Gauss–Newton method, an iterative estimation procedure may be followed, based on the following algorithm [cf. Malinvaud (1966)]:

$$b_{r+1} = b_r + (J'J)^{-1} J'e, \tag{19}$$

where

b = vector to be estimated,
J = Jacobian matrix,
e = vector of residuals.

Unfortunately the estimation of eq. (17) did not converge in our case. A possible improvement might be obtained if the Newton–Raphson procedure were followed [cf. Belsley (1974)]. Instead of this a grid procedure has been applied which minimizes the sum of squared residuals, which is also the philosophy behind eq. (19). This has been done for all nine countries considered in our study. The labour and import figures used relate to the total economy. As to labour, no correction was made for the number of working hours, so the total number of persons employed has been taken. The results obtained are shown in table 16.6.

The deviations shown in the last column are rather small. The value of γ (the elasticity of Q with respect to total labour) is much lower than that found by Carré. This difference is caused by the fact that in our case technical progress makes its own contribution to Q, which is ignored by Carré; technical progress varies from 1.4 percent in the United States to 5.4 percent in Japan. A value for γ greater than one indicates economies of scale; these are important in Japan, Germany, Sweden, the United States and also in Belgium. In contrast, Italy is confronted with diseconomies of scale. The value of π differs very much from country to country, ranging from 0.36 in Germany to 3.27 in Japan, which figures differ from the value of 1.0 arbitrarily imposed by Carré.

The results clearly illustrate the gains that may be obtained from foreign trade.

Table 16.6

Results of predicting gross domestic product from labour employed and real imports.

	γ	π	ρ	k	Average deviation (%)
Belgium	1.085	0.87	0.016	1.25	1.9
France	1.026	1.33	0.035	2.08	2.7
GFR	1.145	0.36	0.046	0.69	3.6
Italy	0.986	1.40	0.043	2.15	3.5
Japan	1.157	3.27	0.054	0.22	3.7
The Netherlands	1.001	0.79	0.017	2.12	1.4
Sweden	1.122	1.07	0.026	1.65	3.7
UK	1.026	1.33	0.018	2.08	1.9
US	1.100	1.71	0.014	2.20	2.4

These gains can be calculated by differentiating eq. (17) with respect to M:

$$\frac{\partial Q}{\partial M} = \left[k^{1/\gamma} y + \pi M^{1/\gamma} \right]^{\gamma-1} \pi M^{(1-\gamma)/\gamma}$$

$$= \left[\left(\frac{k}{M}\right)^{1/\gamma} y + \pi \right]^{\gamma-1} \pi. \tag{20}$$

From this equation it follows that there are decreasing returns to scale: additional imports contribute less, provided that $\gamma > 1$.

The extra amount of gross domestic product resulting from additional imports is shown in table 16.7. Considering the decreasing returns to scale it is not surprising to

Table 16.7[a]

Gains from foreign trade.

	1951	1975
Belgium	0.96	0.91
France	1.40	1.38
GFR	0.49	0.41
Italy	1.35	1.37
Japan	4.94	4.40
The Netherlands	0.79	0.79
Sweden	1.31	1.24
UK	1.38	1.37
US	2.31	2.20

[a] Extra amount of GDP resulting from additional imports (per unit).

see that these gains are especially high in Japan and the United States, but low in Germany and the Netherlands. The *price* of imports has also to be considered. It is clear that this price is influenced to a large extent by the existence of trade barriers. The establishment of the Common Market has led to the abolition of trade barriers and a reduction of international tariffs, thereby lowering import prices and opening new markets.

We have encountered here an important structural factor which probably made a major contribution to the economic expansion of the Sixties. The growth of real exports during the years 1959–1971, compared with the development in the last four years, is shown in table 16.8.

Table 16.8

Yearly growth of real exports (percent).

	1959–71	1971–75
Belgium	9.0	5.1
France	9.7	8.2
GFR	7.7	5.6
Italy	12.1	6.4
Japan	15.4	8.4
The Netherlands	9.2	5.5
Sweden	8.2	4.9
UK	5.3	3.8
US	6.7	8.5

4.3. Capital productivity and foreign trade

Besides the influence of imports on labour productivity, we now intend to introduce the influence on capital productivity. Proposing a Cobb–Douglas production function

$$Q^* = ky^\alpha x^\beta \qquad (21)$$

and including gains from imports we get

$$Q = k(y + \pi_1 y')^\alpha \ (x + \pi_2 x')^\beta, \qquad (22)$$

$$M = k(y')^\alpha \ (x')^\beta. \qquad (23)$$

Equation (22) allows for additional labour (y') and additional capital (x'), the amounts of which become available through eq. (23). The coefficients π_1 and π_2 denote the increase in productivity of labour and capital compared with the initial allocation.

In order to be able to derive the exact amounts of y' and x', information on the capital intensity (x'/y') is required. A computationally attractive assumption takes the capital intensity of the discarded industry to be the same as for the total economy, with a correction for differences in efficiency, so that

$$\frac{x}{y} = \frac{x'}{y'} \frac{\pi_2}{\pi_1}. \tag{24}$$

This condition presumes that the rate of change in marginal productivity is the same for both production factors, i.e.

$$\frac{\partial Q/\partial y'}{\partial Q^*/\partial y} = \frac{\partial Q/\partial x'}{\partial Q^*/\partial x} \tag{25}$$

as can easily be proved by partially differentiating eqs. (21) and (22).

Condition (24) circumvents the delicate problem of identifying different increases in productivity from changes in capital intensity. Substituting eqs. (23) and (24) into (22) results in

$$Q = k \left[y + \left(\frac{\pi_2}{\pi_1} \right)^{-\alpha/(\alpha+\beta)} \pi_2 \left(\frac{M}{k} \right)^{1/(\alpha+\beta)} \left(\frac{y}{x} \right)^{\beta/(\alpha+\beta)} \right]^{\alpha}$$

$$\times \left[x + \left(\frac{\pi_2}{\pi_1} \right)^{-\alpha/(\alpha+\beta)} \pi_2 \left(\frac{M}{k} \right)^{1/(\alpha+\beta)} \left(\frac{y}{x} \right)^{-\alpha/(\alpha+\beta)} \right]^{\beta}. \tag{26}$$

Defining π as geometric average of π_1 and π_2 we get

$$\pi = \left(\frac{\pi_2}{\pi_1} \right)^{-\alpha/(\alpha+\beta)} \pi_2 = \pi_1^{\alpha/(\alpha+\beta)} \pi_2^{\beta/(\alpha+\beta)}. \tag{27}$$

We conclude that the only parameters which have to be estimated are π, α, β and k, so that information on possible differences in π_1 and π_2 or knowledge of the capital intensity is not required. We have circumvented the identification problem in this way, and at the same time gained by discarding two parameters.

A different approach would be to compute x' and y' as the result of a maximization problem with Q as maximand. In the case of a Cobb–Douglas production function, however, this is impossible without indicating realistic limits between which x' and y' may vary – otherwise x' and y' would approach infinity, with Q unbounded.

Figures on gross domestic product, labour, capital and real imports are available for five countries: France, Germany, Sweden, the United Kingdom and the United States. A difficulty arises with regard to the dimension of labour, however. In eq. (21) labour units have to be expressed in the same dimension as gross domestic product and capital. The easiest way would be to multiply the production factors, labour and capital, by their marginal productivity. If the production function is not linearly homogeneous in labour and capital, however, the adding-up of labour income and capital income does not coincide with the magnitude of gross domestic product. But precisely the foreign trade argument is based on possible gains from specialization and economies of scale, so that we must allow for production elasticities which add up to a value greater than one. For that reason labour is expressed in monetary terms by multiplying it by an implicit wage rate (w) obtained by guaranteeing an exact fit of eq. (26) in the base year. It may be verified that this can be done by imposing the condition

$$w_0 y_0 = \left[Q_0^{1/(\alpha + \beta)} - \pi M_0^{1/(\alpha + \beta)} \right]^{(\alpha + \beta)/\alpha} x_0^{-\beta/\alpha}$$

Estimation of the parameters α, β, ρ and π leads to the results shown in table 16.9.

Table 16.9

Results of predicting gross domestic product from labour employed, capital and real imports.

	α	β	ρ	π	Average deviation (%)
France	0.70	0.16	0.040	0	0.9
GFR	1.00	0.20	0.028	0.24	1.3
Sweden	0.80	0.46	0.010	0.34	2.3
UK	1.00	0.12	0.019	0.34	1.3
US	0.90	0	0.022	0.34	2.1

The average deviation found is very low, ranging from 0.9 percent in France to 2.3 per cent in Sweden. Economies of scale exist in Germany, Sweden and the United Kingdom, whereas in France and the United States there are diseconomies of scale. From π we get some insight into the gains in efficiency resulting from foreign trade. Taking Sweden, the United Kingdom and the United States as an example, we find the following combinations of π_1 and π_2 which give rise to the same geometric average of 0.34:

| π_1: | 0.35 | 0.32 | 0.30 | 0.27 | 0.26 |
| π_2: | 0.25 | 0.50 | 1 | 2 | 3 |

Technical progress varies from 1 percent in Sweden to 4 percent in France. In general, these rates are lower than is traditionally the case. Part of technical progress is explained by the gains from imports, while economies of scale also form a substitute for technical progress. In fact, one of the advantages of the introduction of foreign trade is a possible explanation of technical progress. At the same time, however, it may often be difficult to distinguish between them.

5. Sectoral developments

5.1. The three-sector hypothesis

In the sections above we discussed some structural problems, describing the demand side of the economy – consisting of some broad categories of expenditure – and the supply side – consisting of the production factors labour, capital and imports. In reality, however, production takes place within different compartments of production units. From this point of view we now investigate the contribution of major sectors of economic activity to gross domestic product.

The three-sector hypothesis, originally formulated by Clark (1957), Chenery (1960) and Fourastié (1960), is well known. According to this hypothesis, in the course of development the share of agriculture in the gross domestic product decreases until a level of less than 10 percent has been reached. On the other hand, the share of industry would increase to about 50 percent and decline afterwards. Finally, the share of services would rise to a maximum of some 80 percent. In this view the agricultural sector is producing goods for primary needs; after these have been satisfied demand is diverted to industrial goods, yielded by the secondary sector and finally to services, supplied by the tertiary sector. Table 16.10 shows the contribution of each sector to gross domestic product, measured in constant prices, in a number of countries.

Table 16.10

The contribution of major activities to gross domestic product.[a]

	Agriculture		Industry [b]		Services	
	1963	1975	1963	1975	1963	1975
Belgium	5.3	3.3	44.8	43.9	49.9	52.8
France	9.6	6.6	49.8	50.6	40.6	42.8
GFR	4.5	3.7	57.7	58.8	37.8	37.5
Italy	10.7	8.4	41.3	38.8	48.0	52.8
Japan	11.5	5.3	38.8	42.2	49.7	52.5
The Netherlands	7.3	7.7	41.9	44.4	50.8	47.9
Sweden	6.0	5.1	43.2	52.4	50.8	42.5
UK	3.3	3.3	47.6	47.0	49.1	49.7
US	4.6	3.5	40.7	37.9	54.7	58.6

[a] Constant prices of 1970.
[b] Including mining, construction and public utilities.

The countries in the table display more or less the same structure. All belong to the group of highly developed countries with a very low proportion of agriculture and a strong emphasis on industry and services. The share of agriculture is still somewhat high in France, Italy and Japan. On the other hand, in Germany there is considerable stress on industrial products, whereas the service sector is less important than in the other countries.

From the table it appears that the share of each sector is fairly constant. This also applies to the service sector, the share of which was already very high in 1963 and has hardly increased since then. Although it is generally agreed that the share of this sector will continue to increase, this apparently does not apply if gross domestic product is measured in *constant* prices. However, owing to the lower increase in productivity in the service sector the share of services in total *employment* is increasing, and the same applies to the share in gross domestic product measured in *current* prices. The share of each sector in total employment is shown in table 16.11.

Table 16.11

The share of major activities in total employment.

	Agriculture		Industry[a]		Services	
	1963	1975	1963	1975	1963	1975
Belgium	7.4	3.6	46.8	39.9	45.8	56.5
France	21.4	10.0	45.8	45.3	32.8	44.7
GFR	11.9	7.4	48.8	46.0	39.3	46.6
Italy	27.2	15.8	41.0	44.1	31.8	40.1
Japan	26.0	15.2	31.7	33.1	42.3	51.5
The Netherlands	10.2	6.8	41.6	35.5	48.2	57.7
Sweden	12.8	6.4	41.5	36.5	45.7	57.1
UK	4.4	2.7	46.4	40.8	49.2	56.5
US	6.5	3.8	37.5	32.3	56.0	63.9

[a] Including mining, construction and public utilities.

We conclude that the three-sector hypothesis may be accepted when applied to employment or to gross domestic product measured in current prices. In volumes, however, the share of industry and services in gross domestic product seems to remain fairly constant in highly developed countries. It may therefore be worthwhile to make a more detailed study of the industrial sector, as we do in the next section.

5.2. The development of industrial production

Information on the development of world industrial production is shown in table 16.12. The figures in the table generally relate to the development of gross value added expressed in constant 1970 prices.

Table 16.12

The growth of world industry.

ISIC		Annual rate of growth (%)			Relative composition	
		1938–58	1959–74	1938–75	1938	1975
31	food products	3.3	4.6	3.9	0.192	0.128
321	textiles	2.2	4.1	3.1	0.108	0.058
322/24	clothing, etc.	1.9	4.1	2.9	0.084	0.044
33	wood products	3.1	4.9	3.9	0.049	0.034
34	paper, printing	4.6	4.4	4.6	0.060	0.055
35	oil, chemicals	6.5	8.6	7.5	0.087	0.139
36	nonmetallics	4.6	6.6	5.5	0.053	0.055
37	basic metals	3.8	5.4	4.5	0.078	0.064
38	metal products	6.3	7.8	7.0	0.290	0.424
3	total manufacturing	4.5	6.5	5.4		

The average rate of growth of world industry during the period 1938–1975 amounted to 5.4 percent. As could be expected, the following sectors reveal growth rates below average: food, textiles, wood products, paper and basic metals. For these products income elasticities are clearly smaller than one, in accordance with Engel's law. In contrast, the growth rates of chemicals and metal products are far above average.

Comparing the subperiods, it is striking that the period 1938–1958 reveals much lower growth rates than the period 1959–1974 (because of the stagnation of economic growth that suddenly occurred in 1975 we omitted this year from consideration). Differences become even greater if we realize that industrial production probably did not increase during the years 1930–1936, resulting in an average rate of growth of 3.2 percent for the period 1930–1958, just one-half of the growth that took place between 1958 and 1974. It is tempting but it may also be speculative to see in this an illustration of the Kondratieff cycle.

The share of food products in gross domestic product heavily declined, and the same occurred to textiles, clothing, etc., wood products, paper and printing. In contrast, the share of metal products became increasingly important. This group consists of machinery, transport equipment (ships, motor vehicles), etc. The share of the oil and chemical industry also increased very rapidly, but the share in gross domestic product is still moderate. Moreover, because of the relative price decrease in this sector the share becomes even lower when measured in current prices. The same pattern, with minor differences, can be observed for the individual countries, as is shown in Appendix B.

Countries which have a remarkable share of growing industries have an advantage over other countries. As growing industries we identified the oil and chemical industry and metal products, the share of which in world manufacturing increased greatly between 1938 and 1975. Taking advantage of the growth in the oil and chemical industry are Japan and the Netherlands, joined by France, Germany, Italy, the United Kingdom and the United States in later years. Especially Germany, Sweden, the United Kingdom and the United States took part in the excessive growth of metal products. The position of Japan is very remarkable, where making metal products consisted of only 8 percent of manufacturing in 1938, but increased to as much as 47 percent in 1975. The Netherlands too succeeded in improving its initially weak position.

A stable share in total manufacturing is taken by paper and printing, nonmetallics and basic metals. The relative position of each country with regard to these industries did not change very much, but nevertheless showed a tendency to equalization: weak countries succeeded in improving their backward position at the expense of stronger countries.

Food processing, textiles, clothing, etc., and wood products are declining industries. The shrinking of these industries affected all countries to the same degree. Badly hit were the food industry in Belgium and the Netherlands, the textile industry in Italy and Japan, clothing, etc. in France, Italy and the United States, and wood products in Japan and Sweden.

It is clear that the unequal growth of industries in different countries affects the relative position in world industrial production. In the next section we see whether something more can be said about the development of the share of individual countries in total world production.

6. Country shares in world industry

During the period 1963–1975 the share in total world industry of all countries examined in this study decreased, except for Japan. Table 16.13 shows this share for

Table 16.13

Country shares in world industry (constant prices).[a]

	1963	1975
US	32.3	24.3
Japan	5.1	6.9
European countries	26.2	20.9
Total	63.6	52.1

[a] Excluding People's Republic of China.

the United States, Japan and the European countries combined (i.e. Belgium, France, German Federal Republic, Italy, Netherlands, Sweden and the United Kingdom).

The share in world industry (excluding China) of all countries together amounted to 63.6 percent in 1963, but declined to 52.1 percent in 1975. This clearly demonstrates the tremendous change in economic conditions that has taken place during the last twelve years. Taking advantage of this are the developing countries as well as the socialist countries in Eastern Europe.

Roughly speaking the availability of production factors, together with their productiveness, may explain a country's share in world production. However, it does not seem likely that the situation changed so rapidly during such a short period of time. We have to look for other factors which may explain the rate of change of a country's share in world industry. In this respect it is often propounded that the relative position of a country directly depends on its ability to offer competing prices. We may express this relationship by

$$S_i = S_i^{0} \left(\frac{p_i}{p_w} \right)^{-\varepsilon},$$

(29)

where

S_i = the share of country i in world industry,
S_i^{0} = the country's share as far as explained by constant factors,
p_i = the price demanded by exporters in country i,
p_w = world market price,
ε = elasticity between a country's share and the price ratio.

Differentiating eq. (29) with respect to relative prices, it follows that the increase in S equals

$$\frac{dS_i}{d(p_i/p_w)} = -\varepsilon S_i^0 \left(\frac{p_i}{p_w} \right)^{-\varepsilon-1} = \frac{-\varepsilon S_i}{(p_i/p_w)},$$

so that

$$\frac{dS_i}{S_i} = \varepsilon \left(\frac{dp_w}{p_w} - \frac{dp_i}{p_i} \right).$$

(30)

The price of a product is influenced by the costs necessary to produce it: labour costs, capital costs and the costs of raw materials. As is seen from eq. (30) the rate of change in country *i* depends only on the *difference* between the rate of increase of world prices and the rate of increase of domestic prices. As a first approximation we may expect that the *change* in capital costs and the cost of raw materials does not vary much between different countries over a short period of time. In this case differences in rates of change of prices may be fully explained by differences in the development of unit labour costs. Equation (30) may thus be written as

$$\frac{dS_i}{S_i} = -\varepsilon \left(\frac{\Delta W_i}{W_i} - \frac{\Delta Q_i}{Q_i} + \frac{\Delta Y_i}{Y_i} \right) + \varepsilon_w,$$ (31)

where

W = wage level,
Y = labour employed,
ε_w = change in world unit labour costs.

Some information about the change in unit labour costs in total manufacturing is given in table 16.14. The table shows marked differences in the change of unit labour costs

Table 16.14

Change in unit labour costs 1963–1975 – total manufacturing (percent).

	Hourly wages (national currency)	Production	Number of employees	Unit labour costs (nat. curr.)	Exchange rate	Unit lab. costs (dollars)
Belgium	11.98	3.76	−0.88	7.34	2.70	10.04
France	11.00	3.42	0.69	8.27	0.82	9.09
GFR	8.00	4.29	−0.90	2.81	4.31	7.12
Italy	15.04	3.98	0.59	11.65	−0.38	11.27
Japan	15.12	8.80	1.64	7.96	1.46	9.42
The Netherlands	12.00	5.87	−0.79	5.34	3.01	8.35
Sweden	10.02	4.74	−0.13	5.15	2.02	7.17
UK	12.19	2.26	−0.84	9.09	−1.46	7.63
US	5.75	3.52	0.24	2.47	0	2.47

measured in national currencies. However, it also appears that these differences are mitigated when unit labour costs are measured in dollars. Indeed, a strong correlation exists between changes in the rates of exchange and changes in unit labour costs. Excluding the United States, the regression line fitted is

$$Y = -0.591x + 5.816, \qquad R^2 = 0.738,$$ (32)
$$(0.144) \qquad (1.097)$$

where y = average rate of change of exchange rates (i.e. the dollar price expressed in national currency), and x = average rate of change in unit labour costs (national currency).

In fact, in the case of flexible rates of exchange one would expect perfect correlation. However, owing to market imperfections deviations occur. In Germany, a revaluation of 4.3 percent a year took place. The Common Market countries closely related to Germany seem to maintain a high rate of exchange: in Belgium, France, Italy and the Netherlands the increase in unit labour costs was not fully compensated for by a con-comitant devaluation of the national currency. Compared to the United States, all other countries show an *autonomous* revaluation of 4.4 percent a year, which is probably a reaction to the long period of fixed exchange rates which lasted until 1970.

The fact that unit labour costs measured in national currency are more or less equalized by changes in the rate of exchange makes it clear that no correlation can be established between the rate of change of unit labour costs measured in dollars and the change in the country shares. This fact has also been established by Gross and Keating (1970), who made a study of the engineering industry in Germany.

Another possibility would be to relate national production to world production, trying to look for factors which account for deviations from world development. This may be seen as an application of shift and share analysis, which has already been applied successfully at regional level many times [see, inter alia, Brown (1969)]. According to this line of reasoning we suggest the following relationship:

$$\frac{\Delta Q}{Q_i}_i = a \frac{\Delta Q}{Q_w}_w + b \frac{\Delta W_i}{W_i}_i + c. \tag{33}$$

The rate of change in domestic production is related to the rate of change in world production, while a correction is made depending on the change in the wage level.

As data we took the figures from all nine countries and for all nine industrial sectors. The regression line fitted was

$$\frac{\Delta Q}{Q_i}_i = \underset{(0.148)}{1.118} \frac{\Delta Q}{Q_w}_w + \underset{(0.084)}{0.275} \frac{\Delta W_i}{W_i}_i - \underset{(1.186)}{5.280}, \qquad R^2 = 0.69. \tag{34}$$

Although the correlation coefficient is not so high, the standard errors (in parentheses) nevertheless indicate that the coefficients are reliable. The production level in a country more or less follows the development of world industry, but there is a yearly autonomous decrease of 5.28 percent. Especially important is the positive sign of b, the coefficient belonging to the rate of change of the wage level. Increases in wage rates have two distinct effects: of course, the position on the world market is worsened.

but this fact is apparently more than compensated for by an increase in domestic expenditure induced by higher incomes. This outcome at the same time indicates that we have to be careful about cutting wages, a measure which is often recommended by politicians and professional economists when production falls behind. It is emphasized, however, that the regression above encompasses all countries and all sectors. One might ask whether the same relationship holds for each industrial sector. A possible answer to this question may be obtained by investigating the residuals of eq. (34). If for some sector the influence of $\Delta W_i / W_i$ were negative, *positive* deviations would be observed for most of the countries. This might be the case for food processing (seven positive deviations out of nine) and the paper industry (eight positive deviations).

Appendix A: relative composition of total expenditure

	Private cons.	Governm. exp.	Invest- ments	Exports (goods, serv.)	Imports (goods, serv.)	Index of GDP
Belgium						
Current prices						
1953	0.71	0.13	0.17	0.28	−0.29	100
1955	0.70	0.12	0.17	0.32	−0.31	111
1959	0.70	0.13	0.18	0.31	−0.32	131
1963	0.67	0.13	0.21	0.35	−0.36	170
1967	0.63	0.14	0.23	0.36	−0.36	238
1971	0.60	0.14	0.23	0.43	−0.41	344
1975	0.61	0.17	0.22	0.46	−0.46	566
1970 prices						
1953	0.68	0.13	0.18	0.22	−0.22	100
1955	0.68	0.12	0.19	0.26	−0.25	109
1959	0.67	0.13	0.20	0.28	−0.29	118
1963	0.64	0.14	0.21	0.32	−0.32	143
1967	0.61	0.14	0.24	0.36	−0.35	170
1971	0.61	0.14	0.22	0.45	−0.42	209
1975	0.63	0.15	0.21	0.47	−0.46	241
France						
Current prices						
1951	0.64	0.15	0.21	0.15	−0.15	100
1955	0.63	0.15	0.20	0.13	−0.12	139
1959	0.63	0.16	0.20	0.14	−0.12	217
1963	0.62	0.16	0.22	0.13	−0.13	329
1967	0.61	0.16	0.23	0.14	−0.14	458
1971	0.59	0.16	0.24	0.17	−0.16	716
1975	0.63	0.17	0.19	0.21	−0.20	1 146

	Private cons.	Governm. exp.	Invest- ments	Exports (goods, serv.)	Imports (goods, serv.)	Index of GDP
1970 prices						
1951	0.60	0.19	0.19	0.11	−0.09	100
1955	0.62	0.19	0.18	0.11	−0.09	116
1959	0.62	0.18	0.19	0.11	−0.10	136
1963	0.62	0.17	0.21	0.12	−0.12	173
1967	0.61	0.16	0.23	0.14	−0.14	213
1971	0.59	0.15	0.24	0.17	−0.16	267
1975	0.63	0.15	0.20	0.21	−0.20	297
German Federal Republic						
Current prices						
1951	0.61	0.15	0.22	0.16	−0.14	100
1955	0.58	0.13	0.26	0.21	−0.18	151
1959	0.58	0.13	0.25	0.23	−0.20	211
1963	0.57	0.16	0.26	0.19	−0.18	318
1967	0.57	0.16	0.23	0.21	−0.18	419
1971	0.54	0.17	0.27	0.21	−0.19	636
1975	0.56	0.21	0.21	0.25	−0.22	867
1962 prices						
1951	0.57	0.17	0.22	0.13	−0.08	100
1955	0.56	0.14	0.26	0.18	−0.14	140
1959	0.57	0.14	0.25	0.21	−0.17	180
1963	0.58	0.15	0.25	0.20	−0.18	239
1967	0.58	0.14	0.24	0.24	−0.20	282
1971	0.58	0.14	0.27	0.27	−0.25	354
1975	0.60	0.15	0.22	0.31	−0.28	377
Italy						
Current prices						
1951	0.70	0.13	0.19	0.12	−0.13	100
1955	0.67	0.13	0.20	0.11	−0.12	140
1959	0.65	0.14	0.20	0.13	−0.12	187
1963	0.65	0.15	0.23	0.14	−0.17	290
1967	0.65	0.15	0.19	0.17	−0.16	406
1971	0.64	0.16	0.19	0.20	−0.19	588
1975	0.66	0.15	0.19	0.25	−0.25	1 047
1963 prices						
1951	0.68	0.18	0.15	0.06	−0.07	100
1955	0.65	0.17	0.19	0.07	−0.08	124
1959	0.63	0.16	0.20	0.11	−0.10	153
1963	0.65	0.15	0.23	0.14	−0.17	197
1967	0.65	0.14	0.19	0.19	−0.17	237
1971	0.66	0.14	0.18	0.24	−0.22	283
1975	0.66	0.13	0.16	0.27	−0.22	314

Japan

Current prices

1952	0.62	0.17	0.20	0.12	−0.11	100
1955	0.64	0.17	0.18	0.11	−0.10	138
1959	0.60	0.17	0.22	0.11	−0.10	208
1963	0.56	0.18	0.26	0.09	−0.10	395
1967	0.54	0.17	0.28	0.10	−0.10	703
1971	0.53	0.17	0.28	0.12	−0.09	1 261
1975	0.57	0.20	0.23	0.13	−0.13	2 343

1965 prices

1952	0.60	0.22	0.16	0.07	−0.05	100
1955	0.63	0.20	0.16	0.07	−0.06	123
1959	0.62	0.18	0.19	0.09	−0.08	165
1963	0.57	0.19	0.25	0.09	−0.09	257
1967	0.54	0.17	0.29	0.11	−0.10	383
1971	0.50	0.17	0.30	0.14	−0.11	576
1975	0.52	0.17	0.27	0.16	−0.12	700

The Netherlands

Current prices

1951	0.65	0.16	0.21	0.48	−0.50	100
1955	0.60	0.18	0.21	0.48	−0.47	127
1959	0.59	0.18	0.20	0.50	−0.46	160
1963	0.60	0.20	0.20	0.47	−0.48	227
1967	0.58	0.21	0.22	0.43	−0.43	342
1971	0.57	0.22	0.22	0.48	−0.48	527
1975	0.58	0.22	0.17	0.53	−0.50	861

1963 prices

1951	0.60	0.20	0.20	0.31	−0.30	100
1955	0.57	0.21	0.20	0.37	−0.35	121
1959	0.58	0.20	0.19	0.43	−0.40	137
1963	0.61	0.20	0.20	0.47	−0.48	174
1967	0.60	0.18	0.23	0.51	−0.53	215
1971	0.60	0.17	0.24	0.65	−0.65	274
1975	0.60	0.15	0.18	0.71	−0.64	312

Sweden

Current prices

1951	0.61	0.19	0.17	0.30	−0.28	100
1955	0.61	0.24	0.16	0.24	−0.25	128
1959	0.59	0.26	0.15	0.23	−0.23	167
1963	0.58	0.25	0.17	0.22	−0.22	248
1967	0.56	0.27	0.17	0.21	−0.21	358
1971	0.53	0.31	0.15	0.25	−0.24	493
1975	0.52	0.32	0.17	0.29	−0.30	770

1968 prices

1951	0.59	0.26	0.15	0.17	−0.17	100
1955	0.58	0.28	0.15	0.16	−0.17	116

	Private cons.	Governm. exp.	Invest- ments	Exports (goods, serv.)	Imports (goods, serv.)	Index of GDP
1959	0.56	0.30	0.15	0.18	−0.18	134
1963	0.57	0.27	0.16	0.18	−0.18	170
1967	0.56	0.28	0.16	0.21	−0.21	200
1971	0.53	0.30	0.15	0.26	−0.24	232
1975	0.54	0.29	0.17	0.28	−0.28	258

United Kingdom

Current prices

1951	0.70	0.22	0.13	0.25	−0.30	100
1955	0.68	0.21	0.13	0.22	−0.23	133
1959	0.67	0.20	0.13	0.20	−0.20	166
1963	0.66	0.21	0.14	0.19	−0.20	210
1967	0.64	0.23	0.15	0.18	−0.20	277
1971	0.62	0.22	0.14	0.23	−0.21	394
1975	0.62	0.27	0.13	0.26	−0.28	715

1970 prices

1951	0.64	0.26	0.10	0.18	−0.17	100
1955	0.64	0.25	0.11	0.18	−0.17	113
1959	0.66	0.23	0.12	0.18	−0.18	121
1963	0.65	0.23	0.12	0.18	−0.19	138
1967	0.63	0.24	0.14	0.19	−0.20	156
1971	0.62	0.22	0.14	0.24	−0.22	172
1975	0.63	0.23	0.13	0.26	−0.25	184

USA

Current prices

1951	0.63	0.18	0.18	0.05	−0.05	100
1955	0.64	0.19	0.17	0.04	−0.04	121
1959	0.64	0.20	0.16	0.04	−0.05	147
1963	0.63	0.21	0.15	0.05	−0.04	180
1967	0.62	0.23	0.15	0.05	−0.05	241
1971	0.63	0.22	0.15	0.05	−0.06	322
1975	0.64	0.22	0.12	0.09	−0.08	459

1972 prices

1951	0.60	0.23	0.16	0.04	−0.03	100
1955	0.61	0.23	0.16	0.04	−0.04	113
1959	0.62	0.24	0.15	0.04	−0.04	125
1963	0.61	0.25	0.15	0.04	−0.04	144
1967	0.60	0.25	0.15	0.04	−0.05	174
1971	0.63	0.23	0.15	0.05	−0.06	192
1975	0.65	0.22	0.12	0.07	−0.05	207

Appendix B: growth of industrial sectors

ISIC		Annual rate of growth (%)			Relative composition	
		1938–58	1959–75	1938–75	1938	1975

Belgium

ISIC		1938–58	1959–75	1938–75	1938	1975
31	food products	1.4	4.0	2.6	0.246	0.190
321	textiles	1.4	1.7	1.5	0.113	0.060
322/24	clothing, etc.	−1.6	3.3	0.6	0.136	0.051
33	wood products	3.0	7.7	5.2	0.029	0.058
34	paper, printing	3.4	5.4	4.3	0.035	0.051
35	oil, chemicals	4.4	6.8	5.5	0.056	0.125
36	nonmetallics	1.8	4.5	3.0	0.059	0.054
37	basic metals	3.7	3.5	3.6	0.087	0.099
38	metal products	3.4	4.8	4.1	0.238	0.312
3	total manufacturing	2.3	4.5	3.3		

France

ISIC		1938–58	1959–75	1938–75	1938	1975
31	food products	1.0	3.0	1.9	0.257	0.141
321	textiles	0.8	1.3	1.0	0.144	0.057
322/24	clothing, etc.	0.1	0.8	0.4	0.122	0.039
33	wood products	3.5	4.2	3.8	0.034	0.037
34	paper, printing	3.3	4.8	4.0	0.046	0.052
35	oil, chemicals	6.0	7.2	6.5	0.074	0.210
36	nonmetallics	4.1	4.5	4.3	0.038	0.048
37	basic metals	4.1	5.5	4.8	0.037	0.057
38	metal products	5.9	3.1	4.6	0.248	0.359
3	total manufacturing	3.4	3.8	3.6		

German Federal Republic

ISIC		1938–58	1959–75	1938–75	1938	1975
31	food products	3.4	3.6	3.5	0.158	0.148
321	textiles	2.6	2.1	2.4	0.065	0.042
322/24	clothing, etc.	3.9	0.9	2.5	0.052	0.035
33	wood products	1.9	4.3	3.0	0.061	0.009
34	paper, printing	3.1	3.7	3.3	0.063	0.056
35	oil, chemicals	4.3	8.0	6.0	0.072	0.163
36	nonmetallics	2.8	3.9	3.3	0.059	0.052
37	basic metals	2.2	2.5	2.3	0.166	0.103
38	metal products	4.2	4.5	4.4	0.304	0.392
3	total manufacturing	3.4	3.9	3.6		

Italy

ISIC		1938–58	1959–75	1938–75	1938	1975
31	food products	3.2	3.5	3.3	0.143	0.104
321	textiles	1.0	1.9	1.4	0.218	0.079

ISIC		Annual rate of growth (%)			Relative composition	
		1938–58	1959–75	1938–75	1938	1975
322/24	clothing, etc.	0.6	2.1	1.3	0.131	0.046
33	wood products	3.2	4.5	3.8	0.034	0.030
34	paper, printing	2.8	6.2	4.4	0.050	0.052
35	oil, chemicals	6.5	8.7	7.5	0.065	0.201
36	nonmetallics	4.9	6.2	5.5	0.044	0.069
37	basic metals	4.7	7.4	5.9	0.060	0.108
38	metal products	4.5	5.2	4.8	0.256	0.311
3	total manufacturing	3.4	5.3	4.2		

Japan

ISIC		1938–58	1959–75	1938–75	1938	1975
31	food products	1.6	6.2	3.7	0.262	0.088
321	textiles	0.2	6.4	3.0	0.202	0.052
322/24	clothing, etc.	0.5	6.9	3.4	0.050	0.015
33	wood products	4.3	3.0	3.7	0.092	0.030
34	paper, printing	5.6	9.0	7.2	0.057	0.063
35	oil, chemicals	3.8	11.8	7.4	0.119	0.147
36	nonmetallics	3.1	8.9	5.7	0.062	0.041
37	basic metals	3.2	12.4	7.3	0.074	0.089
38	metal products	8.4	16.4	12.0	0.083	0.475
3	total manufacturing	3.3	11.1	6.8		

The Netherlands

ISIC		1938–58	1959–75	1938–75	1938	1975
31	food products	2.2	4.3	3.2	0.351	0.173
321	textiles	2.7	4.3	3.4	0.072	0.029
322/24	clothing, etc.	1.7	5.5	3.5	0.054	0.018
33	wood products	5.6	2.8	4.4	0.042	0.033
34	paper, printing	3.1	7.0	4.9	0.092	0.072
35	oil, chemicals	5.4	9.0	7.1	0.116	0.226
36	nonmetallics	2.1	5.9	3.8	0.072	0.042
37	basic metals	6.5	10.2	8.2	0.018	0.045
38	metal products	4.9	11.4	7.9	0.181	0.362
3	total manufacturing	3.6	7.6	5.4		

Sweden

ISIC		1938–58	1959–75	1938–75	1938	1975
31	food products	2.4	2.6	2.5	0.165	0.094
321	textiles	1.5	1.1	1.3	0.061	0.022
322/24	clothing, etc.	1.7	−1.2	0.3	0.083	0.021
33	wood products	2.2	4.4	3.2	0.101	0.073
34	paper, printing	3.3	3.8	3.5	0.148	0.121
35	oil, chemicals	6.5	7.9	7.2	0.031	0.092
36	nonmetallics	3.2	3.1	3.1	0.050	0.035

37	basic metals	3.8	5.7	4.7	0.071	0.087
38	metal products	4.5	6.3	5.4	0.290	0.453
3	total manufacturing	3.4	4.9	4.1		

United Kingdom

31	food products	2.0	2.5	2.2	0.181	0.134
321	textiles	0.1	1.4	0.7	0.117	0.050
322/24	clothing, etc.	0	2.4	1.1	0.077	0.038
33	wood products	1.5	3.7	2.5	0.035	0.029
34	paper, printing	3.0	2.7	2.8	0.080	0.074
35	oil, chemicals	5.3	6.5	5.8	0.059	0.158
36	nonmetallics	2.5	4.2	3.3	0.039	0.042
37	basic metals	2.3	1.9	2.1	0.088	0.063
38	metal products	3.6	3.8	3.7	0.323	0.411
3	total manufacturing	2.6	3.5	3.0		

United States

31	food products	3.4	3.3	3.4	0.207	0.124
321	textiles	3.7	3.0	3.4	0.061	0.037
322/24	clothing, etc.	1.1	1.2	1.2	0.136	0.037
33	wood products	3.1	2.7	2.9	0.056	0.029
34	paper, printing	4.2	3.2	3.7	0.135	0.092
35	oil, chemicals	8.5	6.6	7.6	0.065	0.172
36	nonmetallics	5.6	2.0	3.9	0.041	0.030
37	basic metals	5.3	2.2	3.9	0.078	0.056
38	metal products	8.4	4.7	6.7	0.222	0.425
3	total manufacturing	5.5	4.1	4.8		

Statistical sources

International

Eurostat, National accounts, several editions (EEC).
Federal Reserve Bank of St. Louis, 1978, Rates of change in economic data for ten industrial countries, Annual data 1958–1977.
ILO, Yearbook of labour statistics, several editions.
OECD, National accounts of OECD countries, several editions.
OECD, Labour force statistics, several editions.
United Nations, Yearbook of national accounts statistics, several editions.
United Nations, The growth of world industry, several editions.

Belgium

Statistisch Jaarboek van België, several editions, Nationaal Instituut voor de Statistiek, Ministerie van Economische Zaken.
Statistisch Tijdschrift, 1970, 1972, Nationaal Instituut voor de Statistiek.

France

Annuaire Statistique de la France, several editions, Institut national de la statistique et des études
économiques.
Les collections de l'INSEE, serie C, no. 7, 8, 11, 13, 29, 30.

German Federal Republic

Bevölkerung und Wirtschaft 1872–1972, Statistisches Bundesamt.
Volkswirtschaftliche Gesamtrechnung, Fachserie N, Statistisches Bundesamt.
Statistisches Jahrbuch, several editions, Statistisches Bundesamt.
Wirtschaft und Statistik, 1960, Statistisches Bundesamt.

Italy

Annuari Statistico Italiano, Instituto Centrale di Statistica, several editions.

Japan

Economic Statistics, several editions, Statistics Department of the Bank of Japan.
Japan, Statistical Yearbook 1978, Bureau of Statistics, Office of the Prime Minister.
Ohkama, T., T. Takamatsu and Yamamoto, eds., 1974, Estimates of long-term statistics of Japan since 1868
(Toyo Keizai Shinposha, Tokyo).

The Netherlands

Central Bureau of Statistics, 1967, Total labour force expressed in man-years 1947–1966.
National accounts, several editions, Central Bureau of Statistics.

Sweden

Sveriges officiella statistika, Statistika Meddelanden, serie N,
   – Capital formation, repair and maintenance and stocks of fixed capital 1950–1974, 1963–1975;
   – Employment 1960–1974;
   – External transactions 1950–1974;
   – Final consumption expenditure 1950–1974;
   – Gross domestic product by expenditure 1950–1963;
   – Standard account 1950–1974.

United Kingdom

Annual abstract of statistics, 1977, Central Statistical Office.
Economic trends, annual supplement, 1977, Central Statistical Office.
Feinstein, H., 1972, Statistical tables on national income, expenditure and output of the United Kingdom,
1855–1965 (Cambridge University Press, London).

United States

Business Statistics, The biennial supplement to the Survey of Current Business, 1975, United States Depart-
ment of Commerce/Bureau of Economic Analysis.
Historical Statistics of the United States, 1975, Colonial Times – 1970, US Department of Commerce,
Bureau of the Census.
Kendrick, J. W., 1976, The national wealth of the United States by major sectors and industry (Conference
Board, New York).

National income and product accounts of the United States, 1929–1974, statistical tables, a supplement to the Survey of Current Business.

Statistical abstract of the United States, 1977 (US Department of Commerce, Bureau of the Census).

References

Belsley, D. A., 1974, Estimation of systems of simultaneous equations and computational specifications of GREMLIN, Annals of Economic and Social Measurement 3, 551–614.

Bergson, A., 1978, Productivity and the social system – the USSR and the West (Harvard University Press, Cambridge, Mass.).

Bolto, A. and M. Keating, 1973, The measurement of domestic fluctuations (OECD Economic Outlook, Paris).

Bombach, G., B. Gahlen and A. E. Ott, 1977, Probleme des Strukturwandels und der Strukturpolitik (J. C. B. Mohr, Tübingen).

Brown, H. J., 1969, Shift and share projections of regional economic growth: An empirical test, Journal of Regional Science 9, 1–18.

Carré, J.-J., P. Dubois and E. Malinvaud, 1976, French economic growth, in: M. Abramowitz and S. Kuznets, eds., Studies of economic growth in industrial countries (Stanford University Press/Oxford University Press, California, London).

Carré, P., 1969, Etudes empirique sur l'évolution des structures d'économies en état de croissance (Editions du Centre National de la Recherche Scientifique, Paris).

Caves, R. E., ed., 1968, Britain's economic prospects (Brookings Institution, Washington).

Chenery, H. B., 1960, Patterns of industrial growth, American Economic Review 50, 624–654.

Clark, C., 1957, The conditions of economic progress (Macmillan, London).

Denison, E. F., 1967, Why growth rates differ (Brookings Institution, Washington).

Fourastié, J., 1960, The causes of wealth (New York).

Gehrig, G. and K. C. Kuhlo, 1972, Überprüfung der ökonometrischen Projektion von 1962 (Ifo-Studien, Berlin, München).

Gross, R. and M. Keating, 1970, Analysis of competition in export and domestic markets, OECD Economic Outlook, Occasional Studies (OECD, Paris).

Malinvaud, E., 1966, Statistical methods of econometrics (North-Holland, Amsterdam).

Peaker, A., 1974, Economic growth in modern Britain (Macmillan, London).

Phillips, G. A. and R. T. Maddock, 1973, The growth of the British economy 1918–1968 (Allen & Unwin, London).

Rostow, W. W., 1978, The world economy, history and prospect (Macmillan, London).

Schatz, K.-W., 1974, Wachstum und Strukturwandel der westdeutschen Wirtschaft im internationalen Verbund (J. C. B. Mohr, Tübingen).

Chapter 17   *p. 141 :*

COMMENT ON MULLER AND ZWEZERIJNEN'S PAPER

TH. VAN DE KLUNDERT   *173-75*

University of Tilburg

There is a growing interest in an empirically orientated approach to the problems of economic growth and development. Recent indications of stagnation and decline call for a rethinking of problems which seemed outdated only a few years ago. Neoclassical growth theory offers no solutions to the questions asked about the causes of stagflation and the determinants of technical change. However, a well-developed theoretical alternative is not available. Under these circumstances the danger of relapse into historicism is not entirely imaginary.

Muller and Zwezerijnen are well aware of this danger, but in their view we have to wait for the construction of an "all-embracing multisector model". In the meantime partial theories and data analysis are the order of the day. I cannot agree with this solution in the present situation. The construction of multisector models, though useful in their own right, is in my opinion not the main task that has to be performed in the near future. Instead, I should like to focus on a few very promising studies at a more aggregate level, like Lamfalussy (1963) explaining the growth performance of the United Kingdom in relation to other European countries, and more recently Cornwall (1977) analysing economic growth along the lines set out by Kaldor (1967).

In these books an attempt is made to construct unconventional models of economic growth on the basis of observed, so-called "stylized", facts. Without such an effort to explain reality in a consistent way, empirical studies are not very satisfying. I am afraid that the paper by Muller and Zwezerijnen leaves something to be desired in this connection. This does not alter the fact that the authors deserve credit for their effort to arrange a large amount of statistical data in such a way that useful cross-country analysis becomes possible. For lack of some overall view or general theory I have to confine myself to a few remarks on the different topics treated in the paper.

Section 2 starts with a rather puzzling correlation between the average rate of

Prospects of Economic Growth, edited by S. K. Kuipers and G. J. Lanjouw
© *North-Holland Publishing Company*

growth and a measure of the fluctuations of economic activity in each country. Although different indicators for the cyclical behaviour of the economy are used, it appears that each time the correlation is positive. This leads the authors to the conclusion: "In one way it is disappointing that a certain degree of demand pressure does not lead to *higher* growth rates, e.g. by inducing additional investments".

I do not think that the correlations warrant such a strong conclusion. In the case of substantial demand pressure occasional interruptions may cause a sharp decline in economic activity, followed by a quick recovery. A measure of variation could then give a wrong impression with regard to the structural forces driving the economy. In all cases considered the US was omitted from the sample. The reason for this is not clear.

Section 3 is devoted to the measurement of the capital coefficient. The Harrod–Domar equation is used for computation of capital coefficients (Incremental Capital Output Ratios) of different countries. The ICOR is not an estimate of the technical capital–output ratio for the following reasons:

(a) physical depreciation of capital stock is not taken explicitly into account;

(b) in order to obtain a correct estimate of the coefficient data with regard to production capacity should be used instead of actual production;

(c) the fall in working hours should be dealt with.

Furthermore, results of a direct calculation of capital coefficients are reported. However, we are not told how the capital stocks employed are determined. It seems that the objections (b) and (c) mentioned above hold in this case too.

In section 4.2 Carré's theory on the role of imports is discussed. According to this French economist the volume of imports should appear in the production function relating output and employment. In this way the gains from international trade are captured. The authors change the original specification of Carré by applying the tautological formula (15). It would have been more convincing if they had argued that an extra parameter should be added to establish dimensional homogeneity. In the second instance the analysis is generalized by introducing the production factor capital. A rather complex production function is then estimated for five countries. The resultant rate of technical progress is lower than usual. Part of it is now explained by gains from trade and economies of scale. However, it is not clear to what extent the different factors are interrelated. The authors conclude that it is often difficult to distinguish between gains from trade and technical progress. In this connection mention should be made of an interesting attempt by Carré et al. (1972) to measure the economies of scale due to international specialization. The outcome is not impressive. The same holds with regard to well-known empirical studies on the gains from trade in the case of constant returns to scale. It is conceivable that the third production factor, volume of imports, scores significantly in empirical estimations. However, it remains to be seen whether this is not a statistical artefact. Anyhow, in my opinion these exercises with a third factor in the production function do not seem very promising.

Data on the growth of industrial production are presented in section 5.2. The suggestion that the slow growth in the period 1930–1958 compared with the rapid expansion in the period 1958–1974 could be conceived as an illustration of the Kondratieff cycle is indeed very speculative. It could be questioned whether total world production is the relevant variable for determining cycles of this kind. The remarkable growth in the second period depended among other things on a closing of the gap between existing and potential productivity as determined by application of American technology in Europe and Japan [e.g. Abramovitz (1977) and Cornwall (1977)]. It remains to be seen what this has to do with the idea of a long cycle.

In the last section an explanation is sought for the share of different countries in total world production. As a first approximation it is supposed that changes in these shares can be explained by percentage changes in unit labour costs. However, compensating movements in exchange rates spoil the relation. Hence, something else is tried. The growth rate of domestic production is related to the growth of world production and the percentage change of nominal wages in the country under consideration. A theoretical explanation for this relation is missing. Moreover, the regression equation is applied to "figures from all nine countries and for all nine industrial sectors". This makes it even more difficult to understand what is meant. It appears that the coefficient with regard to changes in nominal wages has a positive sign. The authors provide the following explanation. An increase in wages stimulates domestic demand. This effect overcompensates the negative effect of a wage increase on foreign demand. To establish a conclusion like this some economists would like to have a complete macroeconomic model at their disposal. As a member of the latter group, I do not have much faith in strong conclusions drawn on the basis of a single regression equation which is not based on solid theory.

The critical remarks made may serve as an illustration of the fact that the important issues of economic growth in developed countries are hardly touched upon. No explanation is given of the differences in growth rates between countries. The stagnation problem is not explained. In short, the balance between theory and measurement is not very well maintained, at least in the view of the present commentator.

References

Abramovitz, M., 1977, Rapid growth potential and its realization: The experience of capitalist economies in the post-war period, Paper presented at the Fifth World Congress of the International Economic Association in Tokyo.

Carré, J.-J., P. Dubois and E. Malinvaud, 1972, La croissance française (Editions du Seuil, Paris).

Cornwall, J., 1977, Modern capitalism. Its growth and transformation (Martin Robertson, London).

Kaldor, N., 1967, Strategic factors in economic development (Cornell University, Ithaca).

Lamfalussy, A., 1963, The United Kingdom and the six: An essay on economic growth in Western Europe (Richard Irwin, Homewood, Ill.).

Chapter 18 $p.141:$

COMMENT ON MULLER AND ZWEZERIJNEN'S PAPER

J. A. H. MAKS

University of Groningen $177-81$

While Muller and Zwezerijnen's study is entitled "Sectoral Change and Economic Growth . . .", they in fact analyse structural changes in a broad sense.[1] Only section 5 deals with changes in the sectoral patterns of production in developed economies. From the data given in their table 16.11 for the nine economies analysed, it is obvious that there was a very important shift in the share of total employment from agriculture and industry to the service sector during the period 1963–1975. Furthermore, it appears from the data given in Appendix B that there were substantial changes within the industrial sector for each country in the period 1938–1975. The observed tendencies are in accordance with the findings in the EEC report *Les Mutations sectorielles des Economies Européennes de 1960 à la Recession* (1978) for the six EEC countries included in the analysis of Muller and Zwezerijnen.

These findings lead the authors to the conclusions that

(a) there is no evidence to oppose the hypothesis of Fourastié and Carré when applied to employment ratios (section 5.1); and

(b) the sectoral patterns of the different countries show a tendency towards conformity (section 5.2).[2]

However, they do not analyse the relation between the sectoral developments and the economic growth rate, or the rate of unemployment as, for example, Van den Goorbergh (1975) has done in a three-sector model. Nor do they consider the diminishing growth in the Seventies of the strong growth industries of the Sixties. Moreover, they do not analyse the possible and likely amplification of this phenomenon by the huge rise in oil prices in 1973 or, for that matter, the effect of this price increase on the diminishing growth of employment opportunities in the service sector. It is fairly

---

[1] For two more or less similar studies, see Cripps and Tarling (1973) and Schatz (1974).

[2] This is also the conclusion drawn in the above-mentioned EEC report (1978, pp. 122, 123).

Prospects of Economic Growth, edited by S. K. Kuipers and G. J. Lanjouw
© *North-Holland Publishing Company*

generally assumed that this sector was able to balance the labour market in the Sixties because of high average growth rates in the industry. Nor do Muller and Zwerzerijnen focus attention on policy implications in this line of thought. One may, for example, consider the possible measures to stimulate the re-emergence of fast-growing industries, e.g. "chips" technology, so that the service sector can again play the role it did in the Sixties. A tentative answer to one or more of these questions might have been appropriate in order to analyse sectoral change and economic growth.

The intention of the authors was to "analyse some common factors responsible for the stagnation of economic growth" in all Western economies "during the last few years". They confine themselves to partial theories and data analyses because, in their view, no satisfactory multisector model exists with both a supply and a demand side. Although a partial analysis may very well be justified for the authors' goal, the argument does not give sufficient credit to, inter alia, the study by Barker et al. (1976), which certainly can be considered an excellent attempt to formulate and to estimate such a multisector model on a level of disaggregation that goes beyond the level Muller and Zwezerijnen use for their partial analyses.

In section 2 the authors focus attention on "the level and pattern of growth of gross domestic product" and "the growth of broad categories of expenditure". In table 16.1 they list the average yearly growth rates of gross domestic product and their standard deviations calculated from growth rate figures for the approximate period 1952–1975. On the basis of these data they test the contention that government intervention in the economic process intensifies the fluctuations in economic growth. It is difficult to see how a regression of the average growth rates on their standard deviations can be employed to investigate this contention. Only if one considers the average growth rate a satisfactory proxy for the degree of government intervention does the procedure make sense. Moreover, the regression results are highly dependent on the chosen sample. Without any argument or explanation Muller and Zwezerijnen leave the US out of the sample. But if one brings the US data into the sample and removes Japan a linear regression leads to a determination coefficient of 0.13. So it may be wise to interpret the estimation results of eq. (1) with care.

In table 16.2 the authors list the average idle capacity rates and their standard deviations. With these data and the average growth rates of table 16.1 they endeavour to evaluate the neoclassical conclusion that steady-state growth is not influenced by the level of demand. For this purpose they regress the average yearly growth rates separately on both the average idle capacity rates and their standard deviations. Although in this case one can see a justification of the testing procedures, the results again depend heavily on the sample. Here, too, Muller and Zwezerijnen leave the US data out of the sample; replacing the Japanese by the US data results in a determination coefficient of 0.06 and a negative coefficient for the influence of the excess capacity on the growth rate. Once again it may be wise to interpret eqs. (2) and (3) with care.

In the developments of the broad categories of expenditure Muller and Zwezerijnen observe a "sudden decline in the investment ratio in all countries comparing 1975 with 1971" and "a small increase in the consumption ratio".

In the following two sections (3 and 4) the relation between the input of production factors and the resultant output is investigated. In section 3 it is concluded that little evidence can be brought against the constant capital–output ratio of the Harrod–Domar model. However, not much value is attached to this result. So, in the next section the liberty is taken of estimating a number of nonlinearly homogeneous production functions in which, moreover, the volume of imports is introduced as an explanatory variable. First, the estimation results are given for a Cobb–Douglas production function. The authors report the "very important result" that "the rate of exogenous technical change" tends to zero as a consequence of this introduction. In this way Muller and Zwezerijnen want to account for international specialization as one of the major factors explaining technical progress. However, the very low estimated values of the rate of technical change can be explained quite differently. If we write

$$Q = X^\alpha \; e^{\beta t} \; M^\gamma \; e^{\delta t}, \tag{1}$$

where Q is gross domestic product, X is capital, and M is volume of imports, we have, taking logarithms,

$$\log Q = (\beta + \delta)t + \alpha \log X + \gamma \log m. \tag{2}$$

We see that the time coefficient can be interpreted as the sum of β and δ. The coefficient β reflects the capital-augmenting or diminishing technical change and δ does the same for the imports. For West Germany the estimated value of the time coefficient is -0.034. Because Muller and Zwezerijnen see imports as a major factor explaining technical progress, one may suppose that they assume a value of δ close to zero. Such a value implies a capital-diminishing rate of technical change β close to -0.034. On a priori common-sense grounds this conclusion seems highly implausible. The assumption of a δ value greater than zero implies a still higher rate, in absolute value, of capital-diminishing technical change. However, only a positive value of β seems acceptable. But even if we admit a negative value of β in the interval $(0, -0.034)$ this still implies a negative value for δ, indicating import-diminishing technical change. Therefore, if we accept the estimation results for West Germany obtained from eq. (9), the only plausible conclusion leads to import-diminishing technical change Figure 17.1 may illustrate the argument more generally.

Along the horizontal axis M stands for imports and along the vertical axis Y symbolizes labour and X capital. Capital- or labour-augmenting technical change moves the isoquant from AA to $A'A'$; the import-diminishing technical change pushes it back in the direction of AA. As a consequence the estimation of a Cobb–Douglas production function leads to a small or even negative estimate of the time coefficient.

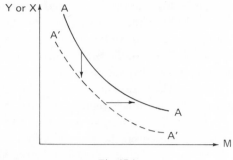

Fig. 17.1

Of course, this reasoning can also be applied to the Cobb–Douglas estimation results for France, Sweden, the United Kingdom and the United States, thereby explaining the low or zero values of the time coefficients.

Two other, nonlinear production functions are estimated in section 4. The first specification uses labour and imports as explanatory variables and specifies Solow-neutral technical change. The other one also includes capital and specifies Hicks-neutral technical change. Here again the estimated values of the time coefficient are lower than normally obtained if imports are not introduced in the production function. Nevertheless, the reasoning given in fig. 17.1 remains basically applicable. The low estimates may be caused by compensating forces of capital- or labour-augmenting technical progress on the one hand and import-diminishing technical change on the other. A consequence of this plausible interpretation is that, instead of explaining the nature and existence of technical change, the introduction of imports may conceal it.

One may add here another argument. As Muller and Zwezerijnen state themselves, one can observe a tendency towards conformity in the production structures of the nine developed economies. This infers that these economies, if they specialize, do not specialize in relation to each other but with respect to, say, the developing economies. If this is the case, we have another empirical argument, apart from the low estimates of the time coefficient, indicating the diminishing technical quality of the imports.

Furthermore, it must be noted that a critical evaluation of the nonlinear estimation results is hardly possible. The data series on which the production functions were estimated are not reproduced. The method of data construction and how the data were made comparable for the different countries are not revealed. No information is given about the nonlinear estimation method, and the determination coefficients, standard errors and other test statistics are not reported.

Combining these arguments, one cannot help feeling that it is premature to share Muller and Zwezerijnen's view that "part of technical progress is explained by the gains from imports".

The most striking conclusion of section 4 is that increasing imports "made a major contribution to the economic expansion of the Sixties". It is also reported in table 16.8 that the yearly growth of real exports in the period 1971–1975 were much lower than in the period 1959–1971. This leads one to the idea that the same may have happened to the growth of real imports (see also table 16.3), and hence to the conclusion that the decline in import growth is an important factor in the explanation of the recent stagnation. However, it may be hazardous to rely on the estimated coefficients of the production functions in this regard. Muller and Zwezerijnen do not report whether 1973 and later years are included in the data. It is generally experienced that the addition of the observed values of these years has a rather strong tendency to upset previously estimated values.

As mentioned above, in section 5 the relation between the sectoral development and economic growth is not considered. In the final section the development in the relative shares of the nine developed countries in world industry is investigated. The estimation results of eq. (34) temptingly lead one to the remarkable suggestion that the decrease in the rate of change of the wage level is an important negative influence on the growth rate of all sectors of industry. And, of course, industrial growth, taken together for all sectors, is a considerable part of total economic growth. Finally, it is emphasized that for the estimation of this equation data are used from "all countries and all sectors". This implies the assumption that every sector in every country reacts identically except for disturbances with zero expectation. This contention can easily be tested. Such a test would almost certainly give negative results for the paper industry and very likely also for food processing. More information about this matter would, of course, have been of great value.

If we try to summarize the most profound conclusions suggested by the study we may list as major factors contributing to the recent stagnation of economic growth: the decline of the investment ratio, the decrease of the growth rate of real imports, and the decrease of the growth rate of the wage level.

References

Barker, T. S., ed., 1976, Economic structure and policy (Chapman and Hall, London).

Cripps, T. F. and R. J. Tarling, 1973, Growth in advanced capitalist economies 1950–1970 (Cambridge University Press, Cambridge).

Goorbergh, W. M. van den, 1975, De structurele vraag naar arbeid in een drie-sectorenmodel, in: Werkloosheid, Preadviezen aan de Vereniging voor de Staathuishoudkunde (Martinus Nijhoff, The Hague).

Rapport du Groupe d'experts d'analyse sectorielles, 1978, Les mutations sectorielles des economies Européennes de 1960 à la recession (Commission des Communautés Européennes, Bruxelles).

Schatz, K.-W., 1974, Wachstum und Strukturwandel der westdeutschen Wirtschaft im internationalen Verbund (J. C. B. Mohr, Tübingen).

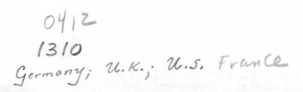

Chapter 19

ON THE ASSESSMENT OF THE
KONDRATIEFF CYCLE AND RELATED ISSUES

/83-222

A. VAN DER ZWAN*

Erasmus University, Rotterdam

This paper is concerned with a twofold problem: (i) the empirical assessment of a long wave in the strict sense as introduced by Kondratieff; and (ii) the underlying causes of major depressions.

For an answer to the first problem a testing procedure is proposed and applied to statistical data for three leading industrial countries and world production and trade. It proved possible to reject Kondratieff's claim of nearly fixed duration and general impact on the basis of the evidence which is presented. An answer to the second problem is sought on the strength of a structuralist approach. A configuration of features of economic growth is outlined in which uneven development over a period of time and disparity between industries play a key role; structural changes accompanying technical change are regarded as the essential phenomena.

1. Introduction

When the editors of the *Review of Economic Statistics*[1] presented Kondratieff's "peculiarly important" article on the long waves in economic life, in translation, they justified this unusual action by the circumstance of an increasing interest in "long waves", combined with the difficulty of securing access to the original article, which was published in German [Kondratieff (1926)]. This original article was published in 1926, while the translation was not presented until 1935 when the notion that a major

* The investigation reported in this paper could not have been performed without research assistance. This was provided by the Centre for Research in Business Economics (CBO) at the Erasmus University. Mr. C. Ouwerkerk of CBO rendered general assistance in the exploration of the literature and data sources. He also supervised the data processing and the production of the statistical results. He did so in close cooperation with Mr. H. Wijnberger who is employed at the Erasmus University as a research assistant.

The first draft of this paper was completed before 1 June 1978. Dr. J. J. van Duijn (Interfaculteit Bedrijfskunde Delft) and Dr. S. K. Kuipers (Rijksuniversiteit Groningen) were so kind as to read the preliminary draft, and they commented on style and content. Owing to their contribution the text could be substantially improved. This involves no responsibility on their part for the stand taken in this paper.

[1] Kondratieff (1935, p. 105).

depression had struck the Western world was generally accepted. It has gradually become a platitude to note that not only economic life is characterized by waves, but also the economic profession in its recognition of real world phenomena. Major economic depressions represent an embarrassment to the economic profession, especially to those branches and schools of thought which take an instrumental view of the economy and believe in its manageability; these have always met the Kondratieff cycle with scepticism. Mainly the Marxist theorists have fully accepted the hypothesis of a long wave and made it a cornerstone of their doctrine.[2] This is not surprising, because the long-term character of this hypothesis fits the Marxist view of the long range remarkably well, while its implied meaning of an "objective trend or tendency", inherent in the capitalist economy, appeals to the Marxist search for "economic laws" that govern society.

Kuznets (1940) has clearly formulated the criteria for the establishment of cycles of a certain type:

(1) the empirical demonstration that fluctuations of a given duration recur with fair simultaneity in the movements of vital aspects of economic life; and

(2) indication of the external factors or the internal economic mechanisms which can be properly account for such recurrent fluctuations.

If we anticipate a further discussion of these formal criteria and emphasize the latter, we may observe that the debate has made hardly any progress. From the beginning the critics of the long wave have pointed out that long waves have usually been explained by external factors and events and have not been related to causes within the economic system itself, so that the problem is only shifted because the recurrent fluctuations in the external factors still have to be elucidated. The supporters of the long wave, notably Kondratieff and his followers, have rejected these objections as invalid by arguing that what the critics look upon as external factors should be regarded as an organic part of a long-cycle characteristic of capitalism. As a matter of fact the protagonists of the long wave internalize the "extra-economic" circumstances and incorporate these into a "meta-theory" [Kondratieff (1935, pp. 112–113)]:

(a) by declaring the development of technology itself part of the rhythm of the long waves;

(b) by fitting wars and revolutions into economic dynamics;

(c) by interpreting the exploitation of new countries, new markets and new sources of raw material as an accelerating factor in the pace of economic development; and

(d) by relating the production of precious metals to more general causes and subordinating it to the rhythm of the long waves.

It cannot be denied that in a long-run analysis the number of "extra-economic" factors that have to be treated endogenously increases while at the same time it must be

---

[2] Cf. Mandel (1972) for a recent elaboration of this thesis. This does not imply unanimity among Marxists. In fact, Kondratieff was heavily attacked by the Soviets.

recognized that a long wave calls for causal factors which display secular movements. But the incorporation of such events as wars and revolutions with economic factors in an interrelated complex which displays acceleration of the pace of development and along with it increased tensions and heightened economic struggle for markets and raw materials, calling for social shocks, and then after a major breakdown a prolonged period of retarded growth, can only be highly speculative.

From the outset it is clear that here we are dealing with a dilemma, because we enter into an argument in which we can choose between two alternatives, each being fatal:

(1) to stick to a more restricted domain of economic phenomena and not be able to assign causal factors which display adequate secular movements; or

(2) to broaden the domain of phenomena and then necessarily arrive at a more speculative theory, which will never meet generally accepted neopositivist standards.

So the long wave constitutes a pre-eminent methodological problem. The reason that it still has such a strong appeal, even for those who are sceptical, can be attributed to its capacity, if not to explain long-term fluctuations which apparently arise, then at least to label our vague notions about tidal variations in economic life. Can we arrive at a more specific judgement and, if so, how should we go about it?

2. The establishment of the long wave: the methodological problem

According to Kuznets (1940) the establishment of cycles of a given type requires the demonstration that fluctuations of that approximate duration occur and an indication of the factors that can properly account for such recurrent movements. These formal and quite general requirements form a suitable starting-point for our exploration of the methodological issues involved.

2.1. The demonstration of the long wave

The statistical evidence put forward by Kondratieff to sustain his hypothesis covered the four industrial countries that were leading at that time. It mainly comprised financial and monetary variables, though it also included a small number of volume series (coal and pig iron production). Burns and Mitchell (1946, p. 431) note that for many years authors in the monetary field had affirmed the existence of long waves in wholesale prices supposed to last at least fifty to sixty years, so it is not surprising that Kondratieff relied heavily on financial and monetary data. Moreover, it is not to be expected that in volume series long cycles will be reflected in the form of actual declines and rises, but rather in retardations and accelerations of growth, while in financial and monetary series these actual declines and rises might be found. Thus the demonstration of the long cycle would be facilitated by the use of price series and the like. Burns and Mitchell verified the long waves in wholesale prices in the US, UK, Germany and France (see table 19.1).

Table 19.1

Peak and trough dates of Kondratieff's long waves and the long waves in wholesale prices of four countries.

Nature of turn	Turns in Kondratieff's long waves	Turns in long waves of wholesale prices			
		United States	Great Britain	Germany	France
Trough	late 1780s–early 1790s	1789	1789	1793	–
Peak	1810–17	1814	1813	1808	1820
Trough	1844–51	1843	1849	1849	1851
Peak	1870–75	1864	1873	1873	1872–73
Trough	1890–96	1896–97	1896	1895	1896
Peak	1914–20	1920	1920	1923	1926
Trough	–	1932	1933	1933	1935

Source: Burns and Mitchell (1946, table 165). See also their comment on these findings.

The similarities among the countries seem to be striking, and most of the turns in the long waves allocated by Burns and Mitchell in the series of wholesale prices appear to fall within the turning zones of the long waves as fixed by Kondratieff. But matters prove to be more complicated than that. Burns and Mitchell's statistical analysis was built around the supposed existence of a long wave in prices and what they actually found is that a movement in prices can be demonstrated that is compatible with the Kondratieff cycle, if mainly judged by movements from trough to peak and from peak to trough of the alleged long waves. When they confronted short-term movements within the Kondratieff zones with the long-term trends, they did not find invariable agreement in direction. Moreover, the long waves back in the 1870s were judged by them as mainly an "optical illusion": "The long waves are clearest in Great Britain; yet one who did not already know these waves in advance might conclude that the trend of prices was not falling from 1823 to 1841, or rising during 1853–1871."[3] So even if we were to accept financial and monetary series as sufficient for the demonstration of the long wave, it can only be regarded as supported relatively convincingly by the facts for the period of decline in prices between 1870–1875 and 1890–1896 and for the period of rising prices between 1890–1896 and 1914–1920.[4] Consequently the evidence put forward by Kondratieff leaves us with the confirmation of what the Anglo-American

[3] Burns and Mitchell (1946, p. 440). It should be noted that their treatise on the business cycles is admirably profound and wide in scope and that their judgements have stayed unchallenged.

[4] The identification of the turn in 1932 is denoted by Burns and Mitchell as uncertain and we leave it out of consideration here. In a more recent study [Broersma (1978)] it is shown that the turn in 1932 can still be

economic historians refer to as the Great Depression (1870–1875 till 1890–1895).

Kuznets (1940, pp. 117–118) has criticized Kondratieff's statistical analysis for the very reason that it relies mainly on price indices, interest rates and activity indices at current prices (value series) which are dominated by strong price movements. Unless it is demonstrated that the Kondratieff cycle is reflected in the movements of various significant aspects of economic life, including the volume of production and employment, it cannot be accepted – according to Kuznets – as affecting economic life at large. To that extent Kuznets is right in stressing this point. But the requirement that the cycle type distinguished should be demonstrated in *volumes* as well as in prices introduces difficulties that might be prohibitive, particularly for long cycles. In the first place it should be noted that the emphasis on prices as main indicators is not uncommon in the analysis of business cycles [e.g. Burns and Mitchell (1946)]. This is due to the greater *sensitivity* of prices (which may show actual increases and declines) as well as to the circumstance that price movements do show a certain similarity among nations. Besides sensitivity crucial price series tend to possess a certain generality. So when we restrict ourselves to price and monetary series we do not run into what can be denoted as *demarcation problems*. From the very moment that we direct our analysis to volume series, we have to single out individual nations, sectors within the economy, industries and goods. The fluctuations in the volume series obtained in this way could to a considerable extent be a function of their demarcation. We may clarify this point by settling the effect of singling out individual nations, sectors, and goods.

Mills (1926), Hoffman (1931) and others have pointed to the impact that the stages in a country's industrial development have on vital characteristics of its economy. Mills (1926) proposed a tentative classification which he applied to four industrial countries that were in a leading position during the interwar period:

A. Early stage of industrialization
   United States: to 1822
   Germany: to 1866.
B. Stage of rapid transition
   England: to 1831
   France: to 1876
   United States: 1822 to date
   Germany: 1866 to date.
C. Stage of economic stability
   England: 1831 to date
   France: 1876 to date.

---

denoted as uncertain as far as the US is concerned. It is noteworthy to mention in this connection that Broersma could convincingly demonstrate the Kondratieff cycle only in US data covering the period 1870–1975 for monetary series. From his analysis we conclude that there seems to be much to be said for a turn in 1938 and we shall accept that accordingly.

Mills's categorization of countries according to the stage of their development can conveniently be checked against a recent breakdown of world exports of manufactured goods and found to be correct up to the interwar period, in which Mills published his article [e.g. Woodruff (1975, table XXII, which covers the period 1899–1970)]. Since then the US happens to have reached maturity while West Germany (together with Japan and Italy) can be regarded as still being in the stage of rapid transition. The relevant point in this connection is that no single leading country has enjoyed a constant share of world exports and could for that reason form a suitably demarcated geographical unit for statistical observation of long-term fluctuations, reflecting movements in the world economy or economic life in the Western world; not even for a period that approximates 50 years, which corresponds to only one full Kondratieff cycle.

When it comes to sectors within the economy we can also observe long-term shifts in the form of an increasing share of producer-goods industries [e.g. Hoffmann (1955, table 3)].

At the level of industries and commodity groups, matters become even more complicated. The textile industry, which stood at the beginning of industrial development, had to yield its place to iron and steel, and at a later stage to the electrical and chemical industries [e.g. Cairncross (1962, table X)]. But the history of industries is far from being uniform among countries. It is conditioned not only by worldwide changes in demand, technology and business organization, but also by *particular national circumstances*. As Kuznets (1929) observed, while Belgian coal output had reached nearly stable levels by the beginning of the twentieth century, American and German coal production was still showing substantial growth.

We come to the conclusion that Kuznets was right in asking for the demonstration of the Kondratieff cycle in terms of volume series. One may wonder, however, whether Kuznets fully anticipated the complications inherent in such a requirement. Long-term movements in volumes of output within nations, sectors and industries reflect many different influences, a number of which are largely specific. These volume series cannot therefore be expected to possess similarity or generality across countries to the same degree as price series do; this will be even more so when the period studied exceeds 50 years. Technically speaking, these specific movements should be removed from series before the long wave can be demonstrated. The greater the amount of specific influences, the more this exercise will be contingent on *maintained* hypotheses and the greater the risk that statistical *artefacts* will be produced. In section 2.3 a procedure will be proposed for overcoming these complications. It will be clear that this procedure can result in only a provisional solution because the problems are of a fundamental nature.

2.2. The causality of the long wave

The method of investigation traditionally followed by students of the long wave consists of an approach in two steps, made explicit by Kuznets in the form of necessary and sufficient requirements. In the first step the demonstration of the existence of long waves is attempted by making use of time series, and notably the variant which Menderhausen (1937) termed as *mechanical*; this mechanical analysis is applied to any series one can lay one's hands on. In the next step an explanation is attempted that is frequently formulated in terms of reference far removed from the empirical data used in step 1 [e.g. Kondratieff (1935)]. The compatibility of the outcome of the two separated steps can then be assured only by the explicit or implicit introduction of "far-reaching" additional hypotheses that are *maintained* throughout the process of investigation.

It cannot be denied that considerable progress has been made, also in economic science, by investigations of a predominantly empirical nature without the previous formulation of hypotheses. The familiar budget analysis still stands out as an example of insight gained by empirical observation that resulted in theory and not vice versa as the textbooks will have it. But this empirical approach will be successful only if in the course of time the gap between the two steps can be bridged and step 2 results in the formulation of the relevant and possibly *direct* criteria that are put to the statistical test in step 1 and give rise to a converging process. It must be noted, however, that the Kondratieff cycle has maintained its status of a "daring" hypothesis just as it had in the Twenties when it was introduced.

2.3. Conclusion

We conclude from our investigation into the methodological issues involved that there are conflicting demands. On the one hand one should require that the long wave be demonstrated in terms of volume series, while on the other hand this requirement tends to be prohibitive. The highest attainable goal in this matter seems to be a pragmatic solution which is based on a "mixed empirical-structural" approach. In this case the use of the method of *split-halves* might be appropriate and is proposed here for that reason. This method implies that one half of the set of economic indicators is used in the phase of *estimation*, notably the identification and dating of the long cycle, while the other half is used in the phase of *testing*, notably the demonstration that the cycle identified in the first phase is reflected in significant economic phenomena.[5] It seems to be appropriate to allocate prices and monetary indicators to the first split-half because

---

[5] The term split-halves should not be taken literally. The split into two separate parts is the essential element. The set of indicators is supposed to be homogeneous. It should be noted that under the Kondratieff hypothesis to be tested, price and volume series may be regarded as such a homogeneous set.

they apparently stand the best chance of showing sensitivity and similarity across countries. The other economic indicators can better be allotted to the second half. From the point of view of explanation it should at least be required that the economic indicators selected for the second split-half bear direct relevance to the proposed theory and should make it possible to judge the scope of the cycle: is it a general or a more differentiated phenomenon? These considerations form the key to our own programme of investigation into the leading question posed by this paper.

3. The establishment of the long wave: testing the Kondratieff cycle as a general phenomenon

The verification of the Kondratieff cycle is taken up by putting to test its presumed general character. The procedure followed is the one proposed at the end of the last section, i.e. starting from the cycle that can be identified and dated on the basis of prices and monetary variables and next testing volume series for the presence of this cycle. Once this approach is accepted, it is natural to rely on the empirical assessment of price movements in the literature (including Kondratieff's work). The dating of the Kondratieff cycle in this restricted sense is pretty well determined and reference has been made above to the work by Burns and Mitchell on this subject. Their scheme will be accepted here and only supplemented by dating the turn during the Thirties in 1938 instead of their provisional estimate (1932). In view of the aim of the test, which is to establish whether the Kondratieff cycle is reflected in volume variables, attention will be paid to broad indicators like production and income as measured in real terms.

Taking the limited availability of statistical records and the world situation during the period mid-nineteenth to the mid-twentieth century into account, the coverage will be limited to the countries that were leading during that period.[6] Fortunately data on the world production of manufactures and on the world trade of primary products during the period concerned are also available. A summary of the main sources of data which will be employed in the testing is given in table 19.2. Volume series covering long periods are dominated by trends and, as far as general indicators such as production and income are concerned, by rising trends. The accepted procedure by authors in this field [e.g. Burns and Mitchell (1946, pp. 427–428)] is to remove these trends as adequately as possible and next to compute five-year averages of the corrected series and to examine the latter for long waves. As a consequence of the point of view taken here, this procedure will not be followed. Instead, two statistical operations will be per-

---

[6] By 1913 the US had become a world power, while Western Europe had maintained its position. The three big European powers – the UK, Germany and France – accounted for more than seven-tenths of Europe's manufacturing capacity and for more than three-quarters of its export trade [e.g. Invar Svennilson (1954, pp. 16–17). France, as a minor European power, is deleted from the analysis because of the restriction mentioned. The period covered (mainly the nineteenth and early twentieth centuries) is regarded by historians as one showing a relatively constant structure and economic system.

Table 19.2

Summary of statistical sources on production and income at the aggregate level to be used in the statistical testing.

Country	Source	Series	Period
US	Frickey (1947)	production	1860–1913
UK	Dean and Cole (1967)	production (industrial)	1800–1938
		income	1855–1959
Germany	Hoffmann (1965)	production (industrial and total)	1850–1934
World	Lewis (1952)	production (manufacturers)	1870–1938
		trade (primary products)	1881–1938

formed which are in line with the utilization of a priori knowledge:

(1) deviations from trends fitted for the *entire* period under consideration will be checked across the predetermined Kondratieff intervals for remaining movements with time; and

(2) growth rates will be estimated *within* each of the predetermined Kondratieff intervals.[7]

Both findings will be tested against the pattern which may be expected on the basis of the hypothesis of the Kondratieff cycle: deviations positively related to time or high rates of growth during intervals of "rise" (upward phase of the cycle) and deviations negatively related to time or low rates of growth during intervals of "decline" (downward phase of the cycle). By these devices full use can be made of the a priori knowledge derived from the price indices and monetary series.

To give the long wave an optimal chance of revealing itself in the volume series studied, the intervals are chosen not only from peaks to troughs of the presumed international long wave and vice versa, but also by country from peak to trough and vice versa with respect to the (national) business cycles that mark the turn of the long wave.[8] The volume indices used throughout the analysis either had already been transformed in the original source into rates of growth (by five-year periods and the like) or have been subjected to a logarithmic transformation[9] before entering into a trend analysis by means of regression methods. This is usual practice and it is employed in view of the fact that volume indices will at best display acceleration and retardation of growth and therefore no actual declines.

In the following tables the results are reported by country. Though the results in

[7] These growth rates will be estimated by fitting a linear trend to the logs of the observed series. Tilanus (1968) has shown that this least squares estimation is superior to estimation by means of averaging annual growth percentages and other estimation procedures.

[8] Burns and Mitchell (1946, table 16). The dating by country on the basis of calendar-year reference dates has been followed where possible (year-to-year series).

[9] Natural logarithms have been employed throughout.

Table 19.3

US: production series and the long wave.[a]

	Entire period [deviations from fitted linear trend related to time within subperiods; estimated by simple correlation coefficients (r)]			Estimated percentage rate of growth	Estimated percentage rate of growth during distinct time intervals (estimated from linear trends)		
	1861–1873	1874–1894	1896–1913	Entire period	1861–1873	1874–1894	1896–1913
Index of production of manufactures among which:	0.66	0.38	0.29	4.84	6.02	5.42	5.28
durables	0.70	0.21	0.31	5.74	8.48	6.45	6.55
nondurables	0.69	0.51	−0.10	4.46	5.97	4.92	4.40
Index of transport and communication	0.80	0.39	0.47	5.68	6.93	6.15	6.17
Combined index of industry and commerce	0.84	0.40	0.37	5.25	6.69	5.75	5.71

[a] The linear trends fitted to the logs of the volume indices for the entire period (1860–1913) provide the following estimates in which a is the regression constant and b the (estimated) rate of growth:

	a	b	$\bar{R}^2$	Test on b (F ratio)
Manufacturing among which:	2.7140	0.04838	0.98816	4425
durables	2.3404	0.05739	0.96412	1425
nondurables	2.8692	0.04465	0.99244	6957
Transport/Comm.	2.4467	0.05684	0.99410	8937
Industry/Commerce	2.5846	0.05254	0.99277	7274

The upward movement of the regression disturbances within the distinct subperiods is also reflected in the upward bias of the rates of growth estimated for the distinct time intervals; these separate estimates exceed the estimate for the entire period.

table 19.3 indicate some general retardation of growth during the whole period[10] and an apparent retardation from the first interval to the second, neither test shows signs of

[10] Frickey (1947) reports contradictory findings. These were based on the estimation of trends in the logs of the volume indices incorporating a quadratic term. The quadratic terms turn out to be nonsignificant. One should bear in mind, however, that the incorporation of a quadratic term introduces multicollinearity which is at the expense of the reliability of the individual regression coefficients from which the significance should be read. Frickey's calculations are not challenged here, merely his interpretation. Comparison of linear trends and quadratic trends fitted to the logs of the volume indices show equally good coefficients of determination after correction for the loss of degrees of freedom ($\bar{R}^2$), while the F ratios are of course much better in the case of the linear trends.

an acceleration of growth following the period of the Great Depression (1873–1896). Frickey also provides volume indices on 34 individual commodities, most of these covering the same period. To all of these items similar tests have been applied. They show the same general pattern, i.e. retardation of growth with hardly any commodity showing accelerated growth during the last interval (1897–1913).[11] The overall conclusion should be that the hypothesis of a decline during the interval 1873–1896 followed by an interval of prosperity – a turn that is so definitely inferred from price movements – is by no means reflected in the volume indices for the US.

The series available for the UK – the first industrialized country – cover very long periods. Real per capita income goes back to 1855, while estimates of the rate of growth of industrial production go back to 1800, spanning the world history of industrialization. Both show marked retardation of growth as a general characteristic for the UK:

$$\ln \text{(real per capita income)} = 2.977 + 0.020t - 0.0000821t^2 \qquad (1)$$
(1855–1959; annual $(F = 303.9)$ $(F = 60.0)$
   figures) $\bar{R}^2 = 0.94624;$

$$\text{Rate of growth of industrial production} = 42.087 - 1.130t \qquad (2)$$
(1800–1938; percentage $(F = 27.1)$
increases per decade, $N = 25$) $\bar{R}^2 = 0.52125$

The UK income series (real per capita income) displays a pattern of development which is completely inconsistent with the alleged long wave (table 19.4). The rate of growth of industrial production (table 19.5) shows a configuration in time which is quite as incompatible with the Kondratieff hypothesis as that of real per capita income.[12]

The German series cover total production and industrial production.[13] These can well be described by a linear trend fitted to the logs of the volume variables:[14]

$$\ln \text{(total production)} = 9.09866 + 0.11166t \qquad (3)$$
(1850–1934; 5-year $(F = 362.2)$
averages, $N = 15$) $\bar{R}^2 = 0.96268;$

[11] One significant exception is the production index of railroad passenger cars, showing successive growth rates of 20.72, 7.91 and 10.29 percent during the distinct intervals.

[12] The fitting of (separate) trends to the observations within the distinct intervals is not optional because of the limited number of observations in this case.

[13] In fact a complete breakdown of production according to eight different sectors is made available by Hoffmann (1965, table 6).

[14] The linear trend is doing quite well. Omitting the last observation, which happens to display a large negative deviation (see the following table) because it is situated in the Thirties with their deep depression, does not disturb the outcome to a great extent. The estimated rate of growth would amount in that case to 12.1 percent (total production) and to 17.4 percent (industrial production). This limited sensitivity to changes in the data set strengthens the reliability of the reported findings. The fitting of a quadratic trend, introducing retarded growth, seems to be unwarranted in this case.

$$\ln \text{(industrial production)} = 7.54747 + 0.15828t \tag{4}$$

(1850–1934; 5-year $(F = 275.2)$

averages, $N = 15$) $\bar{R}^2 = 0.95142.$

Table 19.4

UK: income and the long wave (real per capita income; 1855–1959).

Kondratieff intervals		Deviations from fitted quadratic trend related to time within subperiods; estimated by simple correlation coefficients (r)	Linear trends estimated for distinct intervals			
			a	b	$\bar{R}^2$	Test on b (F ratio)
II Rise	1855–1873	0.29	2.940	0.0202	0.94139	290
II Decline	1874–1996	0.69	2.924	0.0204	0.93670	327
III Rise	1897–1914	−0.86	3.608	0.0049	0.59444	26
III Decline	1920–1939	0.71	2.728	0.0159	0.80041	77
IV Rise	1940–1959	0.14	3.571	0.0066	0.12666	4

a is the regression constant b is the regression coefficient (estimated rate of growth).

Table 19.5

UK: rate of growth of industrial production (percentage increase per decade) and the long wave.

	Deviations from linear trend averaged according to Kondratieff intervals			
	Rise	Number of observations	Decline	Number of observations
I	−14.192	1–2	5.812	3–8
II	3.964	9–13	−5.121	14–17
III	−4.925	18–22	6.268	23–25

During the period of study (1850–1934) industrial production increased by a factor 1.4 higher than total production, implying a growing share of the industrial sector. The deviations from the fitted trends have been related to time according to the Kondratieff scheme (table 19.6). The correlation coefficients seem to point to a configuration which is compatible with the Kondratieff hypothesis. The magnitude of the effect, however, as estimated by the amplitude of the movement around the trend, turns out to be negligible.[15]

Many of the *demarcation* problems noted above can in principle be solved by the

[15] The fitting of (separate) trends to the observations within the distinct intervals is not optional here because of the restricted number of observations in this case.

Table 19.6

Germany: (industrial) production and the long wave; deviations from fitted linear trends related to time; estimated by simple correlation coefficient (r) and amplitude (A).[a]

	Rise				Decline			
	Total production		Industrial production		Total production		Industrial production	
	r	$A(\%)$	r	$A(\%)$	r	$A(\%)$	r	$A(\%)$
II	0.89	0.5	0.88	2.8	0.10	0.1	−0.19	−0.3
III	1.00	0.9	0.96	1.0	b		b	

[a] Amplitude is estimated by taking the difference between the first and the last (predicted) disturbance around the trend values within the distinct time intervals and relating this difference to the trend value in the middle position of the interval.

[b] Not estimated owing to the limited number of observations.

observation of production and trade on a world scale. But the complications in compiling world production and trade series are of course tremendous, because these have to be collected by country and subsequently assembled. One might therefore wonder how accurate and reliable these series are. A complication which is of special interest here is the handling of newcomers on the world scene and how to trace their contribution, especially for the times when these contributions were still insignificant and the quality of the statistical registration possibly likewise. Including a country once it reaches significance introduces bias in the estimates that may disturb the testing for long waves that is attempted here.

The quality of world production and trade series provided by Lewis (1952) is beyond my judgement.[16] World production is provided in two alternative series, one including the US but excluding the USSR, and one excluding both the US and the USSR. The world trade series considered here concerns the volume of primary products entering into international trade. The period covered by the production and trade series ends in 1938 and these may be expected to show *retardation* of growth for that reason only. Special care has to be taken in dealing with this circumstance. To elucidate this point the estimates of the rates of growth for the separate Kondratieff intervals are given in table 19.7.

In the first place there is a striking difference between the two production series which can only underline the seriousness of the depression during the Thirties in the US. In the second place the retardation of growth manifests itself mainly during the last interval (1921–1938), so that the testing should also be directed towards an examina-

---

[16] This remark should not be understood to imply that the quality of the national data *is* within my judgement. But the problems of reliability and accuracy, however, seem to be less urgent in the national context as far as the leading industrial countries are concerned.

Table 19.7

World: rate of growth of production (manufactures) and trade (primary products).

	Linear trends fitted to logs of:								
	Production 1[a]			Production 2[b]			Trade		
	a	b	$\bar{R}^2$	a	b	$\bar{R}^2$	a	b	$\bar{R}^2$
1874–1896	2.924	0.035	0.97	3.115	0.030	0.96			
(1881–1896)							3.204	0.031	0.97
1897–1913	2.877	0.039	0.96	3.083	0.034	0.97	3.239	0.030	0.95
1921–1938	3.545	0.021	0.36	2.906	0.031	0.66	3.556	0.019	0.46

[a] Excluding USSR, including US.
[b] Excluding both USSR and US.

Table 19.8

World: production/trade and the long wave.

Production 1

$\ln y_1 = 2.880 + 0.038t$ $\bar{R}^2 = 0.99107$
(1874–1913) $F = 4330$

		deviations from fitted trend related to time [a]	
		r	$A(\%)$
	1874–1896	−0.48	−2.0
	1897–1913	0.05	0.1

$\ln y_1 = 2.792 + 0.049t - 0.00025t^2$ $\bar{R}^2 = 0.97701$
(1874–1938) $F = 284$ $F = 42$

		deviations from fitted trend related to time [a]	
		r	$A(\%)$
	1874–1896	−0.71	−3.8
	1897–1913	0.71	2.8
	1921–1938	0.08	0.7

Production 2

$\ln y_2 = 3.063 + 0.034t$ $\bar{R}^2 = 0.98930$
(1874–1913) $F = 3608$

deviations from fitted trend related to time [a]

	r	$A(\%)$
1874–1896	−0.53	−2.3
1897–1913	−0.04	−0.1

$\ln y_2 = 3.024 + 0.041t - 0.00018t^2$ $\bar{R}^2 = 0.97145$
(1874–1938) $F = 202$ $F = 24$

deviations from fitted trend
related to time [a]

	r	$A(\%)$
1874–1896	−0.56	−2.7
1897–1913	0.74	2.4
1921–1938	0.50	4.4

Trade

$\ln y_3 = 3.191 + 0.032t$ $\bar{R}^2 = 0.99076$
(1881–1913) $F = 3431$

deviations from fitted trend
related to time [a]

	r	$A(\%)$
1881–1896	−0.17	−0.3
1897–1913	−0.19	−0.5

$\ln y_3 = 3.031 + 0.0465t - 0.00030t^2$ $\bar{R}^2 = 0.96460$
(1881–1938) $F = 176$ $F = 51$

deviations from fitted trend
related to time [a]

	r	$A(\%)$
1881–1896	−0.58	−1.5
1897–1913	0.61	2.1
1921–1938	0.44	3.3

[a] Estimated by simple correlation coefficient (r) and amplitude (A); see table 19.6.

tion of the differences between the first two intervals. This can be realized by the comparison of two alternative trend specifications (table 19.8).

There is no doubt, of course, that the major depression during the Thirties which fits within the Kondratieff scheme is reflected in the volume of world production and trade. Given this fact, the entire period covered by the series can be adequately met only by fitting a trend which contains an element of retarded growth (quadratic trend) or by fitting a linear trend to a shorter period, omitting the postwar years. The statistical fit proves to be very good in both cases. The deviations from these trends as far as production is concerned show some inclination to follow a Kondratieff pattern. The magnitude of the effect, as far as it is consistent, labels it as insignificant.

The period 1874–1913 can be described nearly perfectly as one of constant growth, leaving hardly any room for a turn of a long wave in world production (and trade) during the years 1896–1897.

In conclusion we can say that the overall picture that can be derived from the statistical testing is one that does not support the hypothesis of a long wave in the Kondratieff sense, i.e. a recurrent long cycle affecting economic life at large, which means that it is reflected in crucial volume variables like aggregate production. In particular, the declines between 1870–1875 and 1890–1896 and the following rise between 1890–1896 and 1914–1920 that have been so strikingly inferred from prices and monetary variables appear not to be reflected in the volume of production. This may mean that aggregate production has been free from the hypothesized secular changes, but it may also mean either that the influence of these secular changes has been too small to be detected reliably by means of the data employed or that the secular changes have not followed a general pattern across the leading industrial countries. In either case the claims that are implicit in the Kondratieff cycle – general and substantial impact of recurrent secular changes – should be rejected. Anyone desirous of arguing that the outcome of the testing is sensitive to (normal) deficiencies in the data, the length of the statistical series, a possible lag of volume series with respect to price movements, etc. should realize that this claim is to a large extent self-defeating. It labels the Kondratieff as hardly robust, i.e. a phenomenon well within the range of statistical shortcomings and/or subtle refinements.

4. How to resolve the dilemma? A structuralist approach

In the preceding section it was possible to reject the hypothesis of a Kondratieff cycle employing a formal testing procedure. As Kuznets (1940) has argued, the cycle is essentially a quantitative concept; all of its characteristics can be conceived of as measurable aspects that can be properly assessed only with the aid of quantitative data. In a field where speculation dominates, the use of formal procedures seems to be called for. But one can also become the prisoner of formal methods and drift into a formalistic approach which leads to rigidity. Can it be regarded as an adequate response to reject the Kondratieff in the face of a major depression, while having experienced an even more severe one during the Thirties? Either of these depressions is incontestable, from the point of view both of the generality and the substantiality of its impact on world production and trade. Two issues are involved in this matter. The first seems to be a dominantly academic problem, namely the design of a procedure of investigation into the assessment of the Kondratieff cycle, followed by the actual testing. The second is a problem of much greater scope and momentum, namely what are the causes of the major depressions that have struck the Western world during this century and how these can be overcome and possibly be prevented.

Above we argued (cf. section 1) that in the face of a crisis there is a psychological inclination to look for security. The concept of recurrent movements of an approximately fixed duration seems to offer an element of continuity, while the idea of irregular and therefore totally unpredictable shocks seems to be mentally unacceptable. Apart from the statistical testing in the preceding section, one may wonder, however, what the significance of such a predominantly *mechanical* theory can be. It has a built-in element of "untestability" due to its long-range character; in the long run variability dominates, which is prohibitive from the point of view of testing because testing can only adequately be employed on the basis of a distinction between variable and constant (structural) factors. It also has a built-in element of inevitability and resignation, owing to its implication of fixed duration. The possibility of substantiating this claim can be seriously doubted on a priori grounds; it belongs to the heritage of the nineteenth century in which the notion of the social sciences as "social mechanics" flourished [e.g. Quételet (1869)].

So the conclusion may be that there is much to be said for a farewell to mechanical notions about long-term developments and for relying instead on causal and analytical methods for the explanation of phenomena which obviously manifest themselves. A structuralist approach to these problems is presented in this part of the paper.

4.1. The nature of long-term change

Mitchell (1927, 1946) has asserted that the phenomenon of business cycles does not become a prominent feature of economic life until the stage of monetarization has been reached and economic life has been organized mainly in business enterprises. In other words, not until the division of labour has become a dominant characteristic of economic life. This development is reflected in a sharp decline of the share of agriculture and the domestic services in aggregate production and employment and a marked rise of the manufacturing sector within the economy [e.g. Kuznets (1957, Appendix; tables 2–3)]. The process of industrialization and economic growth is conditioned by three basic, interactive factors:

(1) technological development, the state of the technical arts;

(2) the state of internal organization of the business enterprises as the micro units of economic organization, notably their size, induced by the potential economies of scale; and

(3) the state of external organization of economic life, expressing itself at the industry level in the prevailing competitive conditions and the utilization of capacity and at the macro level in the operation of the market system, interrelations between industries and sectors and the like.

The mainstream of economic theory has tended to assume that developed countries are efficient in their use of resources in each sector and at any point of time, this efficiency being attributable to market competition. As Cripps and Tarling (1973) have claimed, however, the postulate of efficiency in the market economy in this unrestricted sense has to be abandoned if an intelligible and realistic account of the process of economic growth is to be achieved. Economic growth can more adequately be viewed as a process of reallocation of resources, resulting from a complicated interplay between new methods, costs, prices and productivity. As a response to the changing pattern of costs and prices attributable to *uneven* rates of technical change and associated economies of scale *between* industries, we can observe structural changes.

It was Salter (1969) who stressed at an early stage the interindustry differences and resulting structural changes: "... it is much more plausible to think of technical progress and economies of scale as complementary to each other. Economies of scale may be regarded as reinforcing the inter-industry variation in cost and productivity originally attributable to the uneven impact of technical progress. Industries which, in the first instance, are expanding because of improvements in technology, receive an additional stimulus through the realisation of scale economies. Conversely, industries with little stimulus to expansion are handicapped in realising potential scale economies" [Salter (1969, p. 142)].

Salter added to his exploration of uneven development between industries quite a number of facilitating and/or reinforcing dynamic scale and growth economies. In this connection he mentioned the advantages of expanding industries in utilizing new techniques of production enabling them to bridge the gap between best practice and average practice; the high morale in expanding industries favouring the adoption of new methods and the procurement of progressive management and financial means; and the fact that expanding industries provide a good market for capital equipment, fostering the development of special-purpose machinery.

Salter (1969, p. 153) connected his findings with policy recommendations in so far as he defended a flexible economy and rejected artificial support of declining industries as causing misallocation and retarding the growth of production: "The ideal is a highly flexible economy which allows resources to be moved with a minimum of friction from declining to expanding industries where technical change is currently progressing the most rapidly."

The structuralist approach advanced by Salter shows in its elaboration – however admirably well done in itself – nearly complete neglect of the above-mentioned third basic factor, namely the external business organization and prevailing market conditions. Following the structuralist tradition, the present writer has stressed the importance of the environmental factor to long-term economic development. Flexibility may not guarantee efficient allocation and may even cause the reverse. To reap the economies associated with technical change to their full extent, a great many *environmental* barriers have to be overcome and obstacles to be eliminated. Between the anticipated economies of growth and their realization we have to face the interference of the economic environment. This element, in combination with the structuralist approach, has been worked out by the author in the form of an overinvestment hypothesis [Van der Zwan (1975, 1976, 1977a)]. It is the aim of this section to substantiate this hypothesis.

A perfect illustration of what is involved is offered by the automobile industry in the US during its early development (table 19.9). There is a crucial factor in the com-

Table 19.9

Automobile industry in the US (1899–1929).

	Capital-labour ratio (horsepower per worker)	Labour productivity (produced cars per worker)	Scale of production (number of produced cars per unit of production)	Capital productivity (produced cars per horsepower)	Total output (number of cars × 1000)
1899	1.33	1.87	74	1.41	4
1904	0.73	2.23	189	3.04	23
1909	0.97	2.55	494	2.63	131
1914	1.32	7.18	1 674	5.42	569
1919	1.34	9.18	6 138	6.85	1 934
1921	–	11.12	4 146	–	1 597
1923	1.80	16.71	11 493	9.26	4 034
1925	2.58	21.57	14 363	8.37	4 266
1927	3.73	18.10	12 884	4.85	3 401
1929	–	23.76	22 145	–	5 359

Source: Lieftinck (1931, p. 72).

plicated interplay between new methods of production, costs, prices and productivity, on which the mechanism sketched by Salter is dependent. That is the extent to which the scale of production can be enlarged, depending in its turn on the extent to which output can be increased. If output (sales) slackens, the process of improvement breaks down. The steady enlargement of the scale of production, necessarily accompanied by an increase in total output, has a built-in danger of overproduction and excess capacity at industry level. Under certain conditions the existence of excess capacity at industry level can have an impact on economic life at large.

4.2. The basic argument

The basic argument can be summarized in the following hierarchy of observational steps.

(1) Economic growth exemplifies itself to a large extent in the expansion of modern industries, which already have a scale of production considerably larger than that of the more traditional ones, such as clothing, footwear and furniture.

(2) Fast-growing industries with their high rate of gross investment are in a better position to introduce the latest techniques of production and by doing so reduce the gap between best practice and average practice.

(3) Technical progress happens to be size-biased in many industries and the capital-intensive expansion path is associated with this scale-related technology. The minimum efficient scale of production (m.e.s.) tends to increase in time. Although there are large economies of scale for the production of many products, the relationships are far from uniform. For the brick, bicycle, textile, clothing, footwear and furniture industries, the economies for large-scale production are again limited. The type of process in these industries does not allow for great technical economies of scale, nor is the magnitude of initial costs substantial. As a consequence expansion is correlated with the steady enlargement of the scale of production, especially within the cluster of modern and advancing industries, while substitution of capital for labour takes place alongside this technical advance.

(4a) Economies of scale in the technical sense represent potentialities, while their realization within the context of the integral business operation depends on market and other environmental factors, notably: (i) size and rate of growth of the market; (ii) market density and the costs of physical distribution in relation to further market penetration; (iii) marketing costs (including price cuts) that might be preconditions for the increase of sales; and (iv) market conditions and more precisely the chance that competitors might introduce newer types of technology and larger-scale plants even before the economies of existing plants have been fully realized. This puts pressure on all firms in an industry to initiate technical change themselves and closely follow any gesture made by a competitor. These environmental factors can and will take the form of offsetting influences or barriers that have to be overcome in order to reap the potential economies.

(4b) What applies to the expansion of production at industry level (4a), can easily be generalized to the expansion of production at the level of an economy. The potential economies of growth at this level can be realized only within an environment that facilitates the improvement of transport facilities and communications, the adoption of new methods and products, the mobility of labour, the change of customs and traditions. In other words, in an environment that succeeds in maintaining a flexible economy and society which allows resources to be moved with a minimum of friction and also allows change to progress most rapidly. There is no need to underline that such a flexibility and adaptability may not always be sustained (let alone their desirability from the point of view of society); frictions and obstacles may manifest themselves.

(4c) The related processes of change and economic growth do not merely affect industries and the economy at the national level; they also have an international impact. Technical change turns out to be crucially related to international competition, and the rapidly expanding and technically changing industries (cluster of modern and advancing industries) tend to be the internationally "exposed" ones. This implies that the pressure of technical change itself is being felt on an international scale and that major market gestures have international repercussions.

(5) The investment issue to be decided by entrepreneurs in fast-growing and technically rapidly changing industries is not only complex, but also beset by uncertainty. Important considerations in this respect are the following.

(a) The greater the economies of scale for plants, the greater the incentive to anticipate demand by building larger units, although these will not be utilized fully. The real problem for the entrepreneur in this matter is that he will be facing a difficult trade-off between carrying excess capacity, sacrificing economies of scale and price cuts, which might deteriorate overall market conditions.

(b) The relationship between capital costs per unit of capacity and the vintage of plants depends on a number of conflicting influences. Capital charges might, on balance, even be *inversely* related to the vintage of plants, owing to inflationary effects (impact of price inflation on the costs of building plants and the impact of inflation on the user cost of capital).[17] But the entrepreneur has to weigh these effects against the *expected* future rate of inflation and the associated *differential* inflationary effects with respect to wages and prices. In this respect he will thus be faced with a trade-off between anticipated capital charges and labour productivity in the case of building at present against building in the future.

(c) The real problems are even more complicated by the disparity in productivity between sectors and industries within the economy at large. These effects may not always be fully appreciated by entrepreneurs. The lagging behind the trend of economic improvement by the industries outside the cluster of modern and advancing ones leads to an increase in prices in this "backward" sector. As a direct consequence the advancing sector is confronted with rising costs for its inputs, which leaves it with additional demands as far as productivity is concerned. An indirect consequence of the relative price increase in the "backward" sector is the negative impact on purchasing power in the economy at large; this hampers the expansion of the advancing sector on the side of demand.

One may wonder how it is possible that the less productive sector within the economy succeeds in transferring its productivity problems to the highly productive one. This cannot be explained without reference to the market conditions. A clarifying distinction which prevails in the Scandinavian economic literature is that between

---

[17] The cost-of-capital component is the more important, since the real long-term debt-to-equity ratio of firms increases alongside the enlargement of their scale of production.

"sheltered" and "exposed" industries [e.g. Aukrust (1975)]. The former are not exposed to (international) competition to the same extent as the latter. This difference is related to the existence of local/national monopolies in the case of building and services, and the practice of outright protection and imperfections of competition in other cases. The concept of sheltered markets is the economic reflection of environmental barriers to which reference was made above. It may be observed that the advancing industries mainly belong to the "exposed" category, while "backward" industries can be ranked among the "sheltered" ones.

(6) In an expanding economy capital formation plays a key role. A high level of gross investment is an essential condition for the advancement of modernization in production. At the same time the expansion of demand is crucial for the absorption of the enlarged production, which results from a high level of gross investment. This twofold condition gives rise to a process which was labelled by various authors [e.g. Haberler (1937); Salter (1969)] as "cumulative and self-reinforcing". Owing to the uneven rates of technical change and associated economies of scale between industries, environmental obstacles accumulate and the advancing sector has to bear the burden of the productivity demands. In order to meet these demands the scale of production has to be enlarged continuously. This may be an effective response for some time. Once it has become accepted and relied on as normal practice, the anticipation of inflation is incorporated in the decision-making, which means that bills drawn on the future become even more prominent. To stop this practice would, however, raise a cost barrier for the individual entrepreneur who would be ready to consider this alternative; there is no other way than to go on with it. The level of R&D and capital required to stay in business competitively increases substantially. Thus, the volume of sales required to amortize the cost of R&D and capital is steadily increasing, while the time during which this must occur is decreasing. Demand must keep in line with this quickening pace of technological development in order to avoid a situation of overcapacity. To avoid this is difficult not only because of the competitive pressure, but also because it is hard to discriminate between temporary frictions which happen to disappear once demand has built up, and market disturbances of a more lasting nature. Once such structural problems do arise, the economic process is reversed while it remains "cumulative and self-reinforcing". A situation of structural excess capacity deprives firms, even the most efficient, of protection by economies of scale, large plant size, established market and distribution links.

Under normal conditions these advantages can be broken down only by innovations on the part of competitors; if the market deteriorates these advantages cease to be effective. The profit margin is affected by price cuts and capital productivity by underutilization of the capital stock. In either case – and the two may easily go hand in hand – the rate of return is put under pressure. This may lead to a retardation or even decline of economic activity; at first in specific sectors, but with repercussions for the economy at large at a later stage because growth loses its "momentum".

It is essential to recognize that no appeal has to be made to overproduction and excess capacity as an overall phenomenon; it suffices to discern it as a pattern which applies to the advancing sector within the economy. This is all the more important with regard to the future path of investment since the diagnosis implies that economic recovery, notably the recovery of investment at the macro level, will to a large extent be contingent on prospects for the advancing sector.

4.3. The empirical evidence

4.3.1. A note on the availability of empirical evidence

The empirical evidence to sustain the hypothesis proposed in the foregoing section can only be scattered, in the sense that it covers only specific periods and/or countries. This is a serious drawback that any author has to face, because a systematic documentation of capital utilization, for instance, is lacking. To make the best of it, we have tried to rely on empirical findings of a more structural nature such as relationships which happen to be more robust in time and across countries [e.g. Teitel (1975, section IV, table 3) and Banerji (1978, section 4, table 2)]. We shall concentrate on three issues:

(a) growth and the diversity of the manufacturing sector;

(b) the establishment of economies of scale in manufacturing and related issues; and

(c) the behaviour of capital formation in time alongside economic expansion at the macro level.

The first two issues do form indispensable elements with regard to the validity of the hypothesis, while the argument implies that capital formation is the crucial factor in long-term change and we expect to find periods with increasing capital formation to be terminated by a fall in capital productivity and an associated fall in profit rates.

4.3.2. Growth and the interindustry differences

The most direct evidence at this point is provided by Salter (1969) who made the interindustry differences a central issue of his approach and produced striking empirical findings (table 19.10).

Industries prove to differ greatly in their capacity to enlarge production and to improve productivity. The gains from increased productivity tend to be distributed in the long run to customers by means of price reductions, while "industrial backwardness" expresses itself clearly in price increases. Such differentials *reinforce* the interindustry differences in cost and productivity patterns. The impact of these differences may be even more convincingly demonstrated by a comparison of the five or ten industries with the largest increases in output (table 19.11).

Table 19.10

Changes in output, prices and employment, and correlation with movement of output per head (cross section of UK industries 1924–1950).

Changes in	Coefficient of variation across industries (%)	Correlation with output per head (r)
Output	87.2	+0.81
Price	29.1	−0.88
Employment	50.1	+0.61

Source: Salter (1969, table 23).

The advancing industries are responsible for most of the total increase in output and for a large part of the increase in productivity; without their contribution the increase in prices would have been much greater. There is no doubt that the disparity between industries does not fail to affect the price structure. These findings have been fully confirmed by Armstrong [Armstrong (1974, pp. 51–52)]. His sample also refers to the UK, but covers a different period (1948–1969). The general validity of this phenomenon, including the change in the price structure, may be inferred from a study of the sectoral change in six European countries covering the period 1960–1973 [Commission of the EC (1978, pp. 102–114)].

A special role is played by the producer-goods industries.[18] A breakdown of the 28 industries in Salter's cross section for the UK into a sector of consumer-goods and

Table 19.11

Changes in total output, employment, output per head and prices; twenty-eight industries, United Kingdom 1924–1950 (1924 = 100; weight base = 1935).

	Output	Employ-ment	Output per head	Net prices
1. All industries in sample	185	94	196	158
2. Excluding the five industries with the largest increases in output	118	82	145	209
3. Excluding the ten industries with the largest increases in output	103	77	134	236

Source: Salter (1969, table 24).

[18] Of the 28 individual industries reported by Salter, 17 were classified in the category of consumer-goods industries and 11 in the category of producer-goods industries. Consumer goods include all (semi)finished goods which are (largely) bought by consumers for consumption in the home. Producer goods include raw materials, semimanufactured articles and capital goods in the form in which they are used by manufacturers.

producer-goods industries shows a much higher average rate of growth of total output in the producer-goods sector, a (slightly) higher rate of growth of output per head and a lower rate of increase of price. This might be expected on the strength of the observation that it is the technical advance in the producer-goods industries that lowers the price of producer goods relative to labour and induces substitution of producer goods for labour. However, the most striking characteristic is the much greater *variability* of the producer-goods sector in terms of the growth of total output. Special attention to this phenomenon seems appropriate.

We referred above (section 2.1) to the shift within the manufacturing sector from consumer-goods industries to producer-goods industries. These shifts must, of course, be interpreted in terms of higher rates of growth of the producer-goods industries, since the disproportionate development is fully contingent on the expansion of total output. Hoffmann (1955) and Frickey (1947) provide valuable information on the development of individual industries and commodities for long periods. Hoffmann introduced the distinction between producer-goods and consumer-goods industries explicitly and made it a central issue of his analysis. This same distinction can, of course, be applied to the data on individual items provided by Frickey, who did not include this aspect in his investigation. These calculations have been carried out in the context of this analysis with two aims. The first is to check the Kondratieff cycle at the individual commodity level – the results have been reported above – and the second is the breakdown of the manufacturing sector into two subsectors.[19] This can only be achieved with data which are processed at the individual level, enabling a cross-sectional analysis.

As expected, we find a higher mean "coefficient of growth" when we average across producer goods (table 19.12). But the greater diversity of growth patterns for a given period (especially shorter periods) within the producer-goods sector and the pronounced instability of growth patterns in time in that sector are really significant. These features can be explained in terms of shorter lifetimes within the sector of producer goods as the result of heavier substitution pressure. The comparison between established and new industries elucidates this point. In the consumer-goods sector there is virtually no difference between the mean rates of growth and only a limited difference between the coefficients of variation, whereas in the producer-goods sector the new industries reach high mean values, while many established industries decline, thus contributing to a wide variation in growth rates. The same features can be observed for the US as table 19.13 shows.

It is remarkable to note how periods of high rates of growth for producer goods alternate with those of low rates within the distinct sectors. These alternations happen

---

[19] Of the 34 individual commodities reported by Frickey, 16 were classified into the subsector of producer-goods industries and 15 into the subsector of consumer-goods industries, while 3 agricultural producer goods were left out.

Table 19.12

Cross section of UK industries (1819—1935) – mean "coefficients of growth" averaged across individual industries.[a]

	Consumer-goods industries		Producer-goods industries	
	Mean	Coefficient of variation	Mean	Coefficient of variation
1819–1913	1.78 (21)	0.81	2.25 (12)	1.095
1855–1913	1.52 (23)	1.08	2.04 (22)	2.74
1855–1913 (only new industries)	2.20 (2)	0.90	3.23 (10)	2.68
1923–1935	2.30 (25)	1.87	−1.385 (25)	8.96

[a] Number of industries entered in the cross section is reported in the column "Mean" in parentheses.
Source: Hoffmann (1955, table 12).

to compensate each other and therefore leave virtually no traces in the aggregate production indices. Here again the diversity for a given period and the instability in time is much more pronounced for the producer goods. The patterns of growth rates, after averaging across industries, seem to follow a Kondratieff pattern within the producer-goods industries. It should be noted, however, that virtually no *single* index displays this pattern, nor do the aggregate indices, so that the long-wave pattern results

Table 19.13

Cross section of commodities for the US (1861–1913) – rates of growth averaged across individual commodities.[a]

	Consumer goods (N = 15)		Producer goods (N = 16)		Production for manufacture
	Mean	Coefficient of variation	Mean	Coefficient of variation	Aggregate index
1861–1873	9.37	0.548	16.06	0.881	6.02
1874–1894	8.17	0.949	6.83	0.800	5.42
1896–1913	3.96	0.727	10.03	1.623	5.28
1861–1913	5.20	0.625	6.89	0.468	4.82

[a] Rates of growth estimated from linear trends fitted to the logs of the volume indices.
Source: Frickey (1947, table 1 for individual items, table 6 for aggregate index).

from the particular weighting procedure. (Equal weights have been allotted to single commodities.)

We conclude from this section that the interindustry differences can be established beyond doubt. The producer-goods sector proves to be specifically liable to features like diversity and instability in a long-term perspective. It seems plausible enough to look for the expansions and contractions of the producer-goods industries superimposed on the trend of an increasing share of those industries within the manufacturing sector as clues for major movements in the level of economic activity [e.g. Commission of the EC (1978, pp. 69, 108–109)]. This leaves the contribution of the consumer-goods sector, notably the durables, unaffected.

4.3.3. Economies of scale and related issues

Three issues have to be dealt with under this heading, because they play an essential role in the basic argument formulated above.

(1) Economies of scale in production. (a) Their establishment as a significant phenomenon; (b) the change in the values of the minimum efficient scale (m.e.s.) in time; and (c) the (non)uniformity among industries.

(2) The relation between capital intensity and returns to scale.

(3) The relation between technical change and international competition.

(1a) *Economies of scale in production; their establishment.* The economic literature on this subject is not extensive, but in a number of recent publications insight into the matter at hand is provided. The most detailed source of information is to be found in Pratten (1971), the data given by Scherer (1973) refer to different countries, while Teitel (1975) concentrates mainly on process plants. All three sources refer to technical economies, i.e. the cost data to which the estimates relate exclude the cost of marketing and distribution. More detailed information on the coverage of these studies is given in table 19.14. These sources put the matter beyond doubt: economies of scale in production do exist and they are substantial. For process industries the main sources of these economies are the reduction of capital costs per unit of capacity and the lower operating costs for larger units, while for engineering industries the economies are mainly associated with the spread of initial costs of developing new products and with the use of more efficient techniques for longer production runs.

(1b) *Economies of scale in production; increase of m.e.s. in time.* The same sources (see 1a) provide supplementary information on the increase of the value of m.e.s. in time. The range of scale to which economies of scale apply increases in time. Scherer (1973) and Teitel (1975) report supplementary data on a number of cases and find an upward trend. The same holds for Pratten (1971) who, in addition to his own empirical research, made a comparison of his findings with earlier estimates by J. S. Bain for the same industries which confirms the upward trend.

Table 19.14

Coverage of three studies of the economies of scale in production.

	Unit	Country	Period	Number of cases
Pratten (1971)	Production process ("narrow range of products")	UK	1969	25 production processes (with breakdowns into more homogeneous products)
Scherer (1973)	Industry (three-digit)	six countries (North America and Europe)	ca. 1965	12 industries for each of the 6 countries
Teitel (1975)	Products	international (engineering data)	1957–1965	15 products

(1c) *Economies of scale in production; (non)uniformity among industries.* Pratten (1971) is most outspoken on the subject of uniformity among industries: economies of scale are certainly not uniform among industries. For textiles (not the whole range), bricks, bicycles and clothing the economies of scale are severely limited.

The author of the present paper has made a summary of findings on the US consumer-goods industries (three-digit level) reported in the literature [Van der Zwan (1977b)]. The various factors[20] that were taken into account turn out to span an "industry-space" in which a limited number of *clusters* of industries are clearly discernible. One of these clusters can undoubtedly be identified as the group of "backward"[21] industries, as opposed to the cluster of "advanced" industries. The "backward" cluster comprises the same type of industries as identified by Pratten: clothing, footwear, leather products, furniture and the like. Banerji (1978, table 2) produces just the same industries as low-ranking in average plant size among a sample of 20 two-digit level producer-goods and consumer-goods industries. Nonuniformity among industries has been made a key issue in Salter's analysis. He based himself on data restricted to output and inputs. His implications with regard to uneven rates of technical change and associated economies of scale can be considered as fully confirmed by direct observation with regard to the basic underlying industry characteristics.

(2) *The relation between capital intensity and returns to scale.* Banerji (1978) has tested the hypothesis that returns to scale are associated with the capital-intensive expansion path. To this end he has related size of plants (derived from the estimated size distribution within industries) to capital intensity (intraindustry nonwage value

[20] Besides the minimum efficient scale (share of the market corresponding to value measure), growth of demand, absolute capital requirements, concentration, profit rate and cost fixity.

[21] "Backward" industries score low on each of the characteristics employed.

added per employee) in a variation across countries which differ in level of development. The association proves to be statistically significant in an overall sense as well as for a majority of the individual industries in the sample. This result could be expected on the basis of the increase in the value of m.e.s. in time (see 1b), given the fact that capital intensity (also within industries) is positively related to level of development. This movement in plant size with time may be generalized to a variation in level of development on the basis of Banerji's findings and demonstrated by him to be explicitly linked with capital intensity.

(3) *The relation between technical change and international competition.* This relation has not yet received the attention it deserves. Direct evidence can be found in Soete (1978), Hesse (1974) and Commission of the EC (1978), while Cripps and Tarling (1973) and Scherer (1973) present convincing indirect evidence. Soete has shown that the international competition among developed countries has increased considerably since 1960. Foreign penetration of Western domestic markets proves in the first place to be the result of competition among developed countries. "Low wage" competition is still weak except in clothing and resource-intensive industries. In an attempt to discriminate between different explanatory factors, Soete has tested the export performance of 22 developed countries for 40 separate industrial branches against their foreign patenting activity.[22] For many process and engineering industries, notably those where technical change takes place continuously, significant results were obtained. In other industries which rely for their improvement to a great extent on innovation in the capital-goods sector the results were nonsignificant.

In his analysis of intraindustry trade in 52 product classes between 13 industrial countries, Hesse (1974) found that among the determinants product differentiation, technical progress and economies of scale have gained in importance over the period 1953–1970; these factors are able to substantiate a large part of intraindustry trade.

In a report on sectoral change in the European Community [Commission of the EC (1978, pp. 108–114)] it is shown that the advancing manufacturing industries within six European countries are fully exposed to international trade and competition and that this is increasingly the case. From 1960 to 1973 the total volume of exports and imports within these sectors has increased considerably, also in a relative sense.

Cripps and Tarling (1973, pp. 32–33), in search of an explanatory hypothesis compatible with their empirical findings, point to the possible importance of a highly competitive export sector for the achievement of rapid productivity growth. They suppose that the pressure of competition in international trade has increased, especially since 1965, and that the extent to which countries were able to build up such a highly competitive export sector has varied greatly between countries. This hypothesis fits Soete's findings remarkably well.

---

[22] Because of various operational problems this relationship was tested for exports to the US and corresponding patenting activity, thus assuming that the US is the world's leading inventive centre.

Scherer (1973) has demonstrated that international and interindustry plant size variations are associated systematically with the degree to which sales are concentrated in the hands of a few leading producers. This positive link between plant size and concentration exhibits special significance for the European nations. Since one can safely assume that concentration is much higher within the export sector than within the domestic sector of production, plant size and consequently technical change are linked with exposure to international competition.

A large part of the interindustry differences which play a dominant role in the structuralist approach can thus be related to the extent to which industries are "exposed".

4.3.4. Economic development in time perspective

Capital formation can be regarded as the crucial factor in long-term change. On the basis of the hypothesis put forward, we expect to find periods with an increasing capital–labour ratio to be terminated by a fall in capital productivity and an associated fall in profit rates due to excess capacity. We try to verify this statement empirically and turn for that purpose towards long-term data on the capital formation and capital productivity of Germany and the US, and towards data on the more recent international situation.

Evidence on the German development. We present the statistical evidence on the German development first (tables 19.15 and 19.16). We may observe from the data given in table 19.15 that prolonged periods of high investment alternate with prolonged periods of low investment. Major depressions manifest themselves in the investment data for two periods, 1875–1885 and 1925–1938.[23] We find these reflected in declining capital productivity and an increasing wage share. To complete these observations we point out that the wage share of national income is firmly related to the return on capital,[24] so that a rising wage share correlates with a decline in return on capital, as turns out to be the case in the distinct periods. The depressions also reflect themselves in employment, especially in the manufacturing sector, as table 19.16 illustrates.

It can hardly be doubted that this specific configuration of features indicates that the depressions were essentially of an overinvestment type. It should be noted that the period of prolonged high investment (1896–1900 to 1906–1910) that also showed signs of a decline in capital productivity did not display a rise in wage share (on the contrary), nor a decline in return on capital, nor a cut in employment. This period of a rising capital–labour ratio apparently differed from the two that led to major depressions. The difference must be attributed to a disparate situation with regard to

---

[23] The latter depression is beyond further comment. The former one can also be inferred from general data on production and productivity [e.g. Hoffmann (1965, tables 1 and 5a)].

[24] Wage share and return on capital derived from Hoffmann (1965, tables 23 and 34, respectively). First differences of both series during the period 1850–1913 display a coefficient of determination of 0.66.

Table 19.15

Capital formation, capital productivity and wage share of national income 1850–1959 in Germany; deviations from trend.[a]

	Percentage share of net investment in NNP at current prices	Change in labour productivity due to change in capital productivity (differences in constant prices; Mark)	Percentage wage share of national income
	(1)	(2)	(3)
1850–54	0.1		4.6
1855–59	−1.9	−9	0.6
1860–64	1.7 ⎱	14	−1.75
1865–69	−0.8 ⎰		−1.9
1870–74	3.0	24	1.0
1875–79	−0.4	−45	3.35
1880–84	−2.5	−31	0.1
1885–89	−0.6	4	−0.2
1890–94	−0.7	0	−2.2
1895–99	2.0	20	−3.05
1900–04	0.7	−43	−3.4
1905–09	1.8	−15	−4.7
1910–13	1.3	7	−4.85
1925–29	−3.8	60	11.95
1930–34	−13.9	−309	21.85
1935–38	−2.5		3.0
1950–54	0.8		−0.7
1955–59	1.9	227	−1.8

Source: Hoffmann (1965, (1): table 36 (3); (2): table 4 (3) and (3): table 23).

[a] The series given have been derived after correction for a linear trend in time. The following trends have been fitted to the original series in Hoffmann (1965).

(1) $y = 9.32 + 0.35t$; $\bar{R}^2 = 0.56$ (1930–34 observation deleted from the statistical fitting; $N = 17$);

(2) no trend fitted because the series in question does not show a trend;

(3) $y = 77.43 − 0.13t$; $\bar{R}^2 = −0.02$ (1930–34 observation deleted from the statistical fitting; $N = 17$).

In these equations y represents the variables given in the three columns of the table.

capital formation and utilization. A decline in capital productivity can arise from the following two different causes.

(1) The existence of idle capacity of structural dimensions, created either by overambitious investment programmes, induced by the enlargement of the scale of production, or by the penetration of new industries which supersede established industries. Both circumstances find their roots in technological factors. The enlargement of the scale and diversity of production can assume such forms that the market is unable to absorb production at reasonable capacity utilization;

(2) The allocation of capital in the direction of less profitable investment outlets from where a reallocation in more profitable directions remains possible before the situa-

Table 19.16

Employment situation in Germany during periods of investment depressions.[a]

	Manufacturing sector (employment as a percentage share of total working population)			Economy as a whole (working population as a percentage share of total population)		
	Observed	Expected	Deviation	Observed	Expected	Deviation
1871/75–1881/85						
Level	27.95	29.00	−1.05	43.7	44.15	−0.45
Change	+1.90	+3.70	−1.80	+0.7	+0.30	+0.40
1925/27–1931/33						
Level	34.35	36.85	−2.50	45.3	45.80	−0.50
Change	−6.70	−1.30	−5.40	−8.8	+0.20	−9.00

[a] Both variables derived from Hoffmann (1965, table 7, columns 3 and 9). The first variable is related linearly to the inverse of the product (constant prices) per capita [Hoffmann (1965, table 6, column 9 ÷ table 7, column 8/9]: $y = 46.1 - 6907 \, 1/x$; $\bar{R}^2 = 0.86159$. The second variable is related linearly to time: $y = 41.75 + 0.03t$; $\bar{R}^2 = 0.19$. The same phenomenon illustrated in the table can be inferred from Hoffmann (1965, table 1).

tion becomes chronic and the price-cost structure in broad sectors is affected for a longer period.

The latter of these causes fits the case of the period 1896–1910. The fact that Germany managed to enlarge its share of world exports during this same period [Woodruff (1975, table XXII)] is an important factor.

Evidence on the US development. A discussion of the long-term economic developments in the US can take its starting-point in the observation of a trend in two crucial factors of economic growth, namely the capital–labour ratio and the capital productivity index:[25]

$$\ln \text{(capital–labour ratio)} \quad = 4.2796 + 0.0076t, \qquad \bar{R}^2 = 0.6718, \qquad (5)$$
$$(1889\text{–}1955)$$

$$\ln \text{(capital productivity index)} = 4.1772 + 0.0112t, \qquad \bar{R}^2 = 0.7325 \qquad (6)$$
$$(1889\text{–}1955)$$

A positive trend in time in the capital productivity index is a finding which is specific to the US, since in European countries mainly constant capital coefficients are reported [e.g. Hoffman (1965, pp. 21–30) and OECD (1977a, pp. 299–301)].

The positive trends in both indices suggest a positive relation between them, which can in fact be read from the following regression estimate:

[25] Broersma (1978, p. 109). Based on indices derived from Kendrick (1973), included in Broersma (1978, p. 132).

$$\ln (\text{capital productivity index}) = 1.7270 + 0.6238 \ \ln (\text{capital–labour ratio}), \qquad (7)$$
$$\bar{R}^2 = 0.1841.$$

It would be misleading, however, to conclude from this finding that the relation between the two factors is a (weak) positive one. The opposite will prove to be the case. As often occurs in simple correlation analysis, we are confronted with an *induced* relationship, which in this case can obviously be attributed to the common positive trend component. Correction for this component is therefore indicated. Inspection of the scatter diagrams shows that fitting a trend is unsatisfactory because the movements with time are quite heterogeneous; transformation by means of determining the first differences seems to be more effective:

$$\Delta(\text{capital productivity index}) = 1.9181 - 0.9024 \ \Delta(\text{capital–labour ratio}), \qquad (8)$$
(1889–1955 year-to-year $\qquad \bar{R}^2 = 0.6605.$
basis)

Since the first differences have been determined on a year-to-year basis, they still contain many different elements, namely short-term and long-term influences. These have to be separated. With the aid of reference dates of business cycles,[26] the intra- and inter-business cycle movements have been identified by determining first the differences for consecutive peaks and troughs and then for consecutive peaks and consecutive troughs. The first of these differences can be regarded as specifically indicative of business cycle influences, while the latter two can be expected to reflect the long-term influences:

$$\Delta(\text{capital productivity index}) = -0.17902 - 0.6822 \ \Delta(\text{capital–labour ratio}) \quad (9)$$
(from peak to consecutive $\qquad \bar{R}^2 = 0.79721;$
trough; $N = 14$)

$$\Delta(\text{capital productivity index}) = 4.7564 - 0.7983 \ \Delta(\text{capital–labour ratio}) \quad (10)$$
(from peak to consecutive $\qquad \bar{R}^2 = 0.24729;$
peak; $N = 13$)

$$\Delta(\text{capital productivity index}) = 5.0594 - 0.8348 \ \Delta(\text{capital–labour ratio}) \quad (11)$$
(from trough to consecutive $\qquad \bar{R}^2 = 0.87140$
trough; $N = 13$)

It is quite clear that the capital–labour ratio and the capital productivity index are firmly negatively related, both in a short- and a long-term sense. It would be premature,

[26] Burns and Mitchell (1946, table 16, p. 78). This table ends with the trough in 1938. With regard to the period 1889–1938 the capital productivity index proves to be a perfect indicator of business cycles; any of the 14 peaks and troughs which can be observed in this index during that period coincide with the (calendar year) reference dates indicated in the table. Inference of later peaks and troughs from the index itself therefore seems to be warranted.

however, to conclude from this statistical relationship that there is a causal link. The relation is open to ambiguity; the two factors might also reflect a common underlying cause: the level of economic activity. Capital productivity is of course very sensitive to fluctuations in economic activity, while the demand for labour will be adjusted sooner to the level of economic activity than the capital stock, resulting in fluctuations of capital to labour. If we also take the level of economic activity and the movement of the capital stock into account, the situation becomes clearer. Deviations from trend values averaged for five-year periods [e.g. Broersma (1978, pp. 100–111)] give rise to an unambiguous configuration of events: a gradual increase in economic activity and capital formation, accompanied at first (ca. 1900–1920) by a standstill in capital intensity and productivity. During the Twenties economic expansion continued, but with a sharp increase in capital intensity, followed by a dramatic fall in capital productivity and subsequently a complete breakdown, from which a recovery was not possible before the Forties. These long-term movements find their reflection in the relationship between the growth of the capital stock and capital productivity:

$$
\begin{array}{lll}
\text{capital productivity} & = 1.6177 - 0.6178 & \text{capital stock} \\
\text{(deviation from trend,} & & \text{(Id.)} \\
\text{averaged for 5-year} & & \\
\text{periods 1890–1954;} & & \\
N = 13) & & \bar{R}^2 = 0.31674.
\end{array}
\tag{12}
$$

The accompanying movements in the wage share of national income and the profit rate (before the actual depression) can be read from Lieftinck (1931, pp. 361–365) who sought an explanation of these phenomena in the increase of capital intensity giving rise to excess capacity (e.g. p. 202). A more documented survey of the capacity situation within industries before the depression can be found in League of Nations (1931).

Evidence on the recent international situation. Needless to say, we face a major depression of the world economy at the time of writing. There is ample proof of this depression and its international impact; merely as an illustration of this statement we give information on the growth of the national product (volume) for a sample of eight industrial countries (table 19.17). Since it has been realized now that the retardation of growth made itself felt as early as the late Sixties–early Seventies, we make a distinction in periods accordingly.[27]

By way of a preliminary indication of the role played by capital formation, we also provide data on the development of the share of investment in table 19.17. Generally speaking there is, of course, a positive relationship between investment and production,

[27] The employment of such a sample would not be warranted without more thorough background information. This information can be found in Schatz (1974, pp. 122–134), who employed a total sample of 18 countries, from which he derived subsamples. Among these subsamples is the one we present here. Schatz covered the period 1950–1969. We can make use of his findings to check our sample on random fluctuations and subsequently take more recent information into account. We also wish to point out that in OECD (1977a, pp. 295–307), the McCracken report, the same sample is used as the one presented here.

Table 19.17

National product and investment; data for a sample of eight leading industrial countries.[a]

	GNP at constant (1963) prices – average rate of percentage increase; annual figure across countries			Gross investment[b] at factor costs and constant (1963) prices – as a share of GDP		
	Mean (M)	S.D. (σ)	Variation (σ/M)	Mean (M)	S.D. (σ)	Variation (σ/M)
1953–63 (1958–62)	5.05	1.97	0.39	17.6	3.87	0.22
1963–68 (1963–67)	5.5	2.20	0.40	19.3	4.61	0.24
1968–73 (1968–72)	5.3	1.89	0.36	20.6	6.15	0.30
1974	1.5	2.27	1.51			
1975	−1.8	1.69	0.94			

[a] For a list of countries included in the sample, see Table 18.
[b] Investment excluding residential construction.

and table 19.17 exemplifies this as far as the period 1953–1968 is concerned. After 1968 investment still increases significantly, while the rate of growth of production slows and consequently capital productivity declines [e.g. Schatz (1974, table 19; capital coefficients)].

The relation between investment and production may conveniently be checked against the variability between countries within a certain period and also against differences in time between countries. For that purpose we need the data at the level of individual countries (table 19.18). The relation between investment and production can be judged on the basis of the statistical fit of simple linear equations (table 19.19). The outcomes of the cross-sectional and the longitudinal analysis reinforce one another. Between 1953 and 1968 we find a stable relation,[28] implying – roughly speaking – a constant productivity of capital. After 1968 – when investment still expands relative to production – the relation becomes unstable and even vanishes, indicating an apparent decline of capital productivity.

This finding does not stand alone. Data on the rate of return on capital for various countries within the sample show a marked decline from about 1968 [e.g. Van der Zwan (1975) and OECD (1977a, pp. 303–307) for a summary of findings], while capacity utilization rates also decline from 1969–1970, with a temporary recovery in 1972–1973 [e.g. OECD (1977b)]. Further evidence suggests that the rate of scrapping has accelerated and that investment patterns have changed since 1970, showing investment in machinery and equipment rising relative to investment in expansion of capacity [e.g. OECD (1977a, pp. 295–303)]. This configuration of phenomena related to capital

[28] The same holds for the estimates by Schatz (1974, table 21, regression numbers 8–9).

Table 19.18

National product and investment; a moving cross-section of leading industrial countries 1953–1973.

	Gross national product at constant (1963) prices – rate of percentage increase; annual averages			Gross investment as a share of GDP [a]		
	1953–63	1963–68	1968–73	1958–62	1963–67	1968–72
US	2.9	5.1	3.6	13.0	14.2	14.3
Japan	9.2	11.0	9.5	25.9	29.5	35.2
Belgium	3.6	4.2	5.5	16.1	18.0	18.2
The Netherlands	4.5	5.6	5.3	20.8	22.9	23.3
France	5.2	5.3	6.1	15.2	17.9	19.7
Italy	5.8	5.0	4.3	17.1	15.6	15.3
GFR	6.3	4.4	5.1	18.5	19.9	20.9
UK	2.9	3.2	2.8	14.4	16.2	17.8
Average (unweighted)	5.05	5.5	5.3	17.6	19.3	20.6

[a] Investment excluding residential construction; investment and GDP both at factor costs and at constant (1963) prices.

formation points to overinvestment, especially within the advancing sector of the economy [e.g. Commission of the EC (1978, p. 128)].

4.3.5. Conclusion

We feel confident that the empirical evidence on the economic structure and structural change sustains the hypothesis developed in section 4.2; in any case this hypothesis is compatible with the empirical findings.

5. General conclusion

The notion of a long wave which governs economic life at large has always had an appeal. Authors in the monetary field had pointed to cyclical movements of a long-term character long before Kondratieff introduced his formalized cycle with an approximate duration of fifty years. He claimed general significance for this long wave, and in his subsequent explanatory model he sought to endogenize crucial societal developments and related these to economic factors in a fully interdependent system.

Kondratieff's "daring hypothesis" has been questioned ever since its introduction. He has been criticized for a selection bias in demonstrating the cycle, while his explanation has been challenged because of its purely speculative character.

Table 19.19

Relation between investment and production; variation between countries (table 19.18).

Cross-sectional analysis

$y = a + bx$

where

y = rate of increase of GNP
x = investment as a share of GDP

	a	b	R^2	$\bar{R}^2$
1953–63 (1958–62)	−2.616	0.435	0.7294	0.6843
1963–68 (1963–67)	−2.310	0.404	0.7142	0.6666
1968–73 (1968–72)	−0.374	0.274	0.7999	0.7666

Longitudinal analysis

$\Delta y = a + b\Delta x$

where

Δy = change in the rate of change of GNP per country
Δx = change in the rate of investment relative to GDP per country

	a	b	R^2	$\bar{R}^2$
1953/62–1963/67				
including FR	−0.252	0.410	0.2062	0.0739
excluding FR	0.135	0.369	0.3265	0.1918
1963/67–1968/72	0.042	−0.184	0.1129	−0.0349

During the postwar boom not only the economy flourished, but also the idea of its manageability. The conviction gained ground that major cyclical movements had been overcome.

The recent depression has led to a revival of the long wave. This paper is concerned with a twofold problem:

(i) the empirical assessment of a long wave in the strict sense as introduced by Kondratieff; and

(ii) the underlying causes of major depressions.

For an answer to the first problem a testing procedure is proposed and applied to statistical data for three leading industrial countries and world production and trade. It proved possible to reject Kondratieff's claim of nearly fixed duration and general impact on the basis of the evidence which is presented. However, this finding does not imply that the existence of recurrent depressions is questioned, so that the second problem remains topical. An answer to this problem is sought on the strength of a structuralist approach. In this paper an attempt is made to substantiate this approach empirically. A configuration of features of economic growth is outlined in which uneven development in time and disparity between industries play a key role; a picture is given in which structural changes accompanying technical change are considered the essential phenomena. This system of thought draws more on the supply side of the economy for an explanation of the world's contemporary problems [e.g. Klein (1978)]. As a consequence of this view a recovery is not to be expected on the basis of a policy of demand management only. Control of production capacity, especially within the advanced sector of the economy, is a prerequisite for a more lasting improvement of investment expectations.

Lessons from the past are important and continuity in history may be striking, but a simple extrapolation of past evidence seems to lack historical subtlety. It is not impossible that the impact of technical change on economic growth will assume quite another form in the future from that experienced in the past. Microelectronics (microprocessors) for instance seem capable of improving efficiency without the need to enlarge the scale of production. This might open up an alternative route for economic growth, namely upgrading of products and services and levelling of the rate of improvement between industries because of new and more varied means of production control. These changes on the supply side should be matched by a consistent movement towards a greater and more stable awareness of quality on the demand side (i.e. the final consumer) in order to result in more *balanced* growth. The idea that *sustained* growth could thus be realized is a challenging one, not least because it fits into the construct of improved control. But past evidence does not fail to label this idea wishful thinking. We are inclined to agree with Olson (1978, p. 80), who has pointed to a possible contradiction between balance and stability on the one hand and full realization of economic potential on the other. One may wonder whether an attempt to reap the economies of growth fully will be manageable within the limits of control. In the light of the present economic situation it would be fine if another period of more or less controlled growth could be attained, anyhow.

References

Armstrong, A., 1974, A programme for growth, vol. 12, Structural change in the British economy 1948–1968 (Chapman and Hall, London).
Aukrust, O., 1975, Inflation in the open economy: The Norwegian model (Working paper, Central Bureau of Statistics of Norway).
Banerji, R., 1978, Average size of plants in manufacturing and capital intensity, Journal of Development Economics 5, 155–166.
Broersma, Th.J., 1978, De lange golf in het economisch leven (VRB drukkerijen, Groningen).
Burns, A. F. and W. C. Mitchell, 1946, Measuring business cycles (National Bureau of Economic Research, New York).
Cairncross, A. K., 1962, Factors in economic development (Allen and Unwin, London).
Commission of the European Community, 1978, Group of independent experts, Sectoral change in the European Community (EC Directorate General for Industry, Brussels).

Cripps, T. F. and R. J. Tarling, 1973, Growth in advanced capitalist economies 1950–1970 (Cambridge University Press, Cambridge).

Deane, P. and W. A. Cole, 1967, British economic growth 1688–1959 (Cambridge University Press, London).

Frickey, E., 1947, Production in the United States 1860–1914 (Cambridge, Mass.).

Groot, A. D. de, 1961, Methodologie (Mouton, The Hague).

Haberler, G., 1937, Prosperity and depression (League of Nations, Geneva).

Hesse, H., 1974, Hypotheses for the explanation of trade between industrial countries, 1953–1970, in H. Giersch, ed., The international division of labour (J. C. B. Mohr, Tübingen).

Hoffman, W. G., 1931, Stadien und Typen der Industrialisierung (Jena).

Hoffman, W. G., 1955, British industry 1700–1950 (Basil Blackwell, Oxford).

Hoffman, W. G., 1965, Das Wachstum der deutschen Wirthschaft seit der Mitte des 19. Jahrhunderts (Springer-Verlag, Berlin).

Kendrick, J. W., 1973, Postwar productivity trends in the United States (NBER, New York).

Klein, L. R., 1978, The supply side, American Economic Review 68, 1–7.

Kondratieff, N. D., 1926, Die langen Wellen der Konjunktur, Archiv für Sozialwissenschaft und Sozialpolitik 56, 573–609.

Kondratieff, N. D., 1935, The long waves in economic life, Review of Economic Statistics 17, 105–115.

Kuznets, S., 1929, Retardation of industrial growth. Reprinted in: Economic change (Norton & Company, New York, 1953).

Kuznets, S., 1940, Book Review, American Economic Review 30, 250–271.

Kuznets, S., 1957, Quantitative aspects of the economic growth of nations: Industrial distribution of national product and labor force, Economic Development and Cultural Change 5, 3–111.

League of Nations, 1931, Le Cours et les phases de la dépression économique mondiale (Geneva).

Lewis, W. A., 1952, World production, prices and trade, The Manchester School of Economic and Social Studies 20, 105–138.

Lieftinck, P., 1931, Moderne struktuurveranderingen in de industrie in de Verenigde Staten van Amerika (J. B. Wolters, Groningen).

Mandel, E., 1972, Der Spätkapitalismus (Suhrkamp, Frankfurt am Main).

Menderhausen, H., 1937, Methods of computing and eliminating changing seasonal fluctuations, Econometrica 5, 243–262.

Mills, F. C., 1926, A hypothesis concerning the duration of the business cycles, Journal of the American Statistical Association 21, 447–457.

Mitchell, W. C., 1927, Business cycles: The problem and its setting (National Bureau of Economic Research, New York).

Mitchell, W. C., 1946, Measuring business cycles (National Bureau of Economic Research, New York).

OECD, 1977a, A report to the OECD by a group of independent experts, Towards full employment and price stability (OECD, Paris).

OECD, 1977b, Future investment and economic recovery (Secretariat paper CPE/WP2(77)6, Paris).

Olson, M., 1978, The political economy of comparative growth rates (Paper mimeographed, Department of Economics, University of Maryland).

Pratten, C. F., 1971, Economies of scale in manufacturing industry (Cambridge University Press, Cambridge).

Quételet, Ad., 1869, Physique sociale – essai sur le développement des facultés de l'homme (Muquardt, Bruxelles).

Salter, W. E. G., 1969, Productivity and technical change (Cambridge University Press, Cambridge).

Schatz, K.-W., 1974, Kieler Studien vol. 128, Wachstum und Strukturwandel der deutschen Wirtschaft im internationalen Verbund (J. C. B. Mohr, Tübingen).

Scherer, F. M., 1973, The determinants of industrial plant sizes in six nations, Review of Economics and Statistics 55, 135–145.

Soete, Luc, 1978, International competition, innovation and employment (Paper, mimeographed, University of Antwerp).

Svennilson, I., 1954, Growth and stagnation in the European economy (UN Economic Commission for

Europe, Geneva).

Teitel, S., 1975, Economies of scale and size of plant, Journal of Common Market Studies 13, 92–115.

Tilanus, C. B., 1968, Het rekenkundig gemiddeld stijgingspercentage – een ondoelmatige groei-indicator, Statistica Neerlandica 22, 133–139.

Woodruff, W., 1975, America's impact on the world (MacMillan, London).

Zwan, A. van der, 1975, Dalend rendement op geinvesteerd vermogen; conflicterende visies op een omstreden verchijnsel, Economisch-Statistische Berichten 60, 656–660, 680–685.

Zwan, A. van der, 1976, Over de vergroting van de omweg in de produktie, Economisch-Statistische Berichten 61, 60–65, 80–83, 117–122.

Zwan, A. van der, 1977a, Na de smalle marges van het beleid, Economisch-Statistische Berichten 62, 244–248, 268–277, 300–302.

Zwan, A. van der, 1977b, Advertising, market structure and performance: A re-interpretation of empirical findings on the compatibility of advertising and competition, in: C. A. Bochove et al., Modeling for government and business (Martinus Nijhoff, Leiden).

Chapter 20

COMMENT ON VAN DER ZWAN'S PAPER*

J. J. VAN DUIJN

Graduate School of Management, Delft

Professor Van der Zwan's highly interesting and stimulating paper consists of two parts: (a) statistical tests of the long wave as a general phenomenon, and (b) a discussion of the underlying causes of great depressions. His conclusion with respect to (a) is that the existence of a long wave, in the sense of a long cycle of some fifty years, manifesting itself as alternating accelerations and retardations in the growth of aggregate production, should be rejected. Van der Zwan does not find those accelerations and retardations in the time series on industrial production and national income investigated by him for the United States, the United Kingdom and Germany.

I will return to Van der Zwan's test procedure; however, even if we were to accept this procedure and its results, we could not simply forget about the Kondratieff cycle and its underlying hypotheses. In a number of articles in the weekly *Economisch-Statistische Berichten* Van der Zwan has developed his own overinvestment theory,[1] which is itself an explanation of a long wave in aggregate production of Western industrialized countries. Even though the name of Kondratieff is nowhere mentioned by Van der Zwan in these articles, it is clear that he wants to explain why Western economies stagnate after an extended period of growth, knowing that growth retardations similar to the one we are experiencing now have occurred before in the history of the industrialized world.

Van der Zwan uses his paper to present material that is intended as empirical support for his overinvestment theory. This material, partly relating to the time periods of the second and third Kondratieff, does not lead to a rejection of the theory. Does not this imply that there is something to be said in favour of that long-wave hypothesis which posits investment fluctuations as the main "motor" behind the Kondratieff cycle? I think there is and I believe Van der Zwan would be willing to accept the long wave were it not that the automatism and the inevitability – the fatalism some would

---

* Some of the arguments (with accompanying calculations) discussed in this comment have also appeared in Dutch, in Van Duijn (1979).

[1] Van der Zwan (1975, 1976, 1977).

say – that is implicit in the notion of a "cycle" cannot be accepted by him. It should be added that Van der Zwan's own theory concentrates on an explanation of the upper turning-point; he does not explain the lower turning-point and thus one could not blame him for having described a recurrent process while not accepting the cyclical implications of that process. However, not only has the Western world in its two hundred years since the Industrial Revolution suffered from a number of prolonged depressions, it has bounced back from these depressions with periods of even more prolonged expansion. While the depressions cannot be denied, neither can the periods of prosperity. There is reason therefore to take a closer look at the procedure followed by Van der Zwan to ascertain the existence of a Kondratieff cycle in the physical production time series. If periods of depression and periods of prosperity have alternated, it must be possible to trace these alternations in the time series available for core countries such as the United States, Great Britain, Germany and France. The definite way in which the previous sentence is stated may make us overlook a problem that has bothered long-wave authors, from Kondratieff's days to the present time: the defectiveness of the data. Van der Zwan uses only one source per country, but for all four countries mentioned above at least two sources are available for industrial production time series.[2] When one compares two nineteenth-century series on one variable, it is striking to see how much they differ. Data, and certainly the nineteenth-century data, are not all too reliable.

Which data one shall look at obviously depends on the theory one is testing. If one thinks of long waves as being generated by clusters of basic innovations that create new industries and that cause long expansions in the production of capital goods, the Kondratieff cycle should manifest itself first of all in the development of the *index of industrial production*. National income or product is less adequate as a measure, since it contains other components besides industrial production (such as agriculture, trade, domestic services), the development of which is not quite clear in a long-wave context. On top of that, valuation problems are most severe with national product or income. Ideally one should also transform the industrial production series into series on a per capita basis in order to neutralize the effects of internal population growth and migration (e.g. the transatlantic migration waves before 1920!).

A second problem is that of trend elimination. If there is a secular development of a higher order than the Kondratieff, it must be the S-shaped life cycle of economic development of Rostow's five-stages theory,[3] with the "take-off" and the "drive to maturity" in the context of Van der Zwan's paper being the relevant stages. One should not expect that the long-term economic development can be adequately represented by a constant rate of growth during these two stages. If the take-off for a particular coun-

[2] For the United States we have *Long term economic growth 1860–1970* (1973) and Frickey (1947). British industrial production data are contained in Feinstein (1976) and Hoffmann (1955). Sources for French and German data are Lewis (1978) and Mitchell (1975).

[3] Rostow (1966).

try occurs during the expansion phase of the second Kondratieff, one should not expect the same high rates of growth to recur in the third Kondratieff. The consequence of this is that one should not expect, as Van der Zwan did, to find a cycle in the residuals around a log-linear trend.[4]

Whether the addition of a quadratic term to the log-linear equation will solve this problem is questionable; the results will be greatly affected by the nature of the time period covered. My experience is that the pattern of residuals is very sensitive to the trend assumption one makes. It is not difficult to find the low values of the Durbin–Watson coefficients one is looking for, but the blocks of negative and positive residuals are situated differently from case to case. In terms of $\bar{R}^2$ it is hardly possible to prefer one trend specification to another, while the combination of empirical and theoretical knowledge would, as far as I am concerned, indicate only that there is no reason to prefer a log-linear trend to some other trend specification. If one still wishes to use a log-linear trend to test for the existence of a long-wave pattern, it is necessary to impose other requirements on the residuals than Van der Zwan does. An alternative procedure, which also presumes log-linear trend estimation, is presented in Van Duijn (1979).

Next there is the problem of the long-wave turning-points. Here Van der Zwan has imposed on himself a quite unnecessary and theoretically unjustified restriction by taking turning-points in price series as long-wave turning-points. The price series, whose nineteenth-century fluctuations probably have been the prime cause for suspecting a long wave in economic activities at large, but which do not have any further importance in modern long-wave theories, come to the fore again in Van der Zwan's paper. I have no argument with his correct separation of estimation and testing phases, but several objections can be raised to the use of price series in determining long-wave turning-points.

(1) There is no long-wave theory which produces price cycles of some 45–60 years as its major outcome; it might be true that theoretical attempts have been made to explain the nineteenth-century fluctuations in the price level, e.g. by relating them to changes in the gold supply, but for the twentieth century these explanations have no further relevance.[5]

(2) Should one still want to use turning-points in price series as long-wave turning-points, this would clearly lead to absurd results in the twentieth century: an expansion

[4] Fitting a log-linear trend to a really long time series, such as W. G. Hoffmann's industrial production index for Britain over the 1700–1950 interval, one finds only two burning-points: a trough around 1782 and a peak around 1873. This is an interesting result, both in terms of the long-wave hypothesis and in terms of Rostow's stages theory: the years around 1782 can be regarded as the beginning of the first Kondratieff and as the years in which the British economy took off; 1873 marks the upper turning-point of the second Kondratieff and the completion of Britain's drive to maturity.

[5] Lewis (1978, p. 93) argues that changes in the rate of flow of agricultural output were the original cause of the Kondratieff swing between 1870 and 1913. In his view, changes in the rate of flow of gold production were themselves "an accessory to the turn-around of prices rather than its cause".

phase that started in 1932 and that would continue at least into 1978! Such a result would deny both the previous and the current depression. Of course Van der Zwan has realized this, but has reacted by attempting to justify 1938 as a lower turning-point (which it is not) instead of 1932–1933.

(3) Prices are determined by many different factors, some of which are non-economic. International wars have been one such factor. It is not without reason that prices shot up after 1913, only to fall again after the First World War had ended. That, however, does not imply that after 1920 the contraction phase of the third Kondratieff started, if one knows at the same time that one of the basic innovations of the Kondratieff – the automobile – had its years of high growth in postwar America (as Van der Zwan himself demonstrates in a table, adapted from Lieftinck).

(4) The presumed similarity of price movements among nations is not as great as it seems at first sight. Burns and Mitchell's (1946) table (table 19.1 in Van der Zwan's paper) shows spreads of up to ten years for some turning-points.

The objections raised above to Van der Zwan's testing procedure would make me opt for a different approach when the question is to be answered whether or not economic growth occurs with accelerations and decelerations according to a Kondratieff pattern.

Elsewhere[6] I have divided up the time that has elapsed since the Industrial Revolution into Juglars. Kondratieff cycles can then be considered as consisting of a number of phases, the names of which I have adopted from Schumpeter (1939): prosperity, prosperity, recession, depression, recovery. A typical Kondratieff cycle is thus assumed to consist of 5 Juglars, but I hasten to add that this make-up is based on an interpretation of historical material contained in Schumpeter (1939): there is no theoretical reason why Kondratieffs could not consist of, say, 4 or 6 Juglars. In addition, for testing purposes the characteristics of the different phases will have to be specified, and confronted with the observable development of a variable such as industrial production.

As demarcation points between Juglars one should take peak years. In doing so one can calculate annual growth rates of production from peak to peak. The advantages of this approach are: (a) one obtains growth rates over periods that are comparable (five-year periods or decades are not, as they will contain different parts of business cycles); and (b) one does not need any assumptions on the nature of the underlying long-term trend. According to the *innovation life cycle* version of the long-wave theory[7] the following hypothesis with respect to the course of Juglar growth rates γ could be formulated:

$$\gamma_{P_1} > \gamma_{P_1} > \gamma_R > \gamma_D,$$
$$\gamma_D < \gamma_r,$$
$$\gamma_r < \gamma_{P_2} \text{ (next Kondratieff)}. \tag{1a}$$

[6] Van Duijn (1977).
[7] Van Duijn (1977).

Here the subscripts indicate the different Kondratieff phases: $P =$ prosperity; $R =$ recession; $D =$ depression; and $r =$ recovery. Taking into account the long time lag by which the production of (basic) capital reacts to innovation impulses, an alternative hypothesis might be

$$\gamma_{P_1} < \gamma_{P_2},$$
$$\gamma_{P_2} > \gamma_R > \gamma_D,$$
$$\gamma_D < \gamma_{r_1},$$
$$\gamma_r < \gamma_{P_1} \text{ (next Kondratieff)}.$$

(1b)

The assumption (1a) and (1b) is that Juglar growth rates change in time according to a long-wave pattern, with the growth rates of the first and/or second prosperity-Juglar *ex hypothesi* exceeding those of the subsequent recession- and depression-Juglars, and also exceeding those of the previous depression- and recovery-Juglars.

A test of this hypothesis will have to show whether (a) a long-wave pattern in growth rates actually exists; and (b) our "first-round" labelling can be sustained.

Let us turn now to the empirical record. Two preliminary remarks: (a) Van der Zwan has used only a limited number of the available time series on the core countries;[8] and (b) some of his Kondratieff upswing and downswing periods are incomplete, i.e. some of his time series start or end during an upswing or downswing phase. This cannot but weaken his conclusions. I have restricted myself to complete Juglars, the peaks of which were determined by consulting (among other sources) Burns and Mitchell (1946).

First of all the US series (table 20.1). The industrial production index (in the first column) clearly shows a pattern of increasing and decreasing growth rates, albeit that the hypothesized trough rate of growth of the second Kondratieff (1847–1895) does not occur during the depression phase but during the recovery phase. In addition we have no data on the changes in industrial production between 1847 and 1864. The third (1895–1948) and fourth (1948–present) Kondratieff proceed as hypothesized, despite the disturbances of the two world wars. Frickey's series (in the second column) confirms the pattern found in the first column, but is too short. In the series that shows the growth of per capita GNP one can also discern a clear Kondratieff pattern.[9]

To determine the growth of industrial production in Great Britain I employed two sources, Feinstein and Hoffman (see Table 20.2).[10] I left out Deane and Cole's national income series (Van der Zwan's source) for the reason given earlier. In Feinstein's series one can, for the years between 1857 and 1929, recognize the familiar pattern of declining and increasing rates of growth. However, the following depression phase shows a remarkable rise in production (materializing between 1932 and 1937). Postwar

[8] For additional sources refer to footnote 2.

[9] I maintain, however, that for testing purposes industrial production should be preferred to GNP. The third column has been included only because it gives per capita data.

[10] To be precise, Feinstein's data refer to the United Kingdom, Hoffmann's to Great Britain.

Table 20.1

Jugular growth rates, United States, 1864–1973.

Kondratieff phase	Juglar	Ind. prod.[a]	Manuf. prod.[b]	Per capita GNP [c]
Recession	1864–1873	6.2	5.8	
Depression	1873–1882	5.8	5.6	
Recovery	1882–1895	4.0	3.9	
Prosperity	1895–1903	6.4	5.7	2.8
Prosperity	1903–1913	5.3	4.9	1.8
(War)	1913–1920	3.1 ⎫ 4.0		−0.4 ⎫ 1.3
Recession	1920–1929	4.8 ⎭		2.7 ⎭
Depression	1929–1937	0.4		−0.7
Recovery	1937–1948	5.0 ⎫ 4.8		3.1 ⎫ 2.8
Prosperity	1948–1957	4.4 ⎭		2.3 ⎭
Prosperity	1957–1966	5.3		2.4
Recession	1966–1973	3.9		2.3

[a] Industrial production index (NBER and FRB) in: *Long term economic growth 1860–1970* (1973), plus Survey of Current Business, US Department of Commerce for years after 1970.
[b] Index of production for manufacture, in: Frickey (1947).
[c] Per capita GNP, 1958 prices, in: *US historical statistics: Colonial times to 1970* (1975).

developments so far are again as expected.

Just as in the case of the US the industrial production growth rates suggest that our labelling of Kondratieff phases needs some modification: it appears as though the third Kondratieff started with the 1903–1913 Juglar rather than in 1890.

A comparison of Feinstein's and Hoffmann's growth rates shows rather remarkable differences, for which it is unlikely that they can be attributed to the difference in area covered (UK as opposed to Great Britain). At any rate they call for some caution in the interpretation of outcomes based on such historical series. Considering the whole time span between 1782 and 1948, the overwhelming impression is one of gradually decreasing growth rates, an impression which would not conflict with the notion of the S-shaped life cycle of economic development. When industrial production is split into consumer goods and producer goods, a long-wave pattern can be recognized in the latter. Those who claim that the long wave is the result of fluctuations in the production of these producer goods can trace these fluctuations in the fourth column of table 20.2.

However, it should be readily admitted that the historical development of British industrial production, as represented by Hoffmann's index, provides only meagre support for the long-wave hypothesis. For one thing, a depression phase in the first Kondratieff is altogether lacking. There is an explanation for this. The years between 1830 and 1850 are known in Great Britain as "the railway age".[11] This railway age can be seen

[11] Cf. Phyllis Deane: "If there was a period when the rate of capital formation shifted up at all sharply, it was in the railway age, i.e. in the period between 1830 and 1850. This was when the community built up its basic overhead capital, its essential infrastructure" [Deane (1973)].

Table 20.2

Jugular growth rates, Great Britain, 1782–1973.

Kondratieff phase	Juglar	Ind. prod.[a]	Ind. prod.[b]	Cons. goods[c]	Prod. goods[d]
Prosperity	1782–1792		4.8	5.0	3.1
Prosperity	1792–1802		2.4	2.2	3.0
(War)	1802–1815		2.1	2.1	2.1
Recession	1815–1825		3.9	3.8	4.2
Depression	1825–1836		3.7	3.7	3.8
Recovery	1836–1845		3.3	2.9	4.0
Prosperity	1845–1857		3.3	2.3	5.0
Prosperity	1857–1866	3.2	2.1	1.0	3.7
Recession	1866–1873	2.3	3.6	3.5	3.7
Depression	1873–1883	2.2	2.0	1.0	3.3
Recovery	1883–1890	1.6	1.3	1.4	1.2
Prosperity	1890–1903	1.8	1.3	0.9	1.6
Prosperity	1903–1913	2.3	2.6	2.1	3.0
(War)	1913–1920	−0.0	−1.4	−0.8	−1.9
Recession	1920–1929	2.8	1.7	0.8	2.6
Depression	1929–1937	3.3	2.7	1.6*	1.0*
Recovery	1937–1948	1.2	0.8		
Prosperity	1948–1956	3.7			
Prosperity	1956–1965	3.2			
Recession	1965–1973	2.5			

[a] Total industrial production, in: Feinstein (1976); plus own computations (1965–1973).
[b] Total industrial production, excluding building, in: Hoffmann (1955).
[c] Industrial production, consumer goods industries, in: Hoffmann (1955).
[d] Industrial production, producer goods industries, in: Hoffmann (1955).
 * Period 1929–1935.

as a continuation of the Industrial Revolution which had been temporarily interrupted by the economic consequences of the Napoleonic Wars. After the 1845–1857 prosperity–Juglar, producer-goods growth rates decrease, only to rise again briefly at the beginning of the twentieth century.

In France (table 20.3) too the third Kondratieff cycle seems to start with the 1903–1913 Juglar, but from there on the course of the third and fourth Kondratieff is as hypothesized. Prior to 1882 the prosperity–Juglar 1866–1872 (with a virtually stagnating industrial production) is the only irregularity. The depression phase of the first Kondratieff is clearly recognizable. The following recovery (railway building) is stronger than expected. As for Great Britain, it seems more appropriate to label the 1880s as the true depression period of the second Kondratieff. The picture for Germany (table 20.3) shows other peculiarities. High growth rates until 1872, a

Table 20.3

Juglar growth rates, France (1815–1973) and Germany (1850–1973).

Kondratieff phase	France		Germany	
	Juglar	Ind prod.[a]	Juglar	Ind. prod.[b]
Recession	1815–1824	1.4		
Depression	1824–1836	0.5		
Recovery	1836–1847	2.3		
Prosperity	1847–1856	2.8	(1850–1857	3.4)
Prosperity	1856–1866	0.6	1857–1866	3.9
Recession	1866–1872	2.1	1866–1872	5.9
Depression	1872–1882	1.9	1872–1882	1.2
Recovery	1882–1890	0.4	1882–1890	5.0
Prosperity	1890–1903	1.6	1890–1903	3.8
Prosperity	1903–1913	3.5	1903–1913	4.4
(War)	1913–1920	−6.7 ⎫ 1.4	1913–1920 ⎫	
Recession	1920–1929	8.1 ⎭	1920–1929 ⎭	1.1
Depression	1929–1937	−2.6	1929–1937	3.0
Recovery	1937–1948	0.3		
Prosperity	1948–1957	6.6	1948–1957	15.4
Prosperity	1957–1966	6.1	1957–1966	5.8
Recession	1966–1973	5.8	1966–1973	5.2

[a] Mitchell (1975); plus Annuaire Statistique de la France (INSEE) for postwar years;
[b] Mitchell (1975); plus Statistisches Jahrbuch für die Bundesrepublik Deutschland for postwar years.

Table 20.4

Juglar growth rates, four core countries and world (excl. USSR), 1866–1950.

Kondratieff phase	Juglar	Ind. prod. 4 core countries [a]	World prod. (excl. USSR)[b]
Recession	1866–1873	3.7	
Depression	1873–1883	3.5	3.1
Recovery	1883–1892	3.1	3.3
Prosperity	1892–1903	3.5	4.2
Prosperity	1903–1913	3.6	4.0
(War)	1913–1920 ⎫		2.8
Recession	1920–1929 ⎭		
Depression	1929–1937		1.4
Recovery	(1937–1950		2.9)

[a] Industrial production 1865–1913 core countries (US, Great Britain, Germany, France), in: Lewis (1978).
[b] World production (incl. US excl. USSR), in: Lewis (1952).

depression-Juglar, but then a resumption of growth.[12] Our hypotheses (1a) and (1b) are not affirmed by the German data prior to 1948, for one thing because the war preparations in Hitler's Germany quickly undid the production decline of the depression.

Putting together the industrial production of the four core countries (table 20.4), it is not surprising that the 1883–1892 Juglar yields the lowest growth rate (a). The growth pattern of world production (b) is, however, different. For the industrialized world as a whole it seems correct to locate the beginning of the third Kondratieff around 1892. Possibly this difference in phase can be explained by the interaction between the Kondratieff cycle and the stage of economic development according to Rostow's theory. The "take-off" of the four core countries occurred during the first or second Kondratieff and was followed – inevitably – by a retardation of growth and, as now appears to be the case, by a delayed upswing of the third Kondratieff. Other countries entered the circle of industrialized countries at the time that is usually seen as the beginning of the third Kondratieff (around 1896), and this could explain why the growth rates of world production between 1892 and 1913 exceed those of the four core countries.

Do the available industrial production data support the long wave hypothesis?[13] On the basis of hypotheses (1a) and (1b) the following conclusions can be drawn for the four different Kondratieffs that have been recognized so far.

(1) The Industrial Revolution set the first Kondratieff in motion, but this first Kondratieff seems to have been without a depression phase in Great Britain, the only country for which we have available industrial production data from the 1780s

---

[12] That the growth of national product definitely is not the most suitable measure for testing Kondratieff accelerations and decelerations is indicated also in Borchardt (1973, p. 118): "From 1850 to 1873 changes in technology and organization apparently did far more to determine the growth in national product than in later periods. .... One might well single out the two decades after 1850 as a period of especially intensive growth, although their mean rate of growth at 2.4 pct. was lower than in the following decades."

[13] Hypotheses (1a) and (1b) can be formally tested with a small sample sign test based on the binomial distribution. Counting the number of correct order relations between adjacent Juglars in tables 20.1–20.4 the following right-hand tail cumulative binomial probabilities hold for $\pi = 0.5$:

United States, NBER/FRB (8 out of 10 correct)	0.0547
United Kingdom, Feinstein (5 out of 14)	0.9104
Great Britain, Hoffmann (7 out of 11)	0.2745
France (12 out of 15)	0.0176
Germany (6 out of 9)	0.2539
Ind. prod. core countries (3 out of 4)	0.3125
World production (6 out of 6)	0.0156

At the 5 percent level the null hypothesis is only rejected for France and for world production in favour of the Kondratieff-hypothesis. The US probability is just over 5 percent. The industrial production core countries series is just too short. In a binomial distribution even a perfect score of 4 out of 4 has a probability of 0.0625.

onwards. War activities interrupted growth, but railway construction in Britain forms a continuation of the Industrial Revolution. In France, on the other hand, industrial production virtually stagnated between 1815 and 1836 (annual rate of growth: 0.9), and in comparison to the subsequent revival this period could be interpreted as a Kondratieff downswing.

(2) The second Kondratieff is usually associated with railways and iron. However, railway construction did not occur simultaneously in all four core countries, and the start of the second Kondratieff may vary accordingly. In the US, Britain and France the Juglar which I had initially labelled recovery-Juglar appears to have been the true depression-Juglar of that Kondratieff, and it may be more appropriate to locate the beginning of the third Kondratieff around 1903, at least for Britain and France. The growth rates for world production as a whole, however, confirm my initial classification.

(3) The US and world growth rate pattern during the third Kondratieff is – bearing in mind the effects of the First World War – in conformity with the hypothesis of decreasing growth rates through the depression phase, and recovery after that. For Great Britain and Germany the Great Depression of the 1930s has been rendered invisible in our figures by the vigorous growth of industrial production after 1932–1933.

(4) The expansion phase of the fourth Kondratieff (1948–1973) has been as hypothesized by (1a) in Britain, France and West Germany. In the US (a country virtually without physical war damage and consequently lacking a reconstruction impulse) growth rates developed according to hypothesis (1b).

References

Borchardt, K., 1973, The Industrial Revolution in Germany 1700–1914, in: C. M. Cipolla, ed., The emergence of industrial societies (Fontana Economic History of Europe, London).

Burns, A. F. and W. C. Mitchell, 1946, Measuring business cycles (National Bureau of Economic Research, New York).

Deane, Ph., 1973, The Industrial Revolution in Great Britain, in: C. M. Cipolla, ed., The emergence of industrial societies (Fontana Economic History of Europe, London).

Duijn, J. J. van, 1977, The long wave in economic life, De Economist 125, 544–576.

Duijn, J. J. van, 1979, De lange golf in de economie (Van Gorcum, Assen).

Feinstein, C. H., 1976, Statistical tables of national income, expenditure and output of the UK 1855–1965 (Cambridge University Press, London).

Frickey, E., 1947, Production in the United States 1860–1914 (Harvard University Press, Cambridge).

Hoffmann, W. G., 1955, British industry 1700–1950 (Basil Blackwell, Oxford).

Lewis, W. A., 1952, World production, prices and trade 1870–1960, Manchester School of Economic and Social Studies 20, 105–138.

Lewis, W. A., 1978, Growth and fluctuations 1870–1913 (Allen & Unwin, London).

Long term economic growth 1860–1970, 1973 (US Department of Commerce, Washington DC).

Mitchell, B. R., 1975, European historical statistics 1750–1970 (Macmillan, London).

Rostow, W. W., 1960, The stages of economic growth (Cambridge University Press, London).

Schumpeter, J. A., 1939, Business cycles (McGraw-Hill, New York).

US historical statistics: Colonial times to 1970, 1975 (US Department of Commerce, Washington DC).

Zwan, A van der, 1975, Dalend rendement op geïnvesteerd vermogen, Economisch-Statistische Berichten 60, 656–660, 680–685.

Zwan, A. van der, 1976, Over de vergroting van de omweg in de produktie, Economisch-Statistische Berichten 61, 60–65, 80–83, 117–122.

Zwan, A. van der, 1977, Na de smalle marges van het beleid, Economisch-Statistische Berichten 62, 244–248, 268–277, 300–302.

Chapter 21   *p. 183 =*

COMMENT ON VAN DER ZWAN'S PAPER

D. B. J. SCHOUTEN

University of Tilburg   *235·37*

Van der Zwan thinks that recurrent depressions exist that can be explained by some overinvestment theory. In his paper he does not quite reveal the precise content of this theory. The uneven development in time between industries plays a key role in his analysis. But, as Van den Goorbergh (1976) has shown, an uneven technological development in time between sectors with corresponding differences of price fluctuations (see table 19.11 in Van der Zwan's paper) does not necessarily imply that there will be special problems of the overinvestment type or of any type of cyclical theory as long as real wages are properly set. Only the structural ratios change over time: the ratios between prices, between wages and added value, between consumption and investment expenditures. The nature of these changes is a matter not only of uneven technological development, but also of changes in preferences.

In this respect there will be problems only if the price system cannot perform its function of clearing the market. Under these circumstances a situation of overinvestment can be defined as a situation in which the available capacity can be fully absorbed only by means of sales at nonprofitable prices. If the price level remains too high, potential supply will not be met by demand. Underutilization or idle capacity of machinery and labour is the result of prices that are too high or wages that are too low. Under these circumstances losses due to underutilization, low sales (production) per unit of invested capital and a low rate of return are the logical consequences.

Decreasing prices would have been logical as well if the absolute value of the price elasticity were more than one, for in this case the proceeds of more sales (= more production) could increase, provided that the excess of labour that had not yet been shaken out and the existing stock of materials allowed for this situation. If labour and materials have already been disposed of, marginal proceeds should be compared to marginal costs in the usual way; in the latter case the price elasticity should be higher

Prospects of Economic Growth, edited by S. K. Kuipers and G. J. Lanjouw

than in the former case for production to be increased. If it is not sufficiently high, the situation of overinvestment can be regarded as an error of estimation by the relevant investor through lack of perfect foresight. Such estimation errors are made continuously, but they can be neutralized by opposite errors of estimation by other investors. The latter group experiences a situation of more than normal utilization of capacity and consequently a high capital productivity and a high rate of return. As has been said before, those who have overinvested encounter the opposite results. Everything is very differentiated then, but there is no reason why a depression should occur.

Only if cases of overinvestment outnumber cases of underinvestment to a considerable extent do things grow askew, but this has not been proved by the empirical data given by Van der Zwan.

There is no doubt that periods of an increasing capital–labour ratio can occur. Changes in this ratio may have a structural and technological basis. For instance, the *equilibrium* path of economic growth in a vintage model is characterized by a continuous increase in the capital–labour ratio and in labour productivity in such a way that capital productivity can remain constant. By definition overinvestment is out of the question. It is even possible that for some time the saving and investment ratio increases in such a way that investment in new machinery grows more than normally. Average labour productivity will increase more than normally because of the gradual extra modernization of production capacity. At the same time the life span of machinery can be shortened, because more new jobs are created by new investment, so that old jobs on old machinery can be scrapped sooner without loss of the total desired jobs. Capital productivity in a technical sense can remain constant, but the rate of return will decrease owing to a higher share of wages in total income. This is merely an expression of the decreasing returns to an increase in saving and investment activities: there are limits to modernization!

The opposite can occur too: a low saving and investment ratio causing an increasing life span of machinery and a decreasing share of wages in total income. Perhaps such a development can be expected in the near future. But these *structural* changes have nothing to do with any overinvestment theory in a cyclical sense.

A level of real wages that is not properly adjusted to the cases of equilibrium or disequilibrium growth mentioned above is also a phenomenon. Its consequence is only too many or too few available jobs compared to the total supply of labour. But is it possible to isolate these errors in the level of real wages from the cyclical errors that are made in a situation of general overinvestment? If in general there is too much investment in a certain period, the increase in income is likely to be greater than the increase in capacity, at least in the short run. Moreover, this is possible only if the utilization of production factors can be improved, so that employment increases. I am not sure whether under these boom circumstances the capital–labour ratio will increase more than normally: everything increases in such a boom! But after some time there might . be a chance that the increase in capacity exceeds the increase in income. At that moment real wages should increase at a higher rate or prices should decrease to avoid general overcapacity. It is possible, therefore, that markets are cleared via a well-operating price system. But we all know that the equilibrium level of *real* wages is not always found easily, hence the phenomenon of economic cycles.

Too many investments and thus too much capacity evidently cause, through a lack of sufficient purchasing power, a decline via a decrease of investment activity. But why does the price system not operate properly? Nobody will be worse off if everything that can be produced is in fact produced and sold. So the heart of the matter still is: why do we not create sufficient purchasing power if more goods can be produced than sold at the existing wage and price ratio? This crucial question has not been answered by Van der Zwan either. Nowhere in his paper can I find empirical data on wage and price ratios. There are only data on the share of labour in total income. But the reason why *general* overcapacity arises remains unexplained: are the entrepreneurs in this phase of the cycle afraid of decreasing prices or are trade unions not willing to strive for extra increases in real wages? What is the reason for this? Surely the previous boom is no reason to be afraid of still more purchasing power for the working class.

There is an important qualification to this story. If the ceiling of maximum production capacity is reached during the boom, extra increases in prices cannot be avoided. If wage-earners can defend their incomes against inflation by automatic price compensations, this inflation can only damage real profits. This process can be reinforced by a tight antiinflation monetary policy, by which the burden of interest for entrepreneurs increases. Investment will surely decrease in favour of too much consumption. The resultant decline is not a matter of *over*investment; on the contrary, it is a matter of *not enough* investment through a lack of sufficient capacity. Too little investment implies a shortage of jobs in the future and so structural unemployment. Note that this phenomenon has nothing to do with any kind of *over*investment. On the contrary, investment is not high enough and real wages have not to increase – as in the situation of overinvestment – but on the contrary they have precisely to decrease in order to avoid a structural decline.

In view of the fact that the vintage model has become very popular in this country, so that high real wages have been stressed to demonstrate the lack of production capacity, the Dutch Government seems to have opted for the theory of *under*investment. Consequently, deliberate attempts are made to moderate gross real wages. On the ground of his theory of *over*investment Van der Zwan reaches the opposite conclusion. If he had provided more empirical evidence of a *general* overcapacity of all factors of production, he might have been put in the right!

Reference

Goorbergh, W. M. van den, 1976, Structural demand for labour in a three-sector model, De Economist 124, 116–147.

1324

Chapter 22

LONG-TERM FORECASTING – A PARADOX?

A. BOSMAN   *239-60*

University of Groningen

The hypothesis behind this paper is that for the construction of models describing situations on a long-term basis one should not try to extrapolate through long-term forecasting of the exogenous variables in models specifying the existing situation. It is better to predict the future by defining desired states with the help of scenarios and to investigate whether it is possible to reach these states. It is therefore not only the quality of the long-term forecast that is important, but probably more the quality of the model defining these desired states. In this paper a distinction is made between an econometric and a simulation approach to the construction of mdels. A number of differences between these two approaches will be discussed.

1. Introduction

An inventory and evaluation of the methods and techniques available for long-term forecasting can be supplied in at least two different ways. One can (a) discuss the available methods and techniques and compare them, whether or not by means of a number of criteria; or (b) try to formulate conditions that must be satisfied by methods and techniques for long-term forecasting. I have opted for the approach under (b), for the following reasons.

(1) Good inventories of the available methods and techniques exist [e.g. Clark and Cole (1975); Cole (1977)].

(2) A study of these inventories shows that much of the discussion around the comparisons is determined not by the "technological" merits of these techniques, but by the starting-points selected by the investigators and by the objectives defined by them, explicitly or not. As Mason rightly remarks: "How does one decide on world issues? One method, the dominant one in this collection, is to model the world in some manner and derive the implications of the model. Models, however, have a haunting incompleteness about them. The assumptions that underlie them are seldom explicit. But, more importantly, there is no sure method to guarantee that the assumptions are correct" [Mason (1976, p. 97)].

Prospects of Economic Growth, edited by S. K. Kuipers and G. J. Lanjouw
© *North-Holland Publishing Company*

It is my opinion that one of the most important conditions that has to be satisfied by models in general, and those for long-term forecasts in particular, is that an explicitly defined relation (or relations) is established between the investigator's view of the "world" and the objectives that he pursues on the one hand and the choice of methods and techniques on the other. Attention will be devoted to the possible content of these relations in section 3. In section 4 I discuss a number of problems concerning the compilation of models. The list of problems for discussion has been taken from the literature and is certainly not an exhaustive one. In sections 5 and 6 I try to establish a connection between what has been discussed in sections 3 and 4. I endeavour to formulate a number of conditions to be satisfied by models for making long-term forecasts. A number of concepts are defined in section 2.

2. Some concepts

The word "system" plays an important part in the literature that has been published on model-building in recent years. Since different terms and concepts are usually employed in economics, I define the concept "system" so as to avoid misunderstandings. In emulation of Ackoff I define a system as "a set of interrelated elements. Thus a system is an entity which is composed of at least two elements and a relations that holds between each of its elements and at least one other element in the set" [Ackoff (1971, p. 662)].

A system, S, can be specified as follows:

$$S = \{B, R\}, \tag{1}$$

where $B = \{b_i\}$, a set of b_i elements ($i = 1, 2, \ldots, n$); and $R =$ a collection of relations. The terms "elements" and "relationships" are used in various meanings. In so far as the term "relation" is concerned, the two most common meanings in the literature are the following.

(1) A function, f, specifies a relation between an endogenous variable, y, and one or more exogenous variables, in eq. (2) x and z:

$$y = f(x, z). \tag{2}$$

The term "relation" is used in this sense in general systems theory and, unless otherwise stated, in this paper.

(2) A relation specifies an arrangement between the elements in one or more sets. These relations can be used to give a quantitative substance to the concept "structure"; see also section 4.

The *elements* of a system can be concrete or abstract. If they are concrete, the system is called *concrete* or *real*. If they are abstract, one speaks of an *abstract* system.

The elements of an abstract system may have a varying content. In general systems theory the variables that are used for specifying the abstract system are regarded as the elements of the system. In that specification the general systems theory utilizes the black box approach. This means that a problem is described by utilizing the following kinds of variables (see fig. 22.1).

Fig. 22.1

The variables have the following meaning:

x = an exogenous variable the value of which cannot be influenced by the decision-maker. I call this variable an *environmental variable*;

u = an exogenous variable the value of which, at least within certain limits, *can* be influenced by a decision-maker. I call this variable an *instrumental variable*;

y = the endogenous variable;

s = a state variable which is used for efficient description or effective analysis of the system.

The equations resulting from this description can also be regarded as elements of an abstract system. This will particularly be the case when it is desired to divide a system into subsystems, the relations between the subsystems being the subject of research.

Furthermore, the word "system" is often used in a number of approaches from the philosophy of science, whose essence can be represented by the fact that they reject as inadequate the tackling of problems along subject-matter-linked or monodisciplinary lines. This is known as the *systems approach* [see e.g. Churchman (1968); Boguslaw (1965); Laszlo (1973); Ackoff (1974)]. The mutiplicity of definitions used for the concept "system" is largely a result of this systems approach. Although its influence should not be underrated, it can also be stated that in general the systems approach has an inadequate methodological basis [e.g. Bosman (1977, 1978)].

The word "model" is also used in various meanings [e.g. Blalock (1968)]. By establishing a relation between the model and abstract systems it is possible to give both an unequivocal meaning. Here I use the word "model" in the sense of "serve as a model for" and an abstract system as the product of the research. In that sense an abstract system can be a symbolic model of reality. However, it is also possible for a concrete system to be an analogous model of reality or of an abstract system. In this paper the terms "forecasting" and "prediction" are used as synonyms.

3. Conceptual models and paradigms

Science studies problems by means of systems that serve as models for those problems. In many sciences, particularly economics, a certain procedure has been followed in the construction of systems that is disputable on a number of points. To sketch this procedure I make use of fig. 22.2 [Sagasti and Mitroff (1973)] where four stages or phases of research are distinguished that are connected to one another by activities to be performed. Loops can be constructed in fig. 22.2 in various ways.

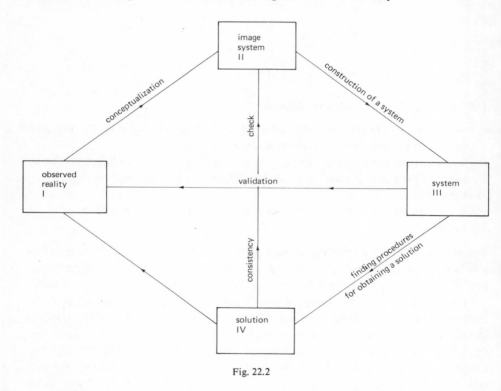

Fig. 22.2

The problem that I wish to discuss in this section relates above all to the connection between phases I, II and III in fig. 22.2 and in particular to the connection between phases I and II. The following two quotations, I hope, outline the problem concerned.

To a large extent, the difference between "reality" and the "conceptual model" would correspond to that customarily made between "data" and "information"....
The fact that many conceptual models may correspond to a given problem situation poses the additional problem of deciding how to build a "good" or workable concep-

tual model and how to determine its characteristics. There are few scientists who propose rules on how to construct conceptual models and/or provide criteria for evaluating alternative conceptual models for a given reality [Sagasti and Mitroff (1973, pp. 700–701)].

The problem broached by Sagasti and Mitroff has been described by Jantsch as follows when the construction of world or global models is concerned.

What is badly missing so far is a useful concept for the mutation of values, or, in more general terms, for the formation of new cultural paradigms and complex systems of such paradigms (religions, ideologies, myths, world views, etc.) – in other words a model of the "Zeitgeist" – as well as a concept for the mode of communication which leads to a wide sharing of these paradigms and beliefs [Jantsch (1976, p. 94)].

The problem highlighted in the two quotations has been the focus of attention in recent years. As with every new subject, it is brought forward under a variety of names, such as conceptual models, paradigms and meta-theories. Although there are differences of emphasis in the problems broached under these various names and in particular in the way in which they are dealt with, the same common theme runs through all these problems. This theme is formed by endorsement of one or more of the following propositions:

(a) objective reality does not exist;

(b) a subject-matter approach to a problem does not lead to an abstract system capable of validation;

(c) the distinction between an explanatory and an applied science is non-sense – these are two sides of the same coin;

(d) the degree of generalization of the usual theories is so great that they say everything about nothing;

(e) the usual methods and techniques for empirical research proceed from a collection of assumptions that are hardly satisfied in practice;

(f) the use of data is at variance with the subject-matter approach. As Churchman pithily puts it: "In other words, we don't know how to collect data for decision making models, world or noworld, many researchers must sense the paradox of data collection: in order to collect the relevant data one has to comprehend the whole system, which is the aim of the model. In order to escape this paradox, one may assume that the past was well managed; a reduction to the absurd" [Churchman (1976, p. 160)].

In fig. 22.2 I have described the problem just broached by the term "conceptualization", leading to a result in the form of an "image system". In themselves these names say little about the content of the activity of conceptualization. I shall try to define the activity of conceptualization in more concrete terms and show its relevance to economic theory and economic research, especially with regard to long-term forecasting. In doing so I use an approach applied by Mitroff and Betz (1972).

Procedures for the construction of an image system are sometimes given the name "theory about a theory". In emulation of Mitroff and Betz I call such a theory a meta-theory [Mitroff and Betz (1972, p. 12)]. The purpose of a meta-theory is to give guidelines for making decisions at relevant points in the process of constructing a system – stage III in fig. 22.2. The following relevant points can be distinguished:

(a) which points of departure – or, if one wishes, paradigms – can be distinguished at an overall level for the design of image systems;

(b) which model cycles can be used at a detailed level to arrive at a system;

(c) establishing relations between the specifications at overall and detailed level; and

(d) criteria for making a choice from the large number of possibilities of constructing a system.

In this section I devote attention to the role of some paradigms in economics and their characteristics for the construction of an image system. In the next section I deal with a number of problems regarding the choice of a model cycle. In section 5 I establish some relations between the specification at an overall and at a detailed level. In section 6 I try to derive some criteria for the construction of systems in which long-term forecasting plays an important role.

Until recently hardly any attention was devoted to the problem of constructing an image system in economics. Image systems were not constructed in economics, they were postulated by means of axioms. Proceeding from Kuhn's methodology, it may be asked what paradigm or paradigms economics has known as a science. To answer this I quote Blaug:

> What are the ruling "paradigms" in the history of economic thought? According to Gordon, "Smith's postulate of the maximizing individual in a relatively free market . . . is our basic paradigm"; "economics has never had a major revolution; its basic maximizing model has never been replaced . . . it is, I think, remarkable when compared to the physical sciences that an economist's fundamental way of viewing the world has remained unchanged since the eighteenth century". Likewise Coats asserts that economics has been dominated throughout its history by a single paradigm – the theory of economic equilibrium via the market mechanism [Blaug (1976, p. 160)].

I agree with the two authors cited by Blaug, though I should like to add the following remarks.

(a) I would like to replace the maximizing individual by the axiom of unbounded or substantive rationality [Simon (1976)]. Unbounded rationality does not explain how a decision-maker – consumer or producer – behaves, it prescribes how he should behave trying to reach an optimum assuming that he knows all the alternatives.

(b) Economics is not interested in how decision-makers behave, but it studies institutions, in particular markets, which as it were coordinate the interests of individuals as impersonal referees. Individual behaviour is made economically (i.e. seen from a point of view of allocating scarce resources) acceptable at an aggregated level through the existence of these institutions. The most important criterion of this acceptability is then an assumed equilibrium. If, however, individual decision-makers do not know all alternatives and do not pursue an optimum, it is questionable whether the joint behaviour of these decision-makers leads to a situation balanced from a social but also from a personal point of view, let alone an optimal economic one. Macroeconomics, therefore, does not proceed from unbounded rationality, but from what De Jong calls modal or average rationality of individuals [De Jong (1949)]. In that case equilibrium is no longer what microeconomics understands by it, but a specification of a number of conditions that have to be satisfied by the solution of the abstract macroeconomic system. In certain cases these conditions can be derived theoretically. In the event of data-bound systems the conditions will usually be determined by means of the solution found. Tinbergen propagated this approach years ago [Tinbergen (1952)].

In conclusion it can be stated that the general paradigm used in economics is the axiom of unbounded rationality, leading to the construction of a system following the loop between stages II, III, IV and II in fig. 22.2. In macroeconomics, especially in data-bound econometric specification, the axiom of unbounded rationality is usually implicitly replaced by one that could be called average rationality. This replacement leads to the construction of a system through a loop between stages, I, II, III and I in fig. 22.2. The connection assumed in such a situation between microeconomics and macroeconomics is an artificial one. Its main disadvantage is that it obviates the formulation of separate paradigms for macroeconomics.

As already stated, one of the main characteristics of the axiom of unbounded rationality is that the behaviour of a decision-maker is not described, but prescribed. The resultant system is normative. The word "behaviour", like the word "system", has come to be increasingly used in recent years. One speaks about the behaviour of a system as one does about the behaviour of a human being or animal. However, this association is incorrect and soon gives rise to misunderstandings, especially among outsiders. When we speak of human behaviour, we mean a description in which human actions take pride of place. When we speak of the behaviour of a system, this is defined by means of endogenous variables that usually traverse a trajectory in time. These endogenous variables may relate to two different objects described as behaviour 1 and behaviour 2 in fig. 22.3. Behaviour 1 is the output – the decision – of a process of decision-making, action 1 in fig. 22.3. In general a decision leads to the implementation of that decision, and this to the performance of certain activities, action 2 in fig. 22.3. Usually economics as a science pays little attention to this kind of action. However, since action 2 means the use of scarce resources, the implementation of a decision is measured and recorded, behaviour 2 in fig. 22.3. The data that are usually available are related to decisions; they do not measure the decision itself but rather the consequences of implementing these decisions.

The axiom of unbounded rationality assumes a one-to-one relationship between action 1 and behaviour 1. It does not describe the process of decision-making, it

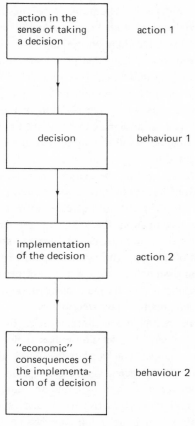

Fig. 22.3

prescribes *what* rules have to be used, given a certain type of decision. If one postulates a one-to-many relationship between action 1 and behaviour 1, it becomes necessary to describe the process of decision-making. Instead of what, the question of *how* becomes important [Simon (1978)]. A paradigm that gives a possibility of answering this question is that of bounded or procedural rationality [Simon (1976)]. The introduction of bounded rationality has consequences not only at the level of a decision-maker but also at a meso and a macrolevel of economic research. At these levels economics now assumes, as already stated, average rationality. If one wants in that case to describe future states of affairs the only way to do so is to extrapolate the existing situation. In macroeconomics attention will have to be paid not only to describing present states of affairs, but also to the development and study of desired states of affairs and the alternative ways of arriving at these. The paradigm of bounded rationality gives an opportunity to do this. A desired state can then be regarded as an aspiration level of a state of equilibrium, while the process of how to reach such a state must be defined.

As a further elaboration of this paradigm attention must be paid above all to:

(a) specifying and examining the measures that can and must be taken to attain desired states of affairs; and

(b) defining alternatives from which a choice can be made for the attainment of a desired state of affairs. Or, to put it another way, in addition to the explanation of existing states of affairs economics will also have to pay attention to the principles of design for attaining new, desired states of affairs.

4. Methods and techniques

I make the following distinction between methods and techniques. I call a *method* a collection of procedures, including techniques, for the construction of a system. A *technique* consists of data-processing features and one or more algorithms that yield a certain result. The concept "method" so defined corresponds in this way to the concept "model cycle" [Bosman (1977, pp. 37–61)]. A connection between the choice of a paradigm, methods and techniques is sketched in fig. 22.4. I deal in this section with the problem of choice of method.

As far as the choice of method is concerned economics has only a choice of two possibilities: the econometric method and the simulation method. The *econometric method* proceeds in essence from general systems theory and the corresponding techniques of systems identification. From a methodological point of view the black box approach – see fig. 22.1 – is the starting-point of this method. The basic information on the number of variables, the number of equations and the degree of interdependence is, in the first instance, derived from economic theory. The econometric method adds the algorithms that are needed for working with data. The use of these algorithms generally has consequences for the specification of the abstract system derived from economics – the identification problem. These consequences may lead to changes in the specification of the abstract system.

The *simulation method* is distinguished from the econometric one by the fact that in the specification of the system use is made of information which one has or assumes that one has on the contents of the black box. The big difference between the two

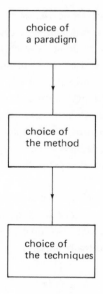

Fig. 22.4

methods is formed by the way in which the connection between the relations is specified. In econometrics the connection, which from now on I term *structure*, is largely the result of the identification procedures. In the simulation method that connection is assumed. The result is a different approach regarding both the way in which possible relations can be defined and the way in which the parameters in the relations have to be estimated. Putting it in very bold terms, one could say that in econometrics the parameters are stochastic and the variables determinate, while exactly the opposite is true using simulation.

The main difference between the two methods is not one of the techniques being used. Once the method has been established the techniques can be chosen, inter alia, on the basis of the individual problem, the objectives of the research, the available data, and the available aids, e.g. computer and software, and other available means. It is my opinion that the techniques do not specifically pertain to one method and that for instance multivariate techniques can be quite well used along with the simulation method, if only to aggregate and to analyse the multiplicity of output. The main difference is between the paradigms that have been chosen as a starting-point for the research. Before I deal with that problem in the next section, I want to illustrate the matter of the choice of the method in more detail by means of a number of problems that are distinguished in the literature on the use of long-term forecasts. These problems are:

(a) the objective of the research;
(b) the specification of the structure;

(c) the degree of abstraction; and

(d) monodisciplinary versus interdisciplinary versus multidisciplinary approaches to problems.

As regards the *objective* of the research in which long-term forecasts play a part, I should like to raise three points. These are:

(a) explaining versus predicting;

(b) the role of the instrumental variables; and

(c) explaining versus planning.

In economics a contrast has long been suggested between explaining and applying or explaining and predicting. My viewpoint is that predicting is only one of the criteria for the validation of a system. In certain cases, depending on the objective of the research, this criterion can play an important part. In this context it is important to make a distinction between two kinds of abstract systems. The one kind is usually the result of application of the econometric method. The abstract system gives a description and thus an explanation of an existing state of affairs based on data obtained from the past. Most econometric models belong to this category. The extent to which this abstract system can also be used for making forecasts in the future depends on:

(a) the extent to which the same variables will continue to play a relevant role in the future; and

(b) the extent to which one is able to predict the development of the influence of the relevant variables in the long term.

I call these systems *explanatory systems*. In addition to the explanatory systems, others can be distinguished the purpose of which is to describe or to predict desirable or undesirable states of affairs in the future. The amount of detail in these systems will in the first instance be determined not by the existing situation but by the expectations entertained about the developments of certain connections in the future. These developments can be described by *scenarios*. In this description use will often be made of the available data, but these can be changed – autonomously or by the system itself – on the basis of the above-mentioned expectations. I call these systems *scenario systems*. It will be clear that these systems do not necessarily explain very much from the existing state of affairs and that it is definitely possible that they predict better than the available explanatory systems. Whether that is in fact the case depends on the answers to the questions asked above under (a) and (b). In any case it can be said that the econometric method is usually unsuitable for the compilation of scenario systems and that the simulation method has to be used for that purpose. Most of the world models, and certainly that of Meadows and Forrester, can be classified as scenario systems.

The role and the function of instrumental variables can be determined only in relation to the question of the purpose for which a system is constructed. As regards the problems with which this paper is concerned, I should like to distinguish only one objective, namely the system must be used in one way or the other for taking better decisions, better in the sense of more efficient, or more effective than would have been possible without the use of this system. On account of the accuracy of forecasting it is often concluded that explanatory systems can be used to solve problems in a short and at most medium term. Scenario systems could then be used in the study and analysis of problems that operate in the long or longer term. I consider this statement incorrect. In my opinion it is not the accuracy of the forecast that must play the decisive role, but the purpose for which the system is to be used. If that purpose is making a choice from alternatives for policy-making – in other words planning – then scenario systems will also have to be compiled for the short and medium term. For explanatory systems often lack relevant alternatives because they have not been performed in the past, while moreover it must be doubted in the alternatives included whether the values of the parameters of the relevant instrument variables correctly reproduce the situation in question.

The purpose of the system can also be described by the contrast between explaining and planning. If one wishes as an economist to exert a deliberate influence at the macro or microlevel, the real economic system cannot be taken as given. If it is desired to consider this system as a variable, measures for changing the system and the possible consequences of this must also be taken into consideration. I call that process the process of planning. *Planning* then comprises three phases:

(a) that of specification of the alternatives;

(b) that of determination of the criteria for choosing and finding an algorithm for making a choice; and

(c) that of compiling a plan and carrying it out.

An elaboration of these three phases makes it clear that only scenario systems can supply simultaneous assistance for each of those three parts [e.g. Bosman (1977, pp. 225–266)]. Forecasting and planning go hand in hand. Planning without forecasting is impossible, since planning has to do with the future and a choice of alternatives is possible only if one is able to indicate which values the exogenous variables will assume in the examined future. This connection between forecasting and planning is at one and the same time the strength and weakness of scenario systems. The strength is that it can be demonstrated by means of sensitivity analysis that most of the exogenous variables do not exert a relevant influence on the results of the process described, i.e. on the endogenous variables. The accuracy of the estimation of these variables is therefore hardly relevant. The weakness is, of course, that the result can never be stronger than the accuracy of the estimation of the relevant exogenous variables and the assumed relations allows. But in this case the simulation method supplies additional technical aids, e.g. by including, instead of a point estimate of a variable, a distribution function of the latter. In addition different relations or different forms of relations can be assumed, and the effect of these differences can be studied.

Once again, to avoid misunderstandings I do not mean to suggest by the latter that the simulation method leads to better predictions. The only thing that I wish to emphasize is that the simulation method, as regards scenario systems,

(a) gives some guarantee that relevant alternatives are not excluded by the simple fact that the researcher himself has to specify the alternatives (I think that this is a better guarantee than finding new alternatives through a process of extrapolating descriptions of existing systems); and

(b) can concentrate attention for estimating exogenous variables on those relevant variables for which accuracy is important.

At the beginning of this section I remarked that a difference between the econometric method and the simulation method can be sought in the concept *structure*. In the econometric method the structure is a datum resulting from the identification process. In the simulation method the structure is a variable. It is therefore important to define structure as a variable and to establish the effect of different structures on the result of the process. In this connection I have made a distinction between an implicit and an explicit specification of structure [Bosman (1977, pp. 114, 122)]. In the latter case the structure is included in the investigation as an exogenous variable. It is possible to assign a value to this or those exogenous variables by using graphs and the (0,1) matrices to be specified with these [e.g. Ozbekham (1976); Betz and de Azvedo (1976)].

The degree of *abstraction* is one of the central problems in the construction of systems, and that applies in particular to the construction of world models. There are at least three problems that have to be considered with respect to this matter and which are, incidentally, not detached from each other. The three problems are the degree of detail applied to the variables, the size of the system, and the structure of the system. Let me begin with the last point. In the case of the simulation method the structure in the system is determined by the researcher himself. In doing so he can choose various points of departure, all of which, however, at least as far as I know, make use in some way or the other of hierarchy. The following quotation from Simon clearly indicates the relevance of the use of hierarchic structures.

If a complex structure is completely unredundant – if no aspect of its structure can be inferred from any other – then it is only its own simplest description. We can exhibit it, but we cannot describe it by a simpler structure. The hierarchic structures we have been discussing have a high degree of redundancy, hence can often be described in economical terms. The redundancy takes a number of forms, of which I shall mention three.

1. Hierarchic systems are usually composed of only a few different kinds of subsystems, in various combinations and arrangements. A familiar example is the proteins, their multitudinous variety arising from arrangements of only twenty different amino acids ... Hence, we can construct our description from a restricted

alphabet of elementary sub-systems from which the complex system is generated.
2. Hierarchic systems are often nearly decomposable. Hence only aggregative properties of their parts enter into the description of the interactions of those parts. A generalization of the notion of near decomposability might be called the "empty world hypothesis". Most things are only connected with most other things; for a tolerable description of reality only a tiny fraction of all possible interactions needs to be taken into account. By adopting a descriptive language that allows the absence of something to go unmentioned a nearly empty world can be described quite concisely ...
3. By appropriate "recoding", the redundancy that is present but unobvious in the structure of a complex system can often be made patent. The commonest recoding of descriptions of dynamic systems consists in replacing of a time path with a description of a differential law that generates that path [Simon (1969, p. 110)].

The three forms mentioned by Simon indicate an equal number of points of departure for structuring. The last point mentioned by Simon is used above all in the construction of explanatory systems; in particular a connection is established by means of aggregation between micro-, meso- and macroeconomic systems. An example of the first form of hierarchy is to be found in Mesarovic's *stratified systems*. Mesarovic et al. (1970) make the following tripartition, see fig. 22.5a. They distinguish at the lowest level a causal stratum that describes the physical processes, at the middle level a decision stratum that defines the relevant decision-making processes and at the top level a normative stratum which as it were establishes the boundaries and the objectives of the system. In fig. 22.5b this structuring is translated into the world model developed by Mesarovic and Pestel [Clark and Cole (1975)]. In the construction of this world model allowance has also been made for the second form of hierarchy mentioned by Simon, namely near decomposability. The world model of Mesarovic and Pestel subdivides the world into ten regions [Cole (1977)]. In the choice of the regions the notion of near decomposability played a part.

It cannot be denied that hierarchy can be used as a guide; however, this guide requires further elaboration. One elaboration has been given by Mesarovic et al. (1970), and others are conceivable. Thus, Hanssmann (1976) and the world model compiled by experts of the UN use input and output models as a basis for the construction of an abstract system. Betz and de Azevado (1976, p. 43) define different strata and a different connection than do Mesarovic and Pestel. It must further be doubted whether the criterion of near decomposability is applicable in all cases. Further research into the possibilities of structuring is a necessity for effective use of the simulation method.

The structuring of all abstract systems has direct consequences for the problem of the size of the system and thus for that of the degree of aggregation. Structuring means distinguishing subsystems that may be regarded as separate modules and therefore can

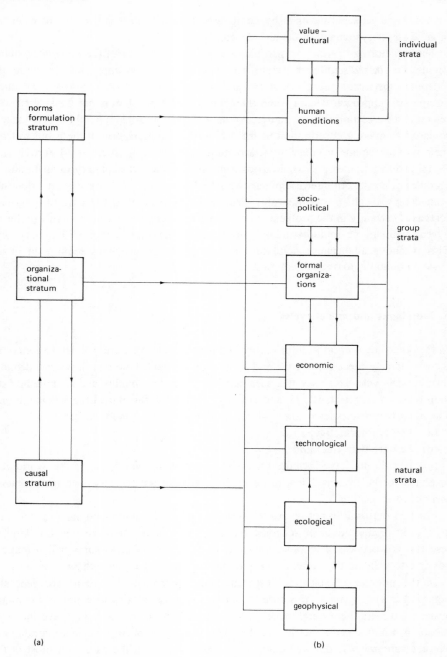

(a) (b)

Fig. 22.5

be processed as separate units by computers. In that way it is possible to calculate large abstract systems with the aid of computers.

The structuring of systems also plays a part in the matter of the *monodisciplinary* versus the *interdisciplinary* versus the *multidisciplinary* approach. I define the difference between interdisciplinary and multidisciplinary as follows. An interdisciplinary approach occurs when the definition of a problem is not considered with reference to a certain subject-matter. An approach to a problem is multidisciplinary if researchers make a contribution to the definition and description of the problem from their monodiscipline or their subject-matter. A structuring such as Mesarovic and Pestel propose makes it possible to concentrate the monodisciplinary contribution in modules or strata. An interdisciplinary approach – see the following section – does not immediately result in a comparable structuring. In general in the case of long-term forecasts, certainly in the problems that are dealt with by the world models, I prefer an interdisciplinary or multidisciplinary approach rather than a monodisciplinary one. This is above all because nondata-free descriptions of problems require an image system not bound to one subject-matter.

5. Paradigms and model cycles

In the preceding section I outlined only two model cycles that are relevant to economic theory, namely the econometric and simulation method. One can, however, define a third model cycle. This uses as a paradigm unbounded rationality and as a method the loop between stages II, III, IV and II in fig. 22.2. I call this model the *axiomatic* one. The main characteristics of the systems resulting from this model cycle are:

(a) they are normative;

(b) they are data-free; and

(c) they do not have facilities to analyse the existing world, unless this world corresponds to the axioms. This, however, is in general not the case, see the problems mentioned in section 3.

For that reason I do not regard the system resulting from the axiomatic model cycle as a valid final product of scientific research. This does not mean that this kind of research is worthless. It should, however, be extended by procedures which make it possible to validate the system. The econometric method supplies these procedures.

In the practice of scientific research image systems and systems are generally regarded as synonyms. In this case the model cycle assumes the function of the image system and meta-theory and model cycle coincide. This is the case, as I have shown in section 4, with the econometric model cycle, where the implicitly specified paradigm of average rationality is not well defined. It is also in general the case with most of the scenario systems that have been used recently for "world model" construction. As someone correctly remarked: "If Forrester were God, his world would be a RLC system" [Rademaker (1976, p. 244)]. The difference between the econometric and the simulation method is, therefore, not only one between an explanatory or a scenario system. The main distinction is what Ackoff calls the difference between reactive and proactive problem-solving. To cite Ackoff:

> In reactive problem solving we walk into the future facing the past – we move away from, rather than toward, something. This often results in unforeseen consequences that are more distasteful than the deficiencies removed. ... Proactive problem solving is always imbedded in a planning process. No problem is treated in isolation, but each problem is formulated as one of a set of interrelated problems that is treated as a whole. Proactive planning consists of designing a desirable future and finding ways of moving toward it as effectively as possible [Ackoff (1978, p. 26)].

It is precisely this distinction between the two methods that yielded the title of this paper. I call long-term forecasting a paradox because the extent to which we are able to solve problems in the long or short run is determined not by the quality of our predictions but by the quality of our systems. The quality of our system depends on the extent to which we are ready and able to devise, to examine and to introduce measures that obviate or solve the problems in question. The quality of the systems to be constructed depends, in my hypothesis (see also the preceding section), on the following factors.

(1) Our ability to analyse existing systems in an interdisciplinary data-bound way.

(2) Our ability to design new systems; for this design we need an understanding of existing systems and a design philosophy.

(3) This philosophy has partly to be constructed with the aid of our ability to solve ill-structured problems.

(4) For the design of new systems we shall have to use planning and scenario systems; the combination of planning and scenario sytems defines the simulation methods.

(5) To specify the simulation method we need paradigms. Only with the help of paradigms can we define the desired state of affairs. The paradigm of bounded rationality, if it can be specified in different ways, open up the possibility of meeting the factors I have just mentioned. Of course, this does not exclude the possibility of defining other paradigms. The important thing, however, is that paradigms should be defined in a way that makes it possible to define *how* people and institutions react. Most of the world models now constructed assume, implicitly, that man as an integrated (seen from a subject-matter point of view) human being changes. What changes are necessary, how they should be reached, how institutional changes are involved and how man as a decision-maker should change, is not defined. This means that the nondefined paradigm of average rationality is extrapolated into the distant future. It also means that we exclude the most relevant variable in the whole system,

namely man as a decision-maker, as an instrumental variable. It is my opinion that this kind of research, as far as a problem in the long run is concerned, is not a valid way of tackling this problem.

I admit that my statements concerning the efficiency and/or the effectiveness of applying the simulation method are of a hypothetical nature. Much research has to be done before the simulation method can compete with the econometric one. However, application of these methods until now, if mostly in the field of management science, has yielded promising results. In the next section I consider some strategies that are possible when constructing abstract systems that need long-term forecasting.

6. Strategies for long-term forecasting

As already stated in section 4, I make a distinction between methods and techniques. A number of techniques that are termed econometric could be applied when using the simulation method and vice versa. Numerous examples can be given of the validity of this statement [e.g. Naylor (1971)]. I agree with Apel when he remarks:

> selbstverständlich darf die Orientierung am besten Modellfit bzw. an der besten Korrelation nicht die einzige Konstruktionsleitlinie bleiben. Das gilt ebenso für eine rein ökonometrische Verfahrenweise wie für eine simulative. Die Entscheidung, wann eine Hypothese als valide angesehen werden kann, muss letzlich unabhängig vom Korrelationsergebnis oder von einem statistischen Test getroffen werden. Hierzu muss das Modellverhalten als ganzes unter Berücksichtigung der Zugrunde gelegten theoretischen Prämissen abgewogen werden. Damit verliert der Unterschied zwischen einem "harten" und einem "weichen" Verfahren an gewicht, der darin besteht, dass im ökonometrische Fall die Eingangshypothese am Datenmaterial scheitert, bevor eine Modellrechnung durchgeführt wird, während im simulativen Fall erst ein Modelllauf getested werden muss [Apel (1977)].

As I have already remarked, the distinction between the econometric and simulation method is one based not on differences in techniques applied, but on differences in the hypothesis chosen.

As far as the problem of long-term forecasting is concerned, both methods are data-bound and need long-term forecasting of the exogenous variables concerned. There is, however, a difference. I agree with Armstrong (1978) when he remarks that the best thing to do is to start with a priori analysis. I do not agree with the following strategy (see table 22.1) which he proposes for conducting research needing long-term forecasting [Armstrong (1978, p. 250)]. His table is a mixture of methods and techniques. Segmentation does not coincide with what I call the simulation method, but simulation as a technique is regarded as a part of the segmentation procedures

Table 22.1

Methods of estimating current status and forecasting change.

Estimating current status	Short-range forecast	Middle-range forecast	Long-range forecast
Judgmental			
Extrapolation			
Econometric		Econometric	
			Segmentation

(pp. 239–240). In fig. 22.6 I try to give a summary using a scheme proposed by Sutherland (1978, p. 6). I distinguish in fig. 22.6 the two-model cycles discussed as different strategies in three phases.

Phase 1 is specified in the first column of boxes. It defines different stages for the construction of systems explaining existing situations. These are explanatory systems. Differences between the econometric and simulation method, if present, are represented by putting the simulation procedures in the boxes with thick black lines.

Phase 2 represents the validation stage. Both methods have a feedback loop that opens up the possibility of redefining the system.

Phase 3 sketches the prediction phase. In this case we have the biggest distinction between the two methods. Only the simulation methods opens up the possibility of specifying new systems with the help of scenarios.

Although not sketched in fig. 22.6, there are also differences in the data we use in both methods [see Armstrong (1978)]. One can conclude that in general the mix between objective and subjective data will in the case of the econometric method be in favour of the objective data and in the case of the simulation methods, especially when used for prediction purposes, will be the other way round. As already stated, there are numerous mixes possible between the two approaches depicted in fig. 22.6. As far as the existing world models are concerned, one can state that they are heavily inclined towards a qualitative – axiomatic – approach. In most cases the conditions that both methods postulate are not met. This means that the methodological basis of these "models" is weak and that they can be regarded only as a first step in the direction of constructing a "sound" a priori qualitative analysis. I repeat that for such an analysis

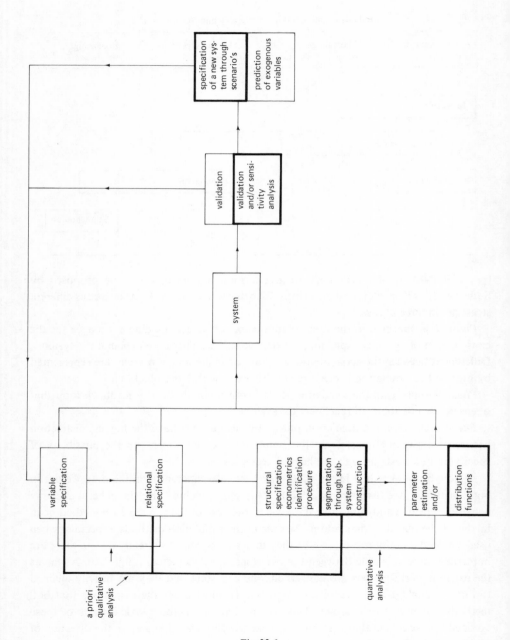

Fig. 22.6

both paradigms and data-bound techniques are necessary. The mixture of these techniques will and must be determined by the paradigm. The paradigms must be specified in such a way that they can perform this task; see the function of a meta-theory discussed in section 3. Only then can world models become more than wishful thinking.

References

Ackoff, R. L., 1971, Towards a system of system concepts, Management Science 17, 661–672.
Ackoff, R. L., 1974, Redesigning the future (John Wiley, New York).
Ackoff, R. L., 1978, The art of problem solving (John Wiley, New York).
Apel, H., 1977, Simulation sozio-ökonomischer Zusammenhänge, Kritik und Modification von "System Dynamics" (Ph.D. thesis, J. W. Goethe University, Frankfurt am Main).
Armstrong, J. S., 1978, Long-range forecasting: From crystal ball to computer (John Wiley, New York).
Betz, F. and J. A. C. de Azevedo, 1976, Structural global models, in: C. W. Churchman and R. O. Mason, eds., World modeling: A dialogue (North-Holland, Amsterdam).
Blalock, H. M., 1968, Theory building and causal interference, in: H. M. Blalock, Jr. and A. B. Blalock, Methodology in social research (McGraw-Hill, New York).
Blaug, M., 1976, Kuhn versus Lakatos or paradigms versus research programmes in the history of economics, in: S. Latsis, ed., Method and appraisal in economics (Cambridge University Press, London).
Boguslaw, R., 1965, The new utopians (Prentice-Hall, Englewood Cliffs).
Bosman, A., 1977, Een metatheorie over het gedrag van organisaties (Stenfert Kroese, Leiden).
Bosman, A., 1978, System identification and simulation, in: Modelling in business (Netherlands IAG, Amsterdam).
Churchman, C. W., 1968, The system approach (Dell, New York).
Churchman, C. W., 1976, The niggling and the grand, in: C. W. Churchman and R. O. Mason, eds., World modeling: A dialogue (North-Holland, Amsterdam).
Clark, J. and S. Cole, 1975, Global simulation models: A comparative study (John Wiley, London).
Cole, S., 1977, Global models and the international economy order (Pergamon, Oxford).
Hanssmann, H., 1976, Systemforschung im Umweltschutz (Schmidt, Berlin).
Jantsch, E., 1976, Modelling the human world: Perspectives, in: C. W. Churchman and R. O. Mason, eds., World modeling: A dialogue (North-Holland, Amsterdam).
Jong, F. J. de, 1949, Over de betekenis van het begrip rationeel handelen in de economie (Bohn, Haarlem).
Laszlo, E., 1973, Introduction to systems philosophy (Harper, New York).
Mason, R. O., 1976, A world issue debate: On assumptions underlying world models, in: C. W. Churchman and R. O. Mason, eds., World modeling: A dialogue (North-Holland, Amsterdam).
Mesarovic, M. D., D. Macko and Y. Takahara, 1970, Theory of hierarchical, multilevel, systems (Academic Press, New York).
Mitroff, I. I. and F. Betz, 1972, Dialectical decision theory: A meta theory of decision making, Management Science 19, 11–25.
Naylor, T. H., 1971, Computer simulation experiments with models of economic systems (John Wiley, New York).
Ozbekhan, H., 1976, The predicament of mankind, in: C. W. Churchman and R. O. Mason, eds., World modeling: A dialogue (North-Holland, Amsterdam).
Rademaker, O., 1976, World models and forecasting: A control engineering perspective, in: G. Broekstra and J. S. Knipscheer, eds., Systemen en toekomstverkenning (Stenfert Kroese, Leiden).
Sagasti, F. R. and I. I. Mitroff, 1973, Operations research from the viewpoint of general systems theory, Omega 1, 695–711.
Simon, H. A., 1969, The sciences of the artificial (MIT Press, Cambridge, Mass.).

Simon, H. A., 1976, From substantive to procedural rationality, in: S. Latsis, ed., Method and appraisal in economics (Cambridge University Press, London).

Simon, H. A., 1978, Rationality as process and as product of thought, American Economic Review, Papers and Proceedings 68, 1–16.

Sutherland, John W., 1978, Societal systems: Methodology, modeling and management (North-Holland, New York).

Tinbergen, J., 1952, On the theory of economic policy (North-Holland, Amsterdam).

Chapter 23   *p. 239 =*

COMMENT ON BOSMAN'S PAPER

C. P. A. BARTELS

University of Groningen

261 - 66

1. Introduction

Long-term forecasting of social systems has become an important field of application for quantitatively orientated system analysts. An intensive use of mathematical models to explore possible patterns of development of large social systems can be noted in recent years. Bosman's contribution aims at indicating conditions for long-term forecasting in this context. He emphasizes the explicit relation between the normative view of a researcher (his paradigm and his own normative goals) on the one hand, and the choice of certain mathematical models on the other. This emphasis results in a number of recommendations, concerning characteristics that have to be present in attempts to forecast the long-term future.

The main recommendations I distil from this paper are the following.

(1) One has to be aware of *the scientific paradigm* underlying the forecasts. In economics, the ruling (neoclassical) paradigm is not realistic. A more realistic set of axioms is required.

(2) There is a strong need for *problem-solving techniques*. Such techniques require an explicit formulation of the desired state of the system, and an indication of alternative ways of reaching this state. Attention to *new* instruments is also needed in this context. This may best be accomplished by formulating alternative *scenarios* for development in the future.

(3) Operational long-term forecasting has to be based on contributions *from several disciplines*. In order to be successful the research has to limit the number of exogenous variables to the really important ones, to be aware of the interdependence of such exogenous variables, and also to consider the structure of the social system as an exogenous variable which can be modified.

Prospects of Economic Growth, edited by S. K. Kuipers and G. J. Lanjouw
© *North-Holland Publishing Company*

(4) Quantitative inquiries into the future may make simultaneous use of the econometric and the simulation method.

Such recommendations are far from new, and in fact several forecasting efforts have already attempted to use such points of departure. In the paper a critical evaluation of such empirical studies is largely absent, except for the attempt to model the world as a system. Instead, the discussion is a rather theoretical one, and hence does not result in a set of clear operational guidelines for successful long-term forecasting of economic variables in social systems. In the continuation of my contribution, I intend to discuss Bosman's recommendations in relation to some experience that has been obtained by several empirical studies. But first a few words on the content and specific characteristics of long-term forecasting of social systems seem in order, since such words are lacking in the paper, while a good understanding of the usefulness of several methods in this field requires explicit attention to these elements.

2. Remarks on long-term forecasting of social systems

Following Rademaker (1975) I define *forecasting* as the process of organized exploratory thinking about the future. *Long-term* forecasting relates to a time horizon in which the system and its goals are completely modifiable. Now it is obvious that each individual in the social system is more or less frequently engaged in such a forecasting process. For our *scientific* discussion of forecasting the future, this latter type of forecast is not informative. Therefore, one may select some *criteria* that a forecast has to satisfy in order to be considered of a scientific nature [cf. Hupkes (1976)]:

(1) the process has to be *controllable*, i.e. repeatable by other people, which implies that a consistent theoretical scheme produces the forecasts;

(2) forecasts have to be stated in *quantitative* terms; and

(3) an indication of *the probability* that a certain situation will arise must be given.

Hupkes considers this last criterion not attainable for long-term forecasts of social systems. The second one too will be hardly met. Thus, a scientific approach to a long-term forecast of social systems is not easily realized. This is caused by a number of *specific characteristics* of this type of forecasting [cf. also Radmaker (1975)]:

(a) social values change in a way difficult to predict;

(b) many exogenous influences can hardly be identified or measured;

(c) unexpected discontinuities, like social or technological innovations, play a major role in the long-term future;

(d) in social systems the goals are pluralistic, conflicting, sometimes ill-defined and partly implicit;

(e) the common problems of empirical economic research can also be mentioned here: lack of good data, weak theory, complexity, impossibility of empirical experimentation.

Given these characteristics, the first question to be answered is: are quantitative models of any use for forecasting the development of complete social systems in the long run? It will be clear that models to accomplish this will have to be essentially of an *integral type*, relating several subsystems to each other.

From Bosman's paper it appears that he seems to believe in the utility of mathematical models for the purpose mentioned above. However, he does not indicate clearly how to deal with the specific characteristics of social systems enumerated above in such forecasting efforts. In the Netherlands, recently, research work was carried out that gives some interesting experience related to this problem. Since Bosman does not refer to this research, I consider it briefly.

3. A long-term forecast for Dutch society

An important experiment with multidisciplinary long-term forecasting of Dutch society has been performed by the Scientific Council for Government Policy [see WRR (1977)]. The report, which resulted from three years of cooperation between experts from several disciplines, contains two variants for the development of Dutch society in the next 25 years. The variants are in fact an amalgamation of the various experts' expectations.

In the report some important points of departure for this research are mentioned:

(a) it was impossible to take new social values into account, since these were considered unpredictable;

(b) it was impossible to indicate the degree of probability of a certain scenario being realized;

(c) an integral model, incorporating all relevant social variables, was unattainable, since not all variables could be quantified. Consequently, a multidisciplinary view of the future could be obtained only by means of an *informal iterative process of discussion* between the experts. (It should be mentioned that at present the Central Planning Bureau is making serious attempts to construct an integral, long-term forecasting model incorporating a large number of social subsystems. The model is not yet operational, however.)

Thus, the forecasts published in the report are only partly presented in quantitative terms, while a complete integration of developments in several subsystems is absent. Therefore, the result does not seem to be a successful attempt at *scientific* multidisciplinary long-term forecasts for a social system (see the remarks in the preceding section). For me it confirms the opinion that forecasts of long-term processes in a social system can hardly be based on a scientific methodology satisfying the criteria

264 *C. P. A. Bartels*

enumerated above. Such a scientific methodology, employing for example the mathematical models discussed by Bosman, seems much better suited to exploring the short- and medium-term future.

4. Methods for exploring the long-term future

The example discussed in the preceding section demonstrated that long-term forecasts may be produced without the use of a mathematical model. It is a drawback of Bosman's paper that the enumeration of forecasting methods has been narrowly limited. I think that the following subdivision of methods, partly derived from Rademaker (1975), gives a more complete picture.

(1) Trend extrapolation of a univariate time series. This method uses historical observations of a variable to predict its future time path. The role of this method in economics has grown considerably through the important work of Box and Jenkins (1970).

(2) *Mathematical multivariate methods* which explicitly formulate relations between variables. In *econometric* models such relations are specified by means of statistical techniques, employing time series, cross-sectional data, or a combination of the two. If relations are not specified by means of such statistical techniques, but by means of point estimates or personal judgement, we use the term *numerical experimentation models* [cf. Varsavsky and Calcagno (1971)]. In practice most models consist of a combination of these two types.

(3) *Methods for coping coherently with extensive information and/or evaluating policies*. Examples of this class of quantitative methods are cost–benefit and cost–effectiveness analysis and multicriteria analysis [see, for example, Van Delft and Nijkamp (1977)].

(4) *Conceptualizing methods*, like Delphi exercises and scenario writing. Given the specific characteristics of social systems, one would like to know what role can be played by mathematical models as compared with the other methods.

5. More specific comments

Thus far my comments have been rather general. Now I return to the four topics mentioned in the introduction.

(1) In my opinion Bosman overestimates the influence of *the traditional paradigm* in economics on applied econometric research. In many empirical studies, certainly for the purpose of long-term forecasting, economic theory is used only to obtain some crude notions about which variables are expected to be interrelated. In the subsequent

stage of statistical estimation, *statistical criteria* are frequently used to specify the final relations [compare, for example, Bartels and Ter Welle (1977)]. Most macro-econometric models seem to follow this sequence [an example in which this is very explicit is Ketellaper et al. (1978)]. In such a situation the content of axioms relating to the economic behaviour of microunits in the system does not directly imply a certain specification of relations at the macro level. Besides, alternative axioms have also been considered in economics. A well-known example is the hypothesis of *satisficing* behaviour of economic agents, which was recently confirmed on the basis of empirical data for consumer behaviour [Kapteyn et al. (1977)].

(2) In the paper it is stated that the scenario approach gives some *guarantee that relevant alternatives are not excluded* by the simple fact that the researcher himself has to specify the alternatives. Evidence on scenarios for long-term developments in fields like energy and environmental quality makes me more critical than Bosman on the extent to which such a guarantee can be present in scenarios. Since alternatives are selected by personal judgement, scenarios considered relevant by other individuals will easily be missing. This is a well-known conflict issue in studies based on the scenario approach [compare Hueting (1978) for a "forgotten" scenario in official studies of the future energy situation].

(3) Bosman seems to promote the development of *integral models* which interrelate the different social subsystems. Given experiences in the past with such integral models, I should like to know the author's opinion on what concrete results we really may expect from such efforts [for a pessimistic view of such efforts see, for example, Klaassen (1977)].

(4) In the preceding section I defined econometric and numerical experimentation models. Both can be used for the simulation of alternative paths that the system may follow. I think this nomenclature is less confusing than the distinction between the econometric and simulation method as made in the paper.

For a good evaluation of both models distinguished above, I think it is required also to keep the following points in mind.

(a) The *econometric* method can be used to estimate a wide variety of models, allowing for changing parameters, parameters incorporating random effects, errors in variables, a priori Bayesian information, etc. These more recent developments extend the usefulness of econometrics a great deal.

(b) The *numerical experimentation model* with a complete a priori specification of parameters and relations can hardly be considered as a serious scientific tool since it offers no possibilities for a good validation of parameter values and specifications of the relations in the model.

6. Final remark

From the comments formulated above it will be clear that I have serious doubts about
the usefulness of integrated mathematical models in the long-term forecasting of social
systems. It seems more appropriate to reserve the mathematical models for forecasts of
the near future which does not display so much variation in the structure of the social
system.

References

Bartels, C. P. A. and H. J. ter Welle, 1977, The functional form of migration relations, Research Memorandum
    no. 34 (Institute of Economic Research, Groningen).
Box, G. E. P. and G. M. Jenkins, 1970, Time series analysis, forecasting and control (Holden-Day, San
    Francisco).
Delft, A. van and P. Nijkamp, 1977, Multi-criteria analysis and regional decision-making (M. Nijhoff,
    Leiden).
Hueting, R., 1978, Kernenergie en produktiegroei, Economisch-Statistische Berichten 63, 292–298.
Hupkes, G., 1976, Toekomstonderzoek, Intermediair 12 (6), 9–11.
Kapteyn, A., T. Wansbeek and J. Buyze, 1977, Maximizing or satisficing? (Report of the Economic Institute
    of Leyden University, Leyden.)
Ketellapper, R. H., B. Bos, M. A. Kooyman and W. Voorhoeve, 1978, A simultaneous econometric model
    for the Dutch economy, Statistica Neerlandica 32, 141–159.
Klaassen, L. H., 1977, Regional science. Some Dutch experiences (Netherlands Economic Institute,
    Rotterdam).
Rademaker, O., 1975, World models and forecasting: A control-engineering perspective, Journal A 16,
    181–195.
Varsavsky, O. and A. E. Calcagno, eds., 1971, America Latina: Modelos matemáticos, Ensayos de
    aplicación de modelos de experimentación numérica a la política económica y las ciencias sociales
    (Editorial Universitaria, Santiago).
WRR, 1977, De komende vijfentwintig jaar. Een toekomstverkenning voor Nederland (Staatsuitgeverij,
    's-Gravenhage).

COMMENT ON BOSMAN'S PAPER

P. S. H. LEEFLANG   *267-70*

University of Groningen

1. Introduction

There are at least two reasons why long-term forecasting can be called a paradox. The first has been put into words by Bosman when he states that: "the extent to which we are able to solve problems in the long or short [sic] term is determined not by the quality of our predictions but by the quality of our systems and the extent to which we are ready and able to devise, to examine and to introduce measures that obviate or solve the problems in question". This can be brought back to a number of other statements that may be found in his contribution[1] in which he endeavours to point out that forecasting is an aid and not an aim in the formulation of economic policy.

A second reason why "long-term forecasting" could be called a paradox, or perhaps rather a contradiction in terms, is that forecasting, at least in the long term, is extremely difficult if not impossible. One of the strong points of Bosman's paper is that he lists a number of drawbacks that are inherent in the use of forecasting methods, in which he considers in particular a number of problems that are connected with the use of what he calls the "econometric method", drawbacks which in all probability are not always known to the users of this "method". These drawbacks, added to others which in my opinion may adhere to the use of the simulation method, may lead after reading Bosman's paper to the question whether long-term forecasting should or should not be called a paradox for *this* reason. Since I share Bosman's opinion (p. 255) that there are numerous possibilities of raising "the quality of our systems", I believe that the answer to the question put above should for the time being be in the negative. Although in this

---

[1] For example, in section 4 "predicting is only one of the criteria for the validation of a system" and, later, "planning without forecasting is impossible".

Prospects of Economic Growth, edited by S. K. Kuipers and G. J. Lanjouw
© *North-Holland Publishing Company*

respect I agree with Bosman, I feel that, also having regard to my terms of reference, I have to differ in opinion with him on a number of points. These points are as follows:

(1) the way in which attention will have to be paid to the designing of systems (section 2);

(2) a number of objections that are made to the "econometric method" (section 3); and

(3) some problems inherent in the use of the "simulation method" (section 4).

2. The design of systems

Bosman's contribution refers at various places to the problems concerning the construction of "image systems" (section 3), in order to arrive at better "abstract systems" via these "image systems". Since the object of these exercises is ultimately to depict reality by which ". . . we are ready and able to devise, to examine and to introduce measures that obviate or solve the problems in question" (section 5), we should also mention other attempts that are being made in this respect, though admittedly in another way. I am referring here to the work that is being done in the field of management science for the purpose of

(1) developing criteria that have to be satisfied by a "good" model; and

(2) modifying the classical model-building process in such a way that the ultimate result is "better" depictions.[2]

In his contribution Bosman completely ignores these attempts and concentrates entirely on contributions from systems theory. Partly because the various concepts that he uses in this context are not clearly defined[3] and make the model-building process (perhaps unnecessarily?) complicated, I feel that this is one more reason to mention the developments in question.

3. Drawbacks of the econometric method

As stated in the introduction, Bosman brings to the fore in his paper a number of drawbacks of the econometric method such as:

(a) the measured effectiveness of instrumental variables represents an average result of non-optimal efforts from the past;

(b) a number of the relevant alternatives may be missing if they have not been performed in the past;

(c) the future values of the (at least non-controllable!) exogenous variables are unknown.

[2] See, for instance, Little (1970), Naert and Leeflang (1978), and Urban (1974).
[3] See, for instance, the definition of the concept "conceptual model" in section 3.

These drawbacks or restrictions could be supplemented by the following:

(d) the number of variables that can be considered should be limited, having regard to the often limited number of observations available; and

(e) extrapolation outside the range of observations of the explanatory variables used to arrive at parameter estimates is particularly dangerous, etc.

Although these drawbacks are correct, Bosman does not go into the attempts that are undertaken to meet them. The following are some examples.

(i) The development of adaptive models which possess the possibility of adapting the values of the parameters to data becoming newly available, and also of modifying the number of variables in the model.[4] In these adaptive models it is possible to make more recent observations weigh more heavily than earlier observations which, in my opinion, might be one of the principles of designing models "for the attainment of a desired state of affairs" (end of section 3).

(ii) Using techniques like progressive time series analysis with which developments in the trend of the parameter values can also be detected.[5]

(iii) The increasing attention being paid to the use of subjective estimates and combinations of subjective estimates and estimates based on "objective" data, with which a number of problems inherent in data-based parameterization can be overcome.[6]

When listing the advantages of the simulation method for drawing up scenario systems, Bosman creates the impression that these "advantages" do not find favour when the econometric method is used, which in my opinion is not correct. Thus, also when the econometric method is used it is possible

(1) with the aid of a sensitivity analysis to determine the influence of the exogenous variables on the results of the process described, by fluctuating the values of the exogenous variables;[7]

(2) to determine the influence of the accuracy of parameter estimation by sampling from the probability distributions of the estimated parameters; and

(3) to assume different relations or different forms of relations and to study the effect of these differences.[8] The structure of the system is indeed not as flexible as in the use of the simulation method, but it is not a datum either (section 4).

4. Drawbacks of the simulation method

In addition to a number of advantages that the simulation method has over the econometric method, it also possesses disadvantages that are almost or entirely ignored

[4] See, for instance, Little (1975a, 1975b) and Naert and Leeflang (1978, p. 105).
[5] See, for an illustration, Leeflang (1977).
[6] See, for instance, Zellner (1971).
[7] See, for an example, Leeflang (1976, pp. 237–244).
[8] See Naert and Leeflang (1978, pp. 106, 114).

in Bosman's contribution. I should like to go into what I consider to be the greatest advantages, namely determination of the connection between variables. As stated by Bosman, these connections are based on expectations that one has about the developments of certain connections of variables in the future. In order to specify these connections use is made of data, "but these can be changed – autonomously or by the system itself – on the basis of the above-mentioned expectations". Since points of departure and criteria that ought to be used in determining these connections are not stated, or perhaps are not known, the construction of systems with the aid of this method can be an extremely precarious undertaking. Only when connections are known on the basis of prior information that can be obtained by means of "laws", "generalizations" or "analogies" will one possess such points of departure.

Something similar to the above can also be said with regard to the structure of the system, as Bosman himself remarks (section 4). I therefore share Bosman's opinion that the econometric and simulation methods both have advantages and disadvantages, only I think that I weigh these advantages and disadvantages differently, as may have become clear from this comment. However, I should like to go a step further than his conclusion, namely not only that both methods can be used *simultaneously*, but also that a *synthesis* of the two methods can be useful in long-term forecasting. The experience being gained with such syntheses may give us a definitive answer to the question whether long-term prediction is or is not a paradox in the second sense formulated by me in the introduction.

References

Little, J. D. C., 1970, Models and managers: The concept of a decision calculus, Management Science 16, B 446–485.

Little, J. D. C., 1975a, BRANDAID: A marketing-mix model, part 1: Structure, Operations Research 23, 628–655.

Little, J. D. C., 1975b, BRANDAID: A marketing-mix model, Part II: Implementation, calibration and case study, Operations Research 23, 656–673.

Leeflang, P. S. H., 1976, Marktonderzoek en marketingmodellen, in: Marktonderzoek en consumentengedrag, Jaarboek Ned. Ver. voor Marktonderzoekers, pp. 217–252.

Leeflang, P. S. H., 1977, De marketing mix III, Bepaling van de effectiviteit der marktinstrumenten, Economisch-Statistische Berichten 62, 549–555.

Naert, Ph.A. and P. S. H. Leeflang, 1978, Building implementable marketing models (Martinus Nijhoff, Leiden/Boston).

Urban, G. L., 1974, Building models for decision makers, Interfaces 4, 1–11.

Zellner, A., 1971, An introduction to Bayesian inference in econometrics (John Wiley and Sons, New York).

Chapter 25

SUMMARY AND EVALUATION OF THE SYMPOSIUM "PROSPECTS OF ECONOMIC GROWTH"

J. WEITENBERG

Central Planning Bureau/University of Groningen

1. General

It has gradually become a tradition for the Groningen Faculty of Economics to organize a symposium on a subject of practical or theoretical interest. Every year the Organizing Committee succeeds in attracting speakers of renown for the subject to be discussed. That has also been the case this year, and that is why we have been able to become acquainted with the views and opinions of the macroeconomists among the Dutch economists. By this remark I do not wish to make light of the contributions from other quarters, but the fact is that the theme of economic growth lies mainly in the field covered by macroeconomics.

I therefore want to compliment the Organizing Committee on its choice of both speakers and subject. A subject which is not only highly topical but also immensely fascinating from a theoretical point of view. This became apparent from the scholarly dissertations which the various speakers had embodied in their papers.

I have been invited to close this symposium with a summary and evaluation. This is not a simple task, given the working method that has been adopted. Bearing in mind the great advantages that may be gained from division of labour, the Organizing Committee has subdivided the general theme into eight subthemes. The various speakers have kept very well to their subject, and it is now for the "summarizer" to try and fit the pieces of the jigsaw puzzle together and form them into a whole. I feel that this is indeed an impossible task, for it would mean that I challenge each speaker on the subject he has presented. I have no such pretensions. That is why I am forced to adopt a selective and subjective course of action and to restrict myself to such matters as seem essential to me in making forecasts about economic growth.

Prospects of Economic Growth, edited by S. K. Kuipers and G. J. Lanjouw
© *North-Holland Publishing Company*

2. Some remarks on methodology

Before taking up this point, a few remarks on methodology would not be out of place. At first sight it looks as if Bosman's paper "Long-term forecasting – a paradox?" falls somewhat outside the framework of the general theme of the symposium. The title suggests more or less that forecasts about future economic developments are impossible to make. However, when studying the paper one finds that it is Bosman's intention to help the researcher – irrespective of his topic of study and his discipline – to maintain the scientific quality of his approach.

Scientists in general, and economists in particular, often seem to handle their methods and techniques rather slovenly, to put it mildly. They frequently display a certain rigidity in their thinking and are reluctant to apply new techniques and methods that have been developed in other disciplines. If I am right, Bosman reproaches the economists in general with paying no attention to the mental conceptualization of the observed reality. Economists are often not aware that their image system is subjectively determined and is a *monodisciplinary* reflection of the observed reality. Moreover, their economic and personally tinged conceptual model is claimed to rest on axioms that hardly differ from those which served as a basis for the classical economists. Such a proposition goes too far for my liking and does not do justice to the developments in economic thinking which started with the Keynesian revolution.

I do agree with Bosman, however, when he points out that the axiom of the *maximization principle* of the economic agents is too broadly defined and that the scientists therefore too easily conclude that economic behaviour will lead to an equilibrium. However, these shortcomings have meanwhile been recognized and are being given sufficient attention in the literature. Thus, for a few years now attention has been paid in the American literature to the problem of incomplete information, with the economic agent choosing from a limited number of alternatives. In the field of disequilibrium analysis we need not go far from home. Both in Groningen and in Rotterdam theses on this subject are at present in the course of preparation.

I could say much more about Bosman's stimulating paper, but will restrict myself to two more points. Bosman is in favour of tackling all kinds of problems on a multidisciplinary scale. I fully agree with him there, for economists all too often ignore the interaction of the various social facets. In his comment Bartels rightly points to the Scientific Council for Government Policy (WRR), a body that has been specially established for the multidisciplinary approach of crucial social problems. He is equally right when he judges the Economic Outlook, which was recently published by the WRR, as immature and even as a failure. I shall refer to this later.

Bosman is also in favour of a more frequent application of simulation methods. He prefers such methods to the less flexible econometric models, which are still widely used. His objections to the econometric method are corroborated by Leeflang in his comment. Yet, in his criticism of the econometric method Leeflang is less severe, and does not feel the need to do away with it for the time being. I agree with Leeflang on this point, and should like to point out in support of his objections to the simulation method that this method is of a more arbitrary character. For, when applying a simulation method we need no longer assume a constant structure; it can also be made endogenous or be adjusted on the basis of expectations. In the latter case the scientist may also have to respect the expectations voiced by politicians. Consequently, he runs the risk of arriving at such solutions and recommendations as will be agreeable to the policy-makers. *Policy-orientated* research would thus change into *policy-maker-orientated* research.

Finally, mention is made in one of the comments (Bartels) of the construction of an *integrated model*, which is being studied by the Central Planning Bureau (CPB). Indeed, for three years people at the CPB have been working on such a model, in which demographic and physical planning and other aspects are incorporated in addition to the economic aspect. For this model intensive use is being made of other methods than the traditional econometric techniques. So Bosman's every wish is attended to. Moreover, a subsequent forecast based on this model may do full justice to the relationships between the various social facets.

3. The economic system within which the future economic development will take place

The growth of the economy does not take place in isolated space, but is embedded in a scheme of social circumstances and institutions. For the sake of brevity this is usually called the economic system within which economic development takes place. This economic system has both a national and an international dimension. Both dimensions may change – in the long term at any rate – and thus influence the volume and the quality of growth.

I want to start by making some remarks on the international order and the international distribution of power. Tinbergen distinguishes at present three power blocs – East, West and South – and notes that a dialogue is in progress. Although he does not express a definite opinion on this point, I have gained the impression that Tinbergen gives preference to a South–West dialogue. Such a dialogue has already been going on for some decades, but has been restricted so far to a transfer of incomes (development aid) and a liberalization of trade policy. This liberalization did not only refer to the economic relations between the two blocs but was concerned particularly with the trade relations within the bloc of Western industrial countries.

As Van Dam has rightly put forward, a standstill, if not a setback, has occurred in both fields since 1970. It is going too far, however, to state (De Haan, Lanjouw) that since Bretton Woods and the first GATT round no real changes have taken place in the international economic order. Moreover, this statement seems to conflict with another proposition made by De Haan and Lanjouw, namely that changes in the international economic order are brought about not only by governmental, but also by private organizations. The phenomena mentioned by them in this connection – the multi-nationals and the opening up of money and capital markets to developing countries – already materialized a long time ago.

Van Dam held the most pronounced, but also the gloomiest, views on the expected future developments in the West–South dialogue (or the North–South dialogue, if you prefer). For he sees the Southern bloc disintegrating into three parts: OPEC, new industrial countries in the take-off stage, and true developing countries. He also foresees that the remaining group of developing countries will shrink continuously, since under the impact of political pride and national prestige more and more countries no longer want to be regarded as developing countries. It is therefore hardly surprising that Van Dam expects little good of a North–South dialogue, especially if a complex of problems were to come up for discussion there.

Tinbergen is more optimistic in this respect, partly because he considers a division of power in favour of the developing countries a vital necessity for maintaining political stability at world level. In Tinbergen's view this division of power implies that in the long term the Third World ought to benefit increasingly from the globally attainable growth. As an additional argument for this opinion he suggests that a more fugal way of life will be indispensable to the West both in view of our health and in view of the credibility of our Western culture. In the short term, however, the growth in the West should be stepped up in order to get out of the present depression.

I feel that in the long run this view of Tinbergen's may play a major role in the North–South relations. As this idea materializes, the growth in our country will not only decelerate, but world trade, too, will be of lesser significance for the realization of this reduced growth. For, as greater emphasis is laid in the West on the output of services, the labour intensity of the output will rise – along with a lesser sensitivity to labour-saving technical progress – while at the same time sales will be increasingly focused on the home market. Moreover, services form a smaller share of imports.

As I mentioned before, the economic order also has a national dimension. Lindbeck's typification of the Western European economies as trilateral power monopolies was generally subscribed to. It was amended on one point, however, namely that no full homogeneity need exist within these power blocs. Centralization–decentralization within the public sector, and the latent struggle for power between separate trade unions and the federations of trade unions, point to sources of conflict within the individual power blocs.

The answer to the question whether our economic order will make growth possible in the future, was less unanimous. Apart from system-linked considerations about raw materials, energy, technology and environment – to which I shall refer later – doubts were expressed about the stability of our economic system. In the discussions, no clear definition was given of the term stability. In my opinion, a stable system is a system that is capable of attaining the desired socio-economic objectives without substantial reforms.

As long as there is a consensus about these objectives, and the objectives themselves do not clash – and this has been the case for a long time – there is less reason to doubt this stability. This situation changes, however, when the objectives rivalize, or when the various groups of social agents have widely divergent opinions on the tenor of the objectives. Particularly when conceptual changes in the existing balance of power are at stake, heavy demands are made of the prevailing system. This is also the case when the system of social security frustrates the free market behaviour of the economic agents.

I feel that we are heading for a period in which the problems of the division of power and the functioning of the labour market will occupy a central place. Whether our present system will be able to cope is a question that cannot simply be answered in the affirmative or in the negative. The opinions on this point are widely divergent.

4. External circumstances and external effects

The conclusions on the availability of raw materials and energy in the coming decades were very clear. In the medium term no bottlenecks need arise *in a technical sense*. This applies to agricultural products, minerals and fossil energy alike. Nor need we fear a physical shortage of foodstuffs and agricultural products for manufacturing purposes over a somewhat longer period. This is different for minerals, where a growing shortage of specific raw materials may well make itself felt in the medium-to-long term. As regards the availability of fossil raw materials the problems threaten to become even more serious. In the medium-to-long term – say a period of between ten and twenty years – bottlenecks are liable to become apparent here unless we can fall back on coal and nuclear fission. Since, for whatever reason, these alternative sources of energy are deemed increasingly unacceptable, this will have a negative effect on growth.

Given our defective knowledge of the world's gas and oil deposits, and in view of the uncertainty about the inventiveness of the technologists who will have to provide solutions for nuclear fusion and solar energy in the long term (around the year 2000), economy will be vital in any case. This conclusion was unanimously agreed, while the argument concerning the future generations and the ecological objections to the use of coal and nuclear energy met with almost universal approval.

I did observe some difference of opinion, though, on the contribution of technology towards the solution of the energy problem. Linnemann felt that optimism on this point was not justified. Van der Grinten, on the other hand, was far more positive in his judgement. He pointed out that the contribution of technology should be directed mainly at individual activities, such as product innovation. He was disappointed that this aspect had not been mentioned in any of the papers.

During the discussion reference was made to the following matters:

(a) technology should be directed more and more toward increasing the productivity of raw materials and energy, so that at the same time less emphasis need be laid on traditional technology, which is usually of a labour-saving character;

(b) in order to achieve this reallocation of research activities, a relative price increase of raw materials and energy would be desirable; thus, future price rises might be anticipated by means of levies, but it goes without saying that this should be done only in an international context.

The objectives of economic growth and a clean environment are highly incompatible, particularly in Hueting's view. He advocates zero growth, and perhaps even negative growth, in order to reduce the burden on the environment. I use the term "reducing the burden" on purpose, because even in the case of negative growth there is a continued accumulation of polluting agents. An interesting contribution in this connection was made by Van der Zwan who pointed out that growth is not necessarily synonymous with imposing an additional burden on the environment. He rightly stated that growth may go hand in hand with a change in the production pattern, by which polluting activities are moved to locations where the self-purifying properties of the natural environment have not yet been affected. Such a spatial reallocation is far from inconceivable, given the growing tendency of the raw-materials-producing countries to process their raw materials on the spot.

Lengthy discussions were held on the question of the extent to which protection of the environment should be regarded as a merit good, on which the government takes the necessary environmental measures, even if this should go against the individual preferences of the citizens. The views on this question, with its ethical overtones, were widely divergent. I personally hold the opinion that it rests with the authorities in the first place to inform the public on these matters. If this works insufficiently or not at all, it is the government's duty – particularly in view of the interests of future generations – to submit its plans to Parliament and to draw the political consequences, if necessary.

The question of the instruments to be chosen was not done sufficient justice. Environmental management calls for the use of scarce resources, which are thus no longer available for the production of other goods. One might say that in this manner the entire problem of the environment is reduced to a problem of weighing priorities. This naturally requires an insight into the costs entailed by the various environmental objectives. It seems to me that the economists have fallen short in this respect until now.

5. The analysis of the growth phenomenon

In his survey Kuipers distinguishes four philosophies – or schools if you prefer – which have dealt in recent years with the growth phenomenon, and particularly with the explanation of the employment trend. When comparing these four types of approach Kuipers comes to the conclusion that the vintage analysis based on neoclassical principles is an adequate method of explaining the national economic development of employment. He attaches little importance to the neo-Keynesian demand analysis, because this approach seems to conflict with the available empirical data.

As a neoclassical macroeconomist, Kuipers has no need of a sectoral approach. Such an approach meets with objections and resistance on his part, a resistance which apparently arises from fear of a loss of position for the macroeconomic discipline. I can sympathize with the objections he raises, such as the disregard of forward and backward linkages between the sectors and the exaggerated fascination for the specific sectoral problems. This does not imply, however, that sectoral analysis should be rejected as a matter of principle.

In my opinion Driehuis takes the right attitude when he points out that a sectoral approach may lead to a deeper and clearer insight into the growth of output and employment at the macroeconomic level. In such an approach we should not lose sight, however, of the interdependences that exist between the sectors, interdependences that grow closer as a more detailed breakdown is adopted. We should also bear in mind that there are no sectoral policy instruments available. Consequently, action focused on specific sectors is not (yet) possible. This does not mean that sectoral analysis would be completely superfluous from the policy angle. Having regard to the fact that the macroeconomic and general policy instruments yield different results for the various sectors, it is not inconceivable that sectoral analysis will lead to a more judicious choice from among the available macroeconomic policy instruments.

Finally, I should like to say that the macroeconomic approach, no matter whether it be based on neo-Keynesian or on neoclassical principles, has not become superfluous, but that it should be complemented by sectoral analyses. Van der Zwan goes even further when he advocates the use of microeconomic analyses. The quartile analyses, initiated some years ago by the CBS, are an important step forward in this direction.

The observation that greater emphasis should be laid on sectoral and microeconomic analyses is not the end of the story. The difficulties encountered by Muller and Zwezerijnen in compiling data on the output trend per sector, let alone sectoral data on plant and equipment, utilization of capacity, technological progress, etc. are a striking example of the scope of the statistical problems. Besides, a breakdown into ten or twenty branches of industry will not be sufficient for this approach. To this it was rightly argued that, even if a further breakdown were feasible, it would still not be possible to distinguish between heavy chemicals and fine chemicals manufacture.

Whereas the statistical work of Muller and Zwezerijnen was greatly appreciated, the opinions on the theories and empirical methods that these two speakers had turned loose on their material were less favourable. Doubts were expressed in particular as to whether the unmistakably increased significance of international trade would have similar effects on the productivity of capital and labour. Van de Klundert doubted whether the procedure followed by the authors would be the right approach for the sectoral analysis of growth and employment. Discussion of this procedure does indeed seem desirable, while at the same time attention might be paid to Van de Klundert's suggestion to adopt a "turnpike" approach.

In addition to the neoclassical and neo-Keynesian schools, Kuipers distinguishes the system approach and the long-term cycle approach. The adherents of the system approach attach great significance to a number of system-linked characteristics of capitalism, which may be held responsible for the recurrent derailment of the Western economies. The supporters of the long-term cycle try to find the causes of the recurrent economic crises in a cyclical movement, the underlying determinants of which are as yet insufficiently understood.

Van der Zwan rejects the long-term Kondratieff cycle because he has been unable to establish either its alleged fixed periodicity or the general and international character of such a long-term cycle. I feel that Van Duyn is right when he objects that in his evaluation method Van der Zwan sets stricter standards for the fixed periodicity of the Kondratieff than those that are normally applied to economic cycles. Furthermore, Van Duyn contends that the national income would be a suitable yardstick. In this connection it might be added that the manufacturing output series may show more variation than the total output series. On the other hand it should be borne in mind that in an economy there are interdependences between the industry and other large sectors. A question which may be brought up in this respect is whether or not mining forms part of industry. Finally, a discussion may arise on the way in which the trend in the series should be eliminated. Depending on the method chosen (linear or nonlinear elimination of the trend) and on the selected intervals, this will yield different residual series and the statistical evaluation of the Kondratieff hypothesis will therefore have different results.

Schouten recognizes on theoretical grounds – indicated as pre-empirical experience – the existence of cyclical movements. He imputes this to a malfunctioning of the market mechanism, the frustrated free market behaviour of the economic agents. He illustrates this thesis by asking why the present general overcapacity does not lead to price reductions, which in their turn would result in a growing demand for consumer goods among wage-earners and in a better utilization of capacity. The fact that this does not occur may have two causes: either there is no general overcapacity, or the market mechanism does not function adequately. Van der Zwan has rightly objected to this argument that in times of crisis different economic mechanisms are called for. As a matter of fact this is proved by historic examples, such as the initiative of the American government in the 1930s to institute price cartels along with output quotas.

Notwithstanding the fundamental differences in theoretical views, the participants were largely unanimous about the therapies to be chosen in the present situation. Among the measures put forward were the general stimulation of demand by increasing the budget deficits, direct innovation measures – the inventions themselves have not come to a standstill, but their application has – and a new industrial policy focused on spearhead industries. In respect of the spearhead industries it will be of particular importance that a certain demand be guaranteed, since a small country like the Netherlands is always in an unfavourable position. All this did not provide an answer to the question of how to prevent general or sectoral overinvestment.

6. Summary and conclusion

What are the expectations of – or rather, for – economic growth? Although not every speaker explicitly said so, the forecasts are generally gloomy. In the coming years some output growth may eventually be realized, even though this will horrify the advocates of a clean environment. Growth of employment, at least in the private sector, seems out of the question. Even with a maximum policy effort and assuming optimum circumstances, both national and international, the employment situation will remain unchanged at most. If this is the case, I foresee that in one of the years to come a symposium will be held on the theme: *How can more people participate in the available employment?*

I should like to close by quoting Schouten: "We did not agree and we have not come to an agreement during this symposium, but we have learned a lot from each other."

AUTHOR INDEX

Entries in the index in bold type indicate contributors' papers or the discussions of their papers

SUBJECT INDEX